Getting Started with
Drones and
Model Airplanes

Patrick Sherman

Getting Started with Drones and Model Airplanes
by Patrick Sherman

Aviation Supplies & Academics, Inc.
7005 132nd Place SE
Newcastle, Washington 98059
asa@asa2fly.com | 425-235-1500 | asa2fly.com

See the Reader Resources at **asa2fly.com/modelair** for additional information and updates related to this book.

ASA-MODEL-AIR
ISBN 978-1-64425-365-6

Additional formats available:
eBook EPUB   ISBN 978-1-64425-366-3
eBook PDF   ISBN 978-1-64425-367-0

Printed in the United States of America
2028   2027   2026   2025   2024   9   8   7   6   5   4   3   2   1

Cover photos: Patrick Sherman

Library of Congress Cataloging-in-Publication Data:
Names: Sherman, Patrick (Drone aircraft specialist), author.
Title: Getting started with drones and model airplanes / Patrick Sherman.
Description: Newcastle, Washington : Aviation Supplies & Academics, Inc., [2024] | Includes index.
Identifiers: LCCN 2023049986 (print) | LCCN 2023049987 (ebook) | ISBN 9781644253656 (trade paperback) | ISBN 9781644253663 (epub) | ISBN 9781644253670 (pdf)
Subjects: LCSH: Drone aircraft—Piloting. | Airplanes—Models—Radio control.
Classification: LCC TL685.35 .S54 2024 (print) | LCC TL685.35 (ebook) | DDC 796.15/4—dc23/eng/20231120
LC record available at https://lccn.loc.gov/2023049986
LC ebook record available at https://lccn.loc.gov/2023049987

For Barbara—the hardest-working writer I know,
and forever an inspiration.

"Any landing you can walk away from is a good landing."

— Chuck Yeager

"Speaking as a drone pilot, I can honestly say that all of my landings have been good landings."

— Patrick Sherman

Contents

Foreword

Although we often think of aviation as arriving on the scene towards the end of the industrial revolution, man's dream of taking flight and soaring with the birds has existed for centuries, perhaps even millennia.

Uncrewed aviation, or what hobbyists refer to as model aviation, predates crewed aviation by several decades. In the fifteenth century, Leonardo da Vinci made the first real studies of flight and had over 200 drawings and sketches that illustrated his theories on flight, most of which were ornithopters—machines that flap their wings, like birds.

Leonardo da Vinci lived centuries before the development of technologies (such as the internal combustion engine) that would have made his imaginings practical. He nevertheless made sketches and built models of flying machines, including this helicopter, that presaged the era of human flight.

In 1878, the Wright brothers' father, Bishop Wright, brought home a rubber band powered toy helicopter designed by the French aeronautical experimenter Alphonse Pénaud. The Wright brothers flew the toy helicopter until it broke, then rebuilt and redesigned the model multiple times as they gained a better understanding of aeronautical design and the theory of flight.

On December 17, 1903, the Wright brothers' experimentation in model aviation resulted in man's first successful powered aircraft flight in the 1903 Wright Flyer with Orville Wright at the controls. In the decades that followed, model aircraft have time and again been employed to prove new aeronautical designs, new flying techniques, and new theories in aerospace science.

Model aviation has not only aided in the development and advancement in aeronautical design and related aviation equipment but has also been instrumental in developing the knowledge, skills, and abilities of thousands of aviators, engineers, mechanics, technicians, and scientist enjoined in the emergent field of aeronautics and aerospace science.

Among the most prominent of these stories is that of Neil Armstrong. Few people on the planet don't recognize Neil Armstrong as an astronaut and commander of the Apollo Lunar Module, *Eagle*, and as the first man to step on the surface of the Moon. However, fewer individuals know that Neil's interest in aviation was spurred by his involvement in model aviation in his youth and during his formative years at Purdue University.

When asked how big of a role aeromodelling played in Neil's endeavors, Neil's brother Dean said, "Enormous!" And, perhaps Neil said it best in his letter to AMA Executive Director John Worth, "My model building and flying activities significantly contributed to my interest in aeronautics and was a primary force in directing my education toward aeronautical engineering."

This is by no means an isolated anecdote. Similar stories are told thousands of times over by aviators, engineers, and aviation career professionals around the country, and it is very much true in my own case. My interest in aviation was stimulated by my father's recounts of his experience as a Flying Fortress B-17 pilot during World War II, and it began in earnest when I flew my first control line model airplane at 6 years old.

This simple beginning led to receiving my first pilot's license upon graduation from high school, followed by a 27-year career in the military, 36 years in civil aviation, and a life-long involvement in the hobby culminating in being elected as president of the Academy of Model Aeronautics.

Model aviation is a hobby that touches the hearts and minds of individuals across the spectrum of life's journey. It's an educational tool in the development of life skills for our youth, it provides a wholesome and productive activity for young adults, it brings families together providing an active and unifying endeavor, and it becomes a social outlet and a therapeutic activity well into the golden years of the aeromodelling enthusiast.

Model aviation also provides a competition platform ranging from local fun flies and sporting events to regional and national competition leading to world-class international competition that climax in podium-level standings in world championship events under the banner of the Fédération Aéronautique Internationale. For more than a hundred years, competition has been the driving force behind innovation and new technologies within the aeromodelling pursuit and has directly translated into advancements in full-scale aviation.

I've known Patrick Sherman for a decade and have worked with him directly in training new entrants into both the uncrewed and crewed aviation arenas. He's a true professional, an ardent educator, and a consummate creator of innovative and effective educational materials. I think you'll find this book to be a treasure trove of concepts and ideas aimed at assisting the novice in getting involved in remote piloting, aeromodelling, and full-scale aviation. Enjoy the read.

Richard Hanson, President
Academy of Model Aeronautics

Preface

You'll figure this out for yourself eventually, so I'm just going to come right out and say it: I am going to deliberately withhold more information than I end up sharing with you. This may not sound like an especially compelling reason to keep reading. However, if you take a moment to consider why I'm making this choice, you might actually agree with me.

I have always believed that the greatest tragedy of the human condition is that we are unable to share wisdom as easily as we are able to share knowledge. If you want to understand how an internal combustion engine works or the history of the British Isles between the Fall of the Roman Empire and the Norman Conquest, I've got some good news for you: We've spent the past several thousand years perfecting techniques that allow us to take what one person knows and instill it in another person.

From the microprocessor to the locomotive and from crop rotation to high-rise architecture, every significant human accomplishment has been built upon understanding what our ancestors understood and then improving on it. This capacity to create and share knowledge—which I would describe as the characteristic that most distinguishes humans from every other life form that we have encountered so far—has enabled our greatest achievements.

However, despite this extraordinary capability, it seems that each new generation must discover wisdom for itself, by trial and error. We can teach people about genetic engineering and orbital mechanics, but as any parent will tell you, we can't teach people that actions have consequences. We can't teach them that bullies are cowards or that thinking about a problem is no substitute for doing the work. It seems that each of us must learn these lessons for ourselves through lived experience—and then watch as the next generation painfully learns those same lessons.

I am not going to propose a solution to this problem: I'll leave that to the philosophers and theologians. I'm just a pilot, these issues are well above my pay grade. Nevertheless, my recognition of this problem has informed the knowledge that I will seek to share with you across these pages. I have taken my best guess about what you need to know as a person who is getting started with drones and model airplanes and eschewed everything that doesn't fulfill that mandate.

Nearly every single sentence you will read between the covers of this book could be expanded upon with a more thorough and comprehensive explanation, each of those explanations could then be expanded upon, as well, again and again, until this book became an encyclopedia. If I were to delve more deeply, however, as a novice I believe you would have trouble distinguishing between those things you need to understand *right now* and those things you can discover for yourself throughout your own journey in aviation.

If a career spent writing has taught me anything, it's that what you don't say is often as important as what you do say. Too much information can be overwhelming, confusing, and ultimately result in less knowledge being meaningfully transmitted to the reader. That's my theory, anyway. You can let me know how it works out for you.

Remember that the only true source of wisdom is experience—and experience is a hard teacher because it gives the test first and the lesson second. My goal, based on my own experience and the insight of many colleagues, is to guide you as to what experiences you should seek out, and those you should seek to avoid.

In keeping with the idea of trying to share wisdom and not just knowledge, I would like to suggest that almost everything you will read in this book has the goal of providing you with *context* for the learning you will do after you are finished reading it. I always tell my students that my goal is not to teach you the rules and the facts: You can look those up for yourself on the Internet in a few seconds. My goal is to teach you how to *think* about the rules and the facts and where to find them when the need arises.

1

First, Do No Harm

The words "first, do no harm" were first spoken nearly 2,500 years ago by the philosopher Hippocrates (Figure 1.1) who was born on the island of Kos in Greece. A physician, by profession, he established the ethical framework that has guided Western medicine for more than two millennia, right down to this very day. Before you flip back to the cover to make sure you're reading the right book, yes, we're here to learn how to fly drones and model airplanes—and neither medical ethics nor Greek philosophy will feature prominently in our discussion moving forward.

1.1 / Although he never saw a flying machine, the wisdom of Greek physician and philosopher Hippocrates is invaluable to us as pilots—or, at the very least, to me.

I learn best if I understand *why* I'm learning something and for me that starts with Hippocrates's famous admonition. Maybe you're different—and that's fine. If you want to jump ahead to another chapter and get into the details of remote piloting, please feel free. My hope is that you will *explore* this book, rather than merely reading it, and that means making your own choices about what is important and what you can save for later.

As a remote pilot, I personally rely on that phrase, "first, do no harm," to remind me about what is important when I go flying—and it isn't me and it certainly isn't my aircraft. What *is* important is the injury and damage my aircraft could inflict on other people and their property. It is a reminder that I have an overriding duty to sacrifice my aircraft without hesitation should it endanger another person, which in itself is a compelling motivation to avoid creating that situation in the first place.

At first glance, the potential hazard may seem quite small. After all, how much damage can a small foam airplane or a palm-sized drone really cause? It turns out that the answer is, "Quite a bit." Studies have revealed that a common drone, the DJI Phantom 4 (Figure 1.2), can inflict a lethal injury on a person *wearing a hardhat* if it falls from an altitude of only 25 feet. Drop almost anything from 400 feet (which, as we'll learn in chapter 2, is the maximum altitude that drones are allowed to fly) and it has the potential to maim or kill.

WHAT DID HIPPOCRATES ACTUALLY SAY?

It turns out that you and I have both been misled by all those medical dramas on television. Not only are those famous words, "first, do no harm," not at the start of the Hippocratic Oath, Hippocrates never even said them. They are most likely the invention of a 19th Century English surgeon named Thomas Inman.

Of course, Hippocrates spoke and wrote ancient Greek, so everything we know of him today is necessarily a translation. He does appear to have put a heavy emphasis on that basic sentiment, requiring physicians to swear, "I will do no harm or injustice to [my patients]." As ever, I suppose it's the thought that counts.

Getting Started With Drones and Model Airplanes

1.2 / Like all but the very smallest and most light-weight drones, the DJI Phantom 4 has the potential to inflict lethal injuries and significant property damage.

Furthermore, the weight and altitude of small aircraft aren't the only threats that they pose. Keep in mind that most of these machines are kept aloft by propellers turning thousands of times per minute. These are capable of inflicting multiple lacerations before a person even knows what is happening, and even before their natural reflexes can move them out of harm's way.

A propeller strike to the soft tissues of the face or other sensitive parts of the body has the potential to blind or disfigure someone for life. To be clear, that someone could be *you*. Remember, you've made a choice to embark upon this journey, and to educate yourself regarding the dangers, but the young couple pushing their newborn baby in a stroller through the park where you happen to be flying has made no such choice. Imagine the long-term impact of an accident on them, then consider the impact on you, your liability, your emotions, your mental health, and your passion for aviation. These losses are unnecessary and avoidable.

I hope you now understand why I begin each flight by reminding myself, "First, do no harm."

SAFETY FIRST

By becoming a remote pilot, even if you are only flying for fun, you are becoming a member of the broader aviation community. Spend any time at all with pilots, airplane mechanics, air traffic controllers, or anyone else associated with this community, and you will quickly find that one overriding goal binds us all together: safety.

Safety is—and must be—the first and last thought of every aviator, and that includes you. In each of the subsequent chapters in this book, you'll see how time and again our conversation turns to safety. The importance of this topic simply cannot be overstated, and if you cannot abide by everything that is required to maintain it, then flying drones and model airplanes might not be the right hobby for you.

That said, safety does not require the complete elimination of all risk, because that would be impossible. The only way to reduce the risk of flying to zero is to not fly at all, and millions of people fly drones and model airplanes every day, and they do it safely. Safe flying requires an understanding of the risks involved and how to mitigate them. Start by following the rules, knowing the environment where you are flying, understanding how your aircraft works and the potential hazards it poses to you and other people, and—the most important of all—recognizing your own limitations. Flying will teach you who you are, along with a great many other things.

> **"Once you have tasted flight, you will forever walk the earth with your eyes turned skyward, for there you have been, and there you will always long to return."**
>
> – Leonardo da Vinci,
> Italian Polymath

Part of being safe also means having a backstop in the event of a catastrophe, both to protect yourself and to make whole, as best as possible, anyone who suffered injuries or losses as a result. Carrying liability insurance that covers the operation of drones and model airplanes provides that protection. The airlines have it, charter operators have it, responsible general aviation pilots have it, and you should, too (it's absurdly cheap).

Since 1937, the *Academy of Model Aeronautics (AMA)* has been the governing body for model aviation in the United States. A private, nonprofit organization, the AMA is led by a board of directors elected by members in 11 regional districts and a president elected by the general membership. Full membership costs less than $100 per year and includes a wealth of benefits, including a monthly magazine, access to local flying fields, and a $2.5 million liability policy.

Set everything else aside and focus on that number for a minute: You get $2.5 million in protection for less than $9 per month. You'd be barking-at-the-moon crazy not to grab hold of a deal like that this instant. Oh, and did I mention that membership (including that necessary insurance) is just $15 a year for children under the age of 19?

Before you ask: Yes, I am a member of the AMA, but I am not a paid spokesperson. If the last couple of paragraphs have come across like a sales pitch, I apologize. But the thought of someone losing their home and their life savings through civil action following an accident involving a drone or model airplane makes me heartsick, as does the possibility of the victim of such an accident having to forego treatment and compensation while waiting for a case to make its way through the courts. If you can afford a drone or a model airplane, you can certainly afford this. 'Nuff said.

IS A MODEL AIRPLANE A DRONE?

It turns out that, from a legal perspective, it's almost impossible to distinguish between a drone and a model airplane—as we will discuss further in Chapter 2. Because of this, the *Federal Aviation Administration (FAA)*, as the regulator charged with maintaining the safety of the United States *National Airspace System (NAS)*, refers to both with a single, catch-all designation: *uncrewed aircraft systems (UAS)*.

So, is a model airplane a drone? Or is a drone a model airplane? The answer is neither, because both are UAS—and most of the time they are *small UAS (sUAS)* because they weigh less than 55 pounds. By the way, professional drone pilots almost never actually use the word "drone" but instead refer to their flying machines as UAS, which I suppose makes them professional UAS pilots.

For the purposes of this text, however, we will eschew jargon and go right on calling drones "drones." With that said, even the term *drone* needs to be refined a little further before we can be sure we're all talking about the same thing. After all, the RQ-4 Global Hawk is an uncrewed aircraft system with a wingspan of 131 feet that weighs 15,000 pounds at takeoff, and it is commonly referred to as a drone (Figure 1.3). However, if you're planning to fly an RQ-4 yourself, you are *definitely* reading the wrong book.

1.3 / No one would dispute that the RQ-4 Global Hawk is a drone. However, if you are planning on flying one, expect you're going to require training that goes well beyond the contents of this book.

Within these pages, when I use the word "drone," I will almost always be referring to a machine with at least four propellers (commonly referred to as multirotor) oriented parallel to the ground that generally flies like a helicopter and carries a camera that sends real-time video back to a pilot on the ground (Figure 1.4). It's important to realize that there are other kinds of drones as well, such as fixed-wing varieties that might almost be mistaken for model airplanes if not for their payloads and price tags (Figure 1.5). These can be valuable tools in the hands of professional UAS pilots, but they have no role in recreational flying and thus will not be a topic of further discussion in this book.

1.4 / When I use the word "drone" in the pages of this book, this is the type of aircraft that I have in mind.

1.5 / Although it may resemble a model airplane, the Parrot Disco has been fitted with specialized sensors that allow it to monitor the health of crops and put it well beyond the budget of most recreational pilots.

1.6 / Part of the fun of aeromodeling is the chance to fly realistic, scale models of actual airplanes, like this T-28 Trojan.

Model airplane people are generally easy-going and are happy to refer to their flying machines as "model airplanes" and "model helicopters." When I use these terms in this book, I will be referring to an uncrewed aircraft that resembles a crewed aircraft of the same configuration. Indeed, particularly among airplanes, these are often scale recreations of specific aircraft, complete with color schemes and markings that are meant to evoke their full-sized counterparts (Figure 1.6). Remote-control helicopters tend to be a little more stylized in their appearance, but you'll never have any doubt about what they are when you're looking at one.

Even this distinction between drones and model aircraft is more slippery than it seems. For example, what happens if you mount a video camera and transmitter on a model airplane and watch the feed from the ground? Does it become a drone? What if you do the same thing with a model helicopter? That would allow you to duplicate all the essential functions of a drone, so does it become a drone at that point, or is it still a model helicopter? What if you remove the camera from a drone and paint it up with a World War II camouflage scheme, is it still a drone or is it now a model aircraft?

The impossibility of parsing these distinctions is why the broader category of UAS was necessary in the first place. Thinking about this stuff too much makes my head hurt, so for our purposes, a drone is a drone, and a model aircraft is a model aircraft. If you're confused about which is what, you're thinking too hard.

WHY DO WE CALL THEM "DRONES," ANYWAY?

If you have even a passing familiarity with entomology, you may already be aware that the word "drone" originally referred to a male bee. It still does, actually. And, as it happens, there is a direction connection between this fact and the reason we call uncrewed aircraft "drones."

Our story begins in the United Kingdom after World War I. The Royal Navy realized that these newfangled airplanes posed a serious threat to its warships, which had allowed Britain to rule the waves for centuries. There was a pressing need to teach antiaircraft gunners how to shoot accurately, but the problem defied an easy solution.

You see, in combat, the deck upon which the guns were mounted would pitch and roll as the ship maneuvered to avoid hostile fire, and the enemy planes would be dodging and weaving for the very same reason. There simply was no way to simulate all the complexities this situation entailed, so the only viable solution was to have trainees shoot at real airplanes from real ships.

Due to a lack of volunteers, the British developed the "Queen Bee"—the world's first remote-control airplane, built from a full-sized trainer, the De Havilland Tiger Moth. Witnessing a training exercise involving the Queen Bee, a visiting American admiral was so impressed with that he ordered one of his subordinates, Lt. Cmdr. Delmar Fahrney, to develop a similar system. Fahrney ended up naming his creation the "drone" as a tip of the hat to its British progenitor, and the name stuck.

Prime Minister Winston Churchill attends the launch of a radio-controlled Queen Bee, from which the modern word "drone" takes its inspiration.

FIRST, HAVE SOME FUN

The primary focus of this book will be on *recreational flying*—that is, simply to enjoy flying for its own sake. As we'll learn in Chapter 2, the FAA makes a fundamental distinction between flying for fun and flying for some economically beneficial purpose like monitoring crop health or selling aerial photographs.

This closely parallels the path taken by crewed aviators, who begin their careers as *private pilots*. Private pilots are prohibited from carrying passengers for hire, for example. Before they can do that, they must first achieve their *Commercial Pilot* Certificate, which requires additional aeronautical knowledge and experience as well as passing another round of tests.

Just because private pilots cannot be hired to fly passengers or cargo doesn't mean the knowledge and experience they gain while flying as a private pilot is any less valuable. Indeed, their logbooks must demonstrate they have flown a specified number of hours under different conditions before they can achieve a commercial pilot certificate.

There is no such requirement when it comes to drones and model airplanes. If you are prepared, you can go out tomorrow and take the test to become a *remote pilot-in-command (RPIC)* under *Part 107*. I hasten to add that the fact you are reading this book suggests you are not prepared, as passing that test requires additional knowledge about the NAS and *Federal Aviation Regulations (FARs)*, among other topics, beyond what we will be discussing here.

If becoming a commercial drone operator is your ultimate goal, this book will help you establish a solid foundation of aeronautical knowledge that will serve you well. The Remote Pilot Certificate with sUAS rating is unique among certifications in that it is the only certificate that doesn't require you to demonstrate any sort of proficiency in the aircraft you intend to fly.

That said, nothing is more embarrassing than being a pilot who doesn't actually know how to fly, so take my word for it, you're starting in the right place. Furthermore, recreational flying offers immense advantages, starting with the fact that it's a lot of fun! Also, you get to take advantage of the low-cost liability insurance provided by the AMA. If you think that's expensive, wait until you're paying for a policy to cover commercial operations—those will take your breath away.

So, start small. Learn your craft, acquire new knowledge and skills, and make some friends along the way. Truth be told, I enjoy my recreational flying much more than my commercial work, because it is the only time I can focus entirely on flying for its own sake, and isn't that opportunity to commune with the air what motivates us to become aviators in the first place?

> "I fly because it releases my mind from the tyranny of petty things."
>
> – Antoine de Saint-Exupery, Pioneering French Aviator and Writer

COMING TO TERMS

Since you're reading a book titled *Getting Started with Drones and Model Airplanes*, I'm going to assume that you are new to flying. Congratulations and welcome to the club. We're glad to have you with us. Now, like any specialized field of human endeavor—be it downhill skiing or organic chemistry—aviation has developed its own unique language to describe what we do.

Right up until this moment in your life, you've never needed formal vocabulary to describe ascending into the air because it's something you've never done before. Furthermore, as we'll learn in Chapter 4, even ordinary words that we think we understand—like *left* and *right*—take on new meaning once we are capable of maneuvering in three dimensions instead of only two.

My point is this: Learning new words, and new meanings for old words, is going to be a crucial component of your journey. The first time I use a word that I believe will be new to you, I will present it in ***bold italic*** type. I assume you know what bold italic type is (that was just an example). Even if it's the exact same word or phrase, I'll do the same thing in every chapter throughout the book.

My goal here is two-fold: First, to facilitate your self-guided exploration of the text. Just because I organized this material in chapters 1 through 10 doesn't mean you need to read it that way. Remember, I'm hoping you *explore* this book and make your own choices about what is important and what you can save for later. Second, I'm hoping to help you understand the connections between these various topics. None of the subjects we will be discussing stands alone. You can't truly understand how the different parts of your aircraft (Chapter 5) allow it to maneuver without understanding aerodynamics (Chapter 4). It's impossible to select a flying site (Chapter 7) unless you understand the rules and regulations that govern remote piloting (Chapter 2).

Most of the time, I will go on to describe the meaning of this new vocabulary as plainly as I am able, so that you can come to understand it yourself. There are a few instances where I will mention a term in bold italic type in passing and *not* define it. This is neither an oversight nor an attempt on my behalf to be deliberately obtuse. Rather, it reflects my judgment that you don't need to understand that term to achieve your goals *right now*. (Though if your curiosity demands, you can look for them in the truncated glossary at the end of the book or for the full glossary check out the Reader Resources available at asa2fly.com/modelair.)

> "There's a big difference between a pilot and an aviator. One is a technician; the other is an artist in love with flight."
>
> – E. B. Jeppesen,
> Pioneering American Aviator

As you gain knowledge and improve your skills as an aviator, you will need to understand these terms and the ideas they represent—but trying to explain them at this juncture would be counterproductive to what we are trying to accomplish here. Think of these as a trail of breadcrumbs that I'm leaving you, to facilitate your continued learning once you have taken all that you can from this book.

One final note on the language of flight: Pilots *love* acronyms. Just consider the few we've surfaced so far in this chapter: AMA, FAA, FARs, NAS, RPIC, sUAS, and UAS, and that's with me doing my best to avoid them! There isn't much more to be said on this point, except that you need to be prepared for a hearty serving of alphabet soup if you want to be a pilot.

CHARTING A COURSE

All that remains now is for you to begin exploring the world of drones and model airplanes. I've done my best to prepare this text so that you can explore these 10 chapters in any order. With that said, I did take care so that if you read through them in the order they are presented, the knowledge you acquire from each one will serve as a foundation for the knowledge you acquire in the next.

That's all well and good, but it also means we don't get around to putting hands on a controller to go flying until Chapter 8. Since you are presumably interested in getting started with drones and model airplanes, I'll understand if you want to skip ahead to the good part. However, I would encourage you to read the first eight chapters before making any big decisions about your career as a remote pilot—like, for example, spending more than $200 on hardware or trying to fly an aircraft that doesn't fit comfortably in the palm of your hand (Figure 1.7).

1.7 / Do us both a favor: Before you purchase a model that costs more than $200, weighs more than 250 grams, or doesn't fit comfortably in the palm of your hand, try to get through at least the first eight chapters in this book.

The last two chapters go beyond the fundamentals and explore specialized activities you might enjoy as a remote pilot. We'll take a look at the basics of aerial photography and how you can begin to capture beautiful images using a flying camera. We'll also look at the wide range of aeromodelling pursuits—from pylon racing to drone soccer—with a particular focus on *first-person view (FPV) flying* (Figure 1.8).

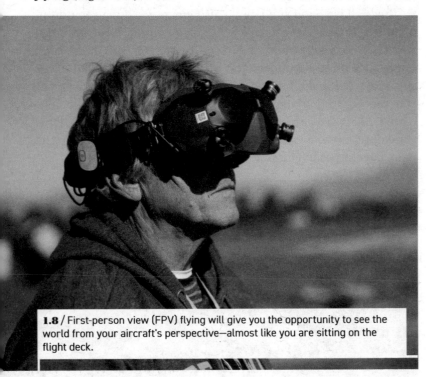

1.8 / First-person view (FPV) flying will give you the opportunity to see the world from your aircraft's perspective—almost like you are sitting on the flight deck.

Here's an outline you can use to chart your course moving forward:

CHAPTER 1—FIRST, DO NO HARM

We will begin by considering the potential hazard remotely piloted aircraft can pose to others and the importance of mitigating… Wait a minute, you just finished reading this chapter, I hope you remember what it was about.

CHAPTER 2—TIME FOR A LITTLE R&R: RULES AND REGULATIONS

It's important to understand the rules that govern the operations of drones and model aircraft because you can be penalized for breaking them and because they have been developed first and foremost with safety in mind. Following the rules means flying safely, and that *must* always be your top priority. This chapter lists and explains the rules you are expected to follow as a recreational remote pilot, including taking a free, online test before you start flying and registering your aircraft. It also describes the resources you have available to make sure you are following the rules, for example, determining whether or not you are in controlled airspace and getting permission to fly there.

CHAPTER 3—THE MANY DIFFERENT TYPES OF AIRCRAFT

Different types of aircraft have different performance characteristics, and as a pilot, it is critical for you to understand the capabilities and limitations of each. This chapter divides the different types of aircraft you are likely to encounter into progressively narrower categories, beginning with top-level distinctions such as lighter-than-air versus heavier-than-air, fixed-wing aircraft versus rotorcraft, and then describing with increasing nuance the differences within each general type. This understanding will allow you to select an aircraft that is appropriate for your flying environment, skill level, and mission.

CHAPTER 4—AERODYNAMICS: A DANGEROUSLY INCOMPLETE EDUCATION

Aerodynamics is the science of flight. As a pilot, it is crucial for you to understand how it is possible for a machine that weighs substantially more than the air it displaces to nevertheless fly as well as the circumstances under which these principles fail, because they are all that distinguish "flying" from "falling." In addition, this chapter will describe the specialized language we use to describe movement through the air and the mechanisms that allow a remote pilot to control an aircraft in flight.

CHAPTER 5—BITS AND PIECES: WHAT'S ON THE INSIDE?

This chapter describes the function of the components that make it possible for a drone or model airplane to fly and maneuver. These include the onboard electronics and sensors and electromechanical systems such as motors and servos and their operating principles. It also examines the use of radio waves to carry command-and-control inputs from the remote pilot to the aircraft and video and telemetry back to the pilot. It concludes with a discussion of *lithium-polymer (LiPo)* batteries and their inherent—and very substantial—hazards.

CHAPTER 6—HOW TO LEARN HOW TO FLY

You can learn how to be a remote pilot in many different ways, and not all of them involve trundling down to the local hobby shop, buying a model, and tossing it into the air. In this chapter, we'll look at how you can use a simulator to begin to develop your piloting skills without putting an aircraft (or anything else) at risk. We'll also look at how you can use electronic and human copilots to help you get out of trouble and, better still, avoid it in the first place. Finally, we'll consider remote piloting as a perishable skill and discuss how to maintain proficiency.

CHAPTER 7—SPACES AND PLACES: CHOOSING WHERE TO FLY

In this chapter, we'll discuss how to select an appropriate flying site, including safety and regulatory compliance, as well as the characteristics of your flying machine and what you are hoping to accomplish by flying in the first place. We'll discuss a range of specific environments, from cities to mountain peaks, from deserts to the seashore, and the potential hazards they pose to you, your aircraft, and the safety of your operations.

CHAPTER 8—HOW DO I WORK THIS THING!?

It's finally time to put our thumbs on the sticks and pilot a machine into the air! First up, we'll learn that it's critical to distinguish between which way you are facing and which way your aircraft is facing. We'll also learn how your aircraft responds to the movement of each stick in each axis and describe a few basic maneuvers and learn what is required to take off and, most especially, to land safely. In addition, we will consider appropriate precautions we can take to mitigate the risk to bystanders.

CHAPTER 9—AERIAL PHOTOGRAPHY PRIMER

The explosion of interest in remote piloting over the past several years is largely owed to the opportunity for anyone (including you) to capture aerial imagery. What was once the purview of a wealthy few is now available to millions. Of course, there is a difference between simply capturing aerial imagery and capturing *good* aerial imagery. In this chapter, we'll take a look at some basic techniques you can use to up your game.

CHAPTER 10—MORE WAYS TO FLY (AND HAVE FUN)

Recreational remote piloting offers plenty of opportunities for excitement, although perhaps none so arresting as ***first-person view (FPV)*** flying: The pilot wears a pair of video goggles and views the world from the perspective of his or her aircraft. It's like being on the flight deck as you experience the speed and thrills of racing other pilots or maneuvering through an obstacle course. We'll also look briefly at traditional aeromodelling activities, including some that don't even involve radio control. And did you know the fastest speed ever recorded for a model airplane wasn't a jet? It was a glider!

That's what you can expect from the pages ahead...let's get started!

2

Time for a Little R&R: Rules and Regulations

Ah, the sky, a boundless realm of humanity's ultimate aspiration: to fly free, like a bird, unconstrained by the petty concerns of those who dwell on the ground below. The only problem is that someone forgot to tell the *Federal Aviation Administration (FAA)*. Although it may be disappointing to learn, there are rules that we must follow even while we fly, and it's crucial for you, as a pilot, to understand them. This is true both because you might face penalties for breaking them but, more importantly, because they have been established to ensure the safety of those above and below.

HAVE A NAS DAY

The best way to begin to understand the expectations that are placed upon you as a recreational remote pilot is by acknowledging that everything that happens in the air is part of a single, coherent structure: the *National Airspace System (NAS)*. From privately built rockets blasting into orbit to your first, tentative flight with a drone or model airplane, all of it takes place within the NAS. Obviously, a very different level of regulatory scrutiny is applied to those two activities, but the key point to understand is that they both exist on a single continuum.

The NAS is a peculiar sort of entity, so much so that it defies easy explanation or understanding through an analogy. At the risk of veering into philosophy, it might be plausible to describe it like a shared vision, or hallucination. You can find physical artifacts connected with it in the real world—colorful maps and rule books and radio beacons and computer servers—but the NAS only truly exists because all of us believe it exists.

Perhaps it's a bit like money: the scraps of paper in your wallet and numbers on a computer screen have no intrinsic value whatsoever, except for the value that we all ascribe to them. If we were to stop believing in their value, chaos and mayhem would surely ensue. So, as a newly minted participant in the NAS, it's your job to believe in it and commit yourself to its continuity and success, because without it, the limitless benefits of aviation would be lost to all of us.

By now, you're probably thinking to yourself, "Well, that's all fine and dandy, but I'd be willing to bet $20 that none of it will be on the test." And, you'd be $20 richer for having made that bet. So, let's take a look at the concrete manifestations of the NAS that you will be interacting with as a recreational remote pilot:

- Rules and regulations
- Certification standards
- Aircraft registration and equipage
- Airspace types and requirements
- Exigent circumstances

We'll spend the rest of this chapter looking at each of these subjects in turn. As we do, keep the concept of ***procedures*** front and center in your mind. A procedure is basically a standardized means of accomplishing a task, and in aviation, boy, do we *love* our procedures (Figure 2.1). Do you want to earn a certification? There's a procedure for that. Do you want to access controlled airspace? There's a procedure for that. Do you need to check for exigent circumstances in your area of operations? There's a procedure for that—and it goes on and on and on…

2.1 / One of the most important procedures in all of aviation, a preflight inspection of the aircraft, is required in both recreational and commercial operations. For professionals, this often entails the use of a printed checklist.

As a recreational remote pilot, your procedures can be pretty informal, except when you are interacting directly with the NAS. Of course, I'll spell out all the details for you as we go, so that you don't miss anything. First and foremost, it's important to understand that procedures are basically the glue that holds the other components of the NAS together—and not all of them are explicitly mandated by the rules. Some have grown up over the decades as norms and customs. A few of those reach across the entire aviation community, but some may be associated with one particular model airplane field or local park where people enjoy flying drones.

Furthermore, developing your own procedures and sticking to them can help improve your own consistency, and therefore safety, as a pilot. From this moment forward, before you do anything involving aviation, stop and ask yourself: Is there a procedure? If so, what is it? If not, should I create my own? Who knows, maybe 100 years from now aviators will be doing something before every flight that you came up with. That's how our community advances, by learning from each other and putting safety first.

FOLLOW THE RULES...BUT WHICH RULES?

So, like driving a car or crossing an international border, there are rules that apply to remote piloting, as well as consequences for violating those rules. Understanding the rules is important, and I'll outline and explain them in a minute. First, I have to let you in on a secret: Remote piloting in the United States isn't governed by one set of rules, there are actually two. Furthermore, which set of rules applies to you depends entirely on what is motivating you to fly at that moment. If you're flying for fun, it's one set; if you're flying professionally, for compensation, it's the other one. It's even possible for the rules to change from one to the other while you are in flight. Crazy, right?

The recreational rules, which will be our primary focus in this book, can be found in *Section 44809 of Title 49 of the United States Code (USC)*, except that instead of actually writing out the word "section" the cool kids use this weird little squiggly mark: "§," so, you typically see this in print as *§44809*. The other set of rules, governing professional operations, is found in *Title 14 of the Code of Federal Regulation (CFR) Part 107*. Because it's a part not a section, it doesn't get a little squiggly, so we just call it *Part 107* for short.

The first thing to know about these two sets of rules is that Part 107 is the default. If you just take a drone and start flying without the slightest attention to any of the rules or regulations and you have the misfortune to draw the gaze of the FAA, your actions will be judged against the standards of Part 107, as that's what Part 107 is: the standard for operating uncrewed aircraft that weigh less than 55 pounds.

> **"Rules are for the obedience of fools and the guidance of wise men."**
>
> – Harry Day,
> Royal Air Force pilot

Generally speaking, Part 107 is stricter than §44809, so this will not work to your advantage. That's a key reason why it's worthwhile to take the necessary steps and follow the rules to fly under §44809. Also, it's much easier to qualify as an operator under §44809 than Part 107, so if recreational flying is your goal, it's the smart move, plain and simple.

The second thing to understand is that recreational operations, as defined by §44809, are extremely limited, and professional operations, as defined under Part 107, are extremely broad. Technically, Part 107 regulates the use of drones for commercial activities, and the word "commercial" is generally understood to involve an exchange of money for goods or services. So, if your neighbor pays you $50 to inspect her roof with your drone, that's obviously a commercial operation because money changed hands.

However, if you offer to inspect your neighbor's roof for free, that *still counts as a commercial operation* because she derives economic value from it. Were it not for your generosity, she would presumably have to pay someone else to do the work. So, §44809 truly is limited to flying for fun. In the words of the regulation itself: "*The aircraft is flown strictly for recreational purposes.*"

USC AND CFR!? ISN'T ONE CODE ENOUGH?

At first glance, having both a United States Code (USC) and a Code of Federal Regulations (CFR) may seem like the height of bureaucratic folly, and one more triumph for the Department of Redundancy Department. However, there is a critical distinction between the two, and it's worth understanding.

The USC is literally the law of the land, as written and passed by Congress and signed by the President. The CFR, however, takes a rather more circuitous route into existence. Sometimes, when dealing with a highly technical subject (like, say, aviation) Congress believes that the legislative process may be too slow to keep up with all the changes.

After all, the FAA is reauthorized by House and Senate once every five years, but significant breakthroughs in drone technology can occur once every five months, or every five minutes. Given that this years-long lag could be lethal to the potential of a new and fast-changing industry, Congress delegates the authority to make rules to a specialized agency of the executive branch, in this case, the FAA.

Congress gives the FAA guidelines regarding what it expects to see in terms of regulation, but the agency makes the rules itself in accordance with the Administrative Procedures Act (APA).

In other words, for the privilege of being allowed to fly in compliance with the rules listed below, your only goal must be your own enjoyment. Do anything else and you're operating under Part 107, for which you are most likely not qualified, and that's a problem.

IS EDUCATION RECREATION? UMM . . . YES?

Clearly, receiving an education creates economic value for the student, perhaps the greatest single source of economic value an individual can realize in their lifetime. Therefore, students flying drones and model airplanes must operate under Part 107, right? Wrong.

Recognizing the incredible value remote piloting can bring to education—both in terms of inspiring students and helping them learn about a diverse range of topics that include aeronautics, mathematics, computers, engineering and so forth—policymakers included a carve-out for education in §44809.

You can find all the legal details about this exception in **Public Law 116-283, Section 10002**, but it basically states: Students who are enrolled in an accredited primary or secondary educational institution, or a Junior Reserve Officer Training Corps (JROTC) program, or any educational program chartered by an FAA-approved **community-based organization (CBO)**, may operate under §44809. Hooray!

Now, what about the teachers who are providing this education using drones or model airplanes, do they need to operate under Part 107? After all, they are realizing economic value from their efforts, in the form of their penurious salaries. The answer to that question is a solid maybe.

Provided that the teacher provides only "minimal assistance" to the student while operating the aircraft, and the course is not itself focused on aircraft operations but instead on the use of the aircraft for another purpose—like environmental monitoring, for example—then the instructor can squeak through under §44809, as well. Otherwise, they are required to hold a current **remote pilot-in-command (RPIC)** certificate under Part 107.

Personally, I'd suggest that teachers conducting any sort of drone or model airplane activities as part of their official duties should be qualified to operate under Part 107 as a matter of best practice. Not only will this ensure they meet a high standard of aeronautical knowledge, but it may also serve to inspire their students to attain certification, as well.

One more thing to be aware of before we launch into a discussion of the recreational rules themselves: They come from two completely difference sources, the FAA and a private, nonprofit organization. I know that this seems like a situation custom-engineered to maximize confusion when all you want to do is go flying. However, this arrangement is actually to your advantage. Allow me to explain.

Model aviation has a long history in the United States, with recreational radio-controlled flight getting its start in the late 1930s. Over the decades, it has enjoyed a remarkable safety record owed entirely to effective self-regulation, such that the FAA never actually imposed any rules on it at all. In 1981, it issued a one-page document *(Advisory Circular 91-57)* that amounted to some good advice for remote pilots, and which largely reflected what they were already doing.

Crucial to this success has been the *Academy of Model Aeronautics (AMA)*. Established in 1936—22 years before the FAA—the AMA has long maintained and published its own safety code for model aviation. Likely this happy arrangement would have continued for many decades more, except for the advent of drones. It turns out that from a regulatory perspective, it's almost impossible to distinguish a drone from a model airplane, but since federal regulation was deemed necessary to curb the enthusiasm of the early drone pioneers, that meant regulating model airplanes, as well.

I'm glossing over about a decade's worth of *sturm und drang* here, but the ultimate solution was to create §44809 and establish the AMA as a *community-based organization (CBO)*. The idea was that the FAA would create the bare minimum regulations and refer remote pilots to the CBO for the rest.

Remember I told you that this whole whackadoodle arrangement was to your advantage? Here's why: As a private organization, the AMA has much greater flexibility than the FAA to make changes to its safety code to keep pace with new technology and new aeromodelling activities. So, thanks to this public–private partnership, you have much greater freedom to fly as a recreational pilot than if the FAA was running the show all by itself.

RULES AND REGULATIONS

So, finally—without any further explanations, digressions, or provisos—here are the rules that govern recreational drone and model aircraft operations in the United States outlined in §44809:

- **The aircraft is flown strictly for recreational purposes.**
- **The aircraft is operated in accordance with or within the programming of a community-based organization's set of safety guidelines that are developed in coordination with the FAA.** Note that it is sufficient to operate "in accordance with" the safety guidelines of a CBO. You don't actually have to be a dues-paying member.
- **The aircraft is operated within visual line of sight of the person operating the aircraft or a visual observer co-located and in direct communication with the operator.** The phrase "visual line of sight" has a specific meaning here that isn't obvious from language or context alone. First of all, it means being able to see the aircraft with your own Mark 1 human eyeballs and without enhancement from anything other than prescription corrective lenses, so, no binoculars or telescopes allowed. Second, it means that you must be able to discern the aircraft's attitude (more on this in Chapter 4) and altitude as well as the surface it is flying above. Finally, a ***visual observer (VO)***, also referred to as a "spotter" in recreational operations, is someone who helps the pilot maintain visual contact with the aircraft (see Chapter 10).
- **The aircraft is operated in a way that does not interfere with and gives way to any [crewed] aircraft.** Like ships passing each other at sea and cars approaching an intersection, specific rules govern which aircraft has the right of way when they approach one another in the sky. The short version is this: Uncrewed aircraft are at the very bottom of the list—we yield to *everybody*. The definition of yielding included in Part 107, by way of reference, reads: "Yielding the right of way means that the small [uncrewed] aircraft must give way to the aircraft or vehicle and may not pass over, under, or ahead of it unless well clear."

- **When operating in [controlled airspace] the operator obtains prior authorization from [air traffic control] before operating and complies with all airspace restrictions and prohibitions.** Controlled airspace and its various classifications are an *extremely* complicated subject, such that you will only have a passing familiarity with it even if you read every word of this book. Heck, if I'm being honest, I didn't fully understand it even after I earned my private pilot's certificate. (Don't tell my pilot examiner, okay?) I'll describe what you need to know about airspace and what you need to do about it under the heading "Airspace Types and Requirements" later in this chapter.

- **The aircraft is flown from the surface to not more than 400 feet above ground level [except when a lower maximum altitude is required by operations occurring in controlled airspace].** The key takeaway from this point is that 400 feet above the ground is as high as drones and model airplanes are allowed to fly. There are, of course, exceptions—both higher and lower, even under the recreational rules—but fix the number "400" in the front of your brain as our general limit. Once again, I'll describe when lower limits are required while flying in controlled airspace in the "Airspace Types and Requirements" section.

- **The operator has passed an aeronautical knowledge and safety test…and maintains proof of test passage to be made available to the [FAA] or law enforcement upon request.** That's right: You're going to have to take a test before you can fly drones or model airplanes for fun, and the best part is that the test has an adorable name, *TRUST*, which is an acronym for *The Recreational UAS Safety Test*. Like I said, adorable! We'll discuss this requirement further in the "Certification Standards" section. Spoiler alert: It's easy.

- **The aircraft is registered and marked [with its registration number], and proof of registration is made available to the [FAA] or law enforcement upon request.** Just like a car, a boat, or a crewed airplane, you have to register your aircraft with the government and put a "license plate" on it. Once again, this isn't nearly as burdensome as it sounds, and we'll take a closer look at it under the heading "Registration and Equipage" in this chapter.

Next up, we're going to look at the requirements the AMA puts forth in its *AMA Member Safety Program Handbook*. It's available as a PDF download, for free, from the AMA's website at modelaircraft.org. Please take the time to read it for yourself as what I'm presenting here is necessarily a summary. Also, a few more notes before we begin:

- First, the safety code incorporates information about aeromodelling activities that do *not* involve radio-controlled aircraft, applications like Free Flight and Control Line. We'll revisit them briefly in Chapter 10, but I've excluded those portions of the safety code below to avoid confusion.
- Second, the AMA presents its rules and guidelines in a couple of different sections throughout the safety code document, which I've consolidated into a single list of bullet points for ease of comprehension.
- Third, the safety code incorporates and re-states every element of §44809 that we've already addressed above, so I've excluded them from the list below to avoid redundant redundancy.

Is all of that clear? Good! Buckle up, here we go:

- **Do not operate an aircraft in a careless or reckless manner.**
- **Do not operate an aircraft while you are under the influence of alcohol, drugs or any substance that could impair your performance.** Pilots of both crewed and uncrewed aircraft use a checklist to ensure that they are mentally prepared to fly, which they remember using the acronym IMSAFE, as in, "I'm safe." Get it?
  - » **Illness**—Am I suffering from any illness or symptoms which would impair my ability to fly safely?
  - » **Medication**—Am I taking any drugs, prescription, over-the-counter, or recreational, that would impact safety?

- » **Stress**—Am I currently experiencing any psychological pressure, related to the upcoming flight or not, which might adversely affect my performance?
- » **Alcohol**—Am I currently under the influence of alcohol?
- » **Fatigue**—Have I had sufficient sleep and adequate rest to perform at my best?
- » **Emotion**—Am I upset or angry?

- **Do not fly over unprotected persons, moving vehicles, or occupied structures.** A critical assumption that all good remote pilots make is that at any point during any fight, their aircraft could be magically transformed into a paperweight without warning and plunge uncontrolled toward the ground. If there are people, moving vehicles, or vulnerable property below it at the instant this happens, that's officially *a bad thing*. The only sure-fire way to prevent this bad thing from happening is to avoid flying over people, moving cars, etc. This rule also reflects an explicit requirement in Part 107.

WHY CAN'T WE FLY OVER MOVING VEHICLES?

It's easy enough to understand why flying a battery-powered weed whacker over people is a bad idea, but why aren't we allowed to fly over moving vehicles? After all, there isn't much chance a one-pound foam airplane is going to punch through somebody's windshield and maul them.

True enough, but that's not the threat that the AMA was seeking to guard against when they established this rule. By the way, the FAA incorporated essentially the same rule in Part 107. In both cases, the reasoning is the same: Most likely, a modern automobile would be able to shrug off a hit from a two-pound aircraft.

However, this won't stop the startled driver from panicking and swerving into a tree following the impact. It's a legitimate concern, and the reason we don't fly over moving vehicles.

- **Do not operate an aircraft that weighs 55 pounds or more, including fuel, unless you are certified through the AMA's Large Model Airplane Program.** Again, this reflects a requirement under Part 107, which explicitly prohibits the operation of aircraft weighing 55 pounds or more. While this requirement can be waived by making an application to the FAA, the AMA offers a much easier path for recreational pilots.
- **Do not operate an aircraft powered by a jet turbine unless you are certified by and in compliance with the AMA's Gas Turbine Program.** We'll talk more about powering model airplanes using an actual, real-life, working jet engine in Chapter 3. Don't expect it's going to be cheap or easy.
- **Do not fly an airplane any closer than 25 feet from any person, excepting yourself and members of your flight crew, unless you are taking off, landing, or performing in accordance with the AMA's competition regulation.** As you are probably beginning to figure out on your own at this point, keeping aircraft and people separated from one another is a fundamental part of any remote pilot's job, because of the harm aircraft can inflict on people. Any doubts? Take an electric weed whacker to your face and see how that feels. The AMA's safety code, even more so than Part 107, lays out explicit measures you are required to take to ensure this separation. Always keep these in the forefront of your mind.
- **Use a safety line, also known as a *flight line*, to separate aircraft operations from spectators and bystanders.** The flight line is the ultimate tool for keeping people and aircraft separate. Go to almost any AMA flying field, and you'll likely find an actual line painted on the tarmac. People stay on one side of that line and aircraft—until they have stopped moving and been powered down—stay on the other side. Part 107 has no equivalent regulation, but it's an idea that I routinely draw upon while conducting professional drone operations. It's simple, and it works.
- **Be aware of and honor no-fly zones, whether they are temporary or permanent.** Some places you're never allowed to fly and other places you're sometimes not allowed to fly.

We'll examine this topic more closely under the heading "Exigent Circumstances."

- **Avoid intruding on the privacy of others while operating an aircraft equipped with a camera, like a drone.** Needless to say, a flying camera is an incredibly powerful tool for surveillance, along with more benign applications like capturing gorgeous aerial photographs. Unless you work in law enforcement and are executing a warrant signed by a judge, *never, ever* use a remotely piloted aircraft to capture imagery of any person where they would have a *reasonable expectation of privacy*. A person walking down a public street has no such expectation; a person standing in their fenced backyard does. If you wouldn't want it done to you, don't do it to anybody else. Exhibitionists need not apply.

- **Before and after each flight, inspect your aircraft to confirm it is in good condition to be operated safely.** This is a requirement in Part 107 and also in crewed aviation. Hopefully, this is tickling your "procedures" antenna, because it's a big one. Both crewed aviators and professional drone pilots use printed checklists to make sure they don't miss anything.

- **Always follow the manufacturer's guidelines regarding proper care and maintenance of your aircraft.** First, if they bothered to write about it in the manual, it's probably important. Second, it's helpful to understand that this is part of a long-standing requirement in crewed aviation: You are literally not allowed to take off unless you've got a copy of the aircraft flight manuals on board—they are that important. Remote piloting, whether recreational or commercial, hasn't quite reached this point yet, but I wouldn't rule it out at some point in the future. The takeaway is: Familiarize yourself with the manual and keep it handy for reference.

- **Fly well away from overhead electrical power lines. If your aircraft becomes entangled in power lines, do not attempt to retrieve it yourself. Contact the local utility for help.** I hope this goes without saying, but transmission lines are not something you want to be playing around with on your own: They can literally make you dead in a heartbeat (Figure 2.2). If you do end up with an aircraft snagged on a wire, I know it's embarrassing, but call the power company and wait for them to show up. They've seen worse—I guarantee it.

- **Devices that propel hazardous projectiles are prohibited.** Don't put a gun—or a missile, or a harpoon, or whatever else you can come up with—on your aircraft. Not only is it a violation of the AMA safety code *and* a spectacularly bad idea, but many states have passed laws against weaponizing remotely piloted aircraft. So, you could find yourself facing some serious criminal charges as a result.

- **Dropping any object that creates a hazard for persons and property on the ground is prohibited.** Notice that you're not allowed to drop an object that "creates a hazard" for persons and property on the ground. So, that means it's actually okay to drop an object from your aircraft provided it is harmless. What would this look like? Maybe you could drop an inert "bomb" during a demonstration with World War II era model airplanes. Use your imagination but be safe.

- **Visual observers, also known as spotters, must maintain their full and complete concentration on the aircraft and**

2.2 / Unless you are a professional doing a job that requires you to operate near power lines, keep well away. They pose a serious risk of collision and bring with them the potential of electromagnetic interference (EMI) to boot.

the surrounding airspace throughout the operation. We'll talk more about VOs in Chapter 10, but for the moment what matters is to realize that it's a full-time gig. If you're acting as a VO, you need to have your head up and your eyes on the sky, watching not only your pilot's aircraft but the surrounding airspace, just in case a Life Flight helicopter pops out from behind that nearby grove of trees.

CERTIFICATION STANDARDS

As a recreational pilot operating a drone or model airplane under §44809, you must pass a basic aeronautical safety test before you fly for the first time. It is known as *The Recreational UAS Safety Test (TRUST)*. The whole notion of taking a test, especially as a beginner, may seem daunting, but, trust me, it really isn't.

Indeed, it's actually a test that you *cannot* fail. It's multiple choice and if you do get a question wrong, you'll be asked the same question again—with the same answers available. A score of 100 percent is required to pass, but you could pass using simple trial and error even if you couldn't read the language being used to ask the questions. So, do *not* be intimidated. What is important is that you recognize the safest practices before your first flight.

Furthermore, the test will give you all the answers in a series of short educational briefings that precede each block of questions. On top of that you—yes, you—will be especially well equipped to take the test because I'm covering all of the material, well beyond the minimum requirements, in this chapter. If, despite that, you take the time to read all of the material closely and carefully think about your answers, the whole thing should take less than an hour.

So, with that pep talk and the realization that failure literally isn't an option, the only question left for a go-getter like you is, "Where do I take the test?" The answer, again, is simplicity itself. It's available online, for free, from a whole bunch of different groups and organizations. At the top of that list is the *AMA* itself, along with the *Boy Scouts of America*, and several other public and private educational organizations. I suppose that if I want my next performance review to go well, I should mention the fact that my employer, *Embry-Riddle Aeronautical University*, is among them.

You don't even need to create an account. Just find the test, click "START" and git 'er done!

Probably the most important part of the whole process comes at the end, when the website will give you the opportunity to download and print a certificate in PDF format, commemorating your accomplishment. This seems a little cheesy, I know, but it's a critical part of the process. You need to have a copy of that certificate with you at all times while you are flying (Figure 2.3). Upon request, you must present it to either an FAA representative or a member of the law enforcement community.

I'll assume you know best how to make this happen. Print it out and keep a copy in your flight bag. Laminate it and keep a copy in your wallet. Save it as an image on your phone. Be sure to keep a backup because, if you lose it, you'll need to take the test *again*! Of course, by then you'll be a seasoned remote pilot and you can bang the whole thing out in 10 minutes, like I did while preparing to write this section.

It's as easy as falling off a log, but without the risk of serious bodily injury. So, finish reading this chapter and go take the test. You'll be fine—TRUST me.

2.3 / The most important part of the TRUST test comes at the very end, when you will get the opportunity to print out or save your certificate. Remember, nobody but you is keeping track of this, so be sure to have backups available.

AIRCRAFT REGISTRATION AND EQUIPAGE

As I mentioned previously, you are *required to register your aircraft with the FAA*. Although, like the TRUST test, this process isn't nearly as rough as it sounds. To accomplish this task, you'll need to visit the ***FAA DroneZone*** on the Internet. The actual URL for the website changes occasionally, so it's probably best that you find it for yourself using a search engine, rather than relying on an address that I provide here, which might go out of date. Just remember that the FAA is a federal agency, so any legitimate website associated with it will end in a ".gov" suffix. If you see anything else, somebody is trying to scam you.

Another thing to watch out for: Some unscrupulous persons will offer to "help" you register your aircraft for a modest fee and will pay to have advertisements for their generous "services" appear above the actual FAA website in your search engine results. Eschew these rascals, you don't need them. The process is cheap and easy, and involving a third party in the process will only serve to increase the expense and likelihood of a problem.

It really is simple. First of all, as a recreational pilot, you only need to register once, no matter how many different aircraft you end up owning. It's different for commercial operators, who must individually register each aircraft in their fleets.

Before you shed too many tears on our behalf, recognize that the cost of registration is $5 and each one is valid for three years. For you, as a recreational pilot, that represents the sum total of your commitment, even if you eventually own 100 different aircraft. Also, if, like me, you end up flying both professionally and for fun, you can still use one registration number for all of your recreational aircraft while registering your commercial aircraft individually.

One final note: If you are flying for fun and your aircraft weighs less than 250 grams (that's 8.81 ounces for our American friends) you are not required to register it. However, if you're flying the same aircraft professionally, you *are* required to register it. I know: Who makes up all of these rules, and who can be expected to remember them all? If you ever have any doubts about whether or not to register, remember this: There is a fine for not registering, but no penalty for just going ahead and paying the $5. Just do it.

By definition, this book is not intended to prepare you to become a certificated **remote pilot-in-command (RPIC)** under Part 107. However, it's only natural that you should be curious about the process, so here is a quick overview.

The primary hurdle you will have to overcome is a 60-question **Airman Knowledge Test (AKT)**, which is administered at an FAA-approved testing center, typically located at smaller, general aviation airports. While obviously being focused on drones, the test shares a fair amount of content in common with the private pilot written exam.

You will have two hours to complete the test, and you'll pay for the privilege. A passing score is 70 percent, and if you don't pass, you'll need to wait two weeks before trying again—and paying again.

Even if you could recite the contents of this book by rote, you would not be prepared to take that test. You will have a strong foundation to move forward, if that's your goal, but you'll need to acquire a more detailed understanding of virtually every topic we cover, specifically the Part 107 rules and airspace.

While the regulatory outlines of §44809 and Part 107 are broadly similar, there are a lot of details about Part 107 that we haven't touched on here because, well, that's not the subject of this book. Also, there are even a few minor points of disagreement between §44809 and Part 107. Beyond that, you'll need to learn how to interpret **sectional charts** and gain a much more thorough understanding of the NAS.

Other requirements for becoming a Part 107 RPIC include:
- Being at least 16 years of age;
- Being able to read, write, and speak English; and,
- Being able to pass a background check by the Transportation Security Administration (TSA).

Anyway, the point is that registration is cheap, easy, and required by law, so find the FAA DroneZone website, create an account using your e-mail address and a password and pay the $5. When you do that, two very important things will happen. First of all, you will be given a registration number. It will be very long, include both letters and numbers, and will most likely start with "FA." You are required to mark this number legibly on an external surface of your aircraft (Figure 2.4).

2.4 / After you register your aircraft, you are required to display its FAA-issued registration number on an external surface. Legibility is mandatory. Using a label printer and matching-color labels is strictly optional.

It is perfectly acceptable to do this with a permanent marker. Obsessive types like me use a label maker to ensure a clean, professional appearance, but this is categorically *not* a requirement, so long as it's clear. By the way, verifying that your registration number is still affixed and legible should be one step in your pre-flight procedures.

At the FAA DroneZone, you will be provided with a registration card in PDF format. You should download this and, like your TRUST completion certificate, keep it with you at all times while you are flying. You are legally required to present your registration to an FAA representative or law enforcement officer upon request.

When it comes to the equipment required on board an aircraft in crewed aviation, the list goes on for pages. However, drones and model airplanes are only required to have one single item: a *remote identification* module. Remote identification, abbreviated *remote ID* or *RID*, is an on-board system that transmits a short-range radio signal—think of something along the lines of Wi-Fi—that includes basic information about your aircraft: a unique identifier for the drone, location, altitude, airspeed, and so forth. This is equivalent to the transponders carried on board crewed aircraft, except that those can be detected for miles around.

The idea is that if somebody gets up to no good with a drone or model airplane (like spying on someone in their back yard, for example) anybody with a cell phone and right app installed can capture that RID signal. The only identifying information your average citizen will be able to extract is that long, nonsensical identification number—basically like the license plate on a car (Figure 2.5).

2.5 / The FAA determined that the approach illustrated above wasn't practical for identifying drones and model airplanes in flight, so the agency settled on a system based on short-range radio transmissions known as remote identification (RID).

However, that person can then share that number with the FAA or law enforcement, who can use the registration database to identify the pilot behind that number and figure out what's happening. All drones and model airplanes manufactured today have a built-in RID capacity. If you're flying an older model, you may need to attach an external RID module. These are generally small enough and light enough that they will not adversely affect flight performance.

A final option when it comes to RID is not to use it at all—although, as you would expect, this requires playing by an entirely different set of rules. Acknowledging that there are many places where remote piloting has been happening for decades without causing any problems, mainly AMA flying fields, the agency created something called *FAA-Recognized Identification Areas (FRIAs)*. The name is somewhat ironic because remote identification is *not* required in these "identification zones," but we'll leave that to better minds than ours to sort out. Establishing a FRIA requires that the site be affiliated with a CBO or an educational institution and make an application to the FAA. Once the FRIA is approved, you can fly there without a RID module.

AIRSPACE TYPES AND REQUIREMENTS

As I alluded to earlier, airspace is a hugely complicated topic that can only be truly mastered through long, diligent study. I'm guessing that you didn't buy a book for beginners because you are interested in long, diligent study. You just want to know enough to be safe and stay out of trouble—and that's perfectly reasonable for a recreational remote pilot who is just getting started.

So, the first thing to know is that every cubic yard of free air above the United States to the edge of the atmosphere belongs to one of six categories of airspace: A, B, C, D, E, and G. That's not a typo—there is no "Class F" airspace.

The truth is a little more complicated than this, but for our purposes, Class A, B, C, D, and E are known collectively as *controlled airspace*. If you wish to fly an aircraft—be it an Airbus A380 or a foam model airplane—in controlled airspace, you must first receive permission from *air traffic control (ATC)*.

Class A airspace only exists above 18,000 feet *mean sea level (MSL)* and is the domain of commercial jetliners, so it is irrelevant for us remote pilots. Class B, C, D, and E airspace surround airports and exist to make safe and efficient use of that airspace for arriving and departing traffic. These four categories are ranked by their size and the volume of traffic they handle. Class B is the busiest, being centered around major international airports, and Class E is the least busy. What they all have in common is that a part of that controlled airspace reaches all the way down to the surface of the earth—specifically, that portion closest to the airport itself—and, in the case of Class B and C airspace, it expands outward at higher altitudes.

Generally speaking (and the word *generally* is doing a lot of heavy lifting here) the surface area of the controlled airspace surrounding an airport is circular and extends between 5 and 12 miles from the airport. Since as remote pilots we are *generally* limited to flying at 400 feet *above ground level (AGL)* or below, this is the only portion of controlled airspace that we *generally* need to worry about. If you want to fly in such a location, you'll need permission. More about how we get that in a minute, I promise.

Class G airspace, on the other hand, is *uncontrolled airspace*. You don't need permission from anybody to fly in Class G airspace. And here's a little more good news: below 700 feet AGL, Class G airspace is by far the most predominant type over the entire land area of United States. The other categories tend to be clustered in urban areas where larger airports are located.

Okay, so now that we understand that there are two basic categories of airspace—*controlled* and *uncontrolled*—the only remaining problem is to identify the boundaries between them. So, how do we do that? Well, crewed aviators and cranky old guys like me rely on *sectional charts*, essentially road maps for the sky. Believe it or not, you can still buy paper copies of them (Figure 2.6).

2.6 / Sectional charts are so densely packed with information that they don't lend themselves to easy interpretation by beginners—or anyone else, for that matter.

As much as I might enjoy it—in an "eat your Brussels sprouts" kind of way—teaching you to interpret sectional charts would probably require an additional book, so we'll put a pin in that for the moment. Instead, we're going to push the "Easy" button and use an app to do it for you. The app is called ***B4UFly*** and is available for free on iOS, Android, and via the web. Through the magic of the Internet, this app will pinpoint your current location and show you all of the surface-level controlled airspace in the vicinity, or across the whole country, if you want. Why don't you go ahead and try it right now? I'll wait.

Back so soon? My, you *are* a quick study! Okay, so now we can distinguish controlled airspace from uncontrolled airspace. How do we get permission to fly in controlled airspace?

To facilitate this process, the FAA has developed what are called **UAS facility maps** (see Figure 2.7) for hundreds of airports across the country. Basically, these take the controlled airspace surrounding each of these airports and chop it up into one-square-mile grids. Then, each grid square is assigned a maximum altitude AGL between 400 and zero. That is as high as you are allowed to fly a drone or model airplane anywhere in that square *with permission* from ATC, but without the need for further safety analysis by the FAA.

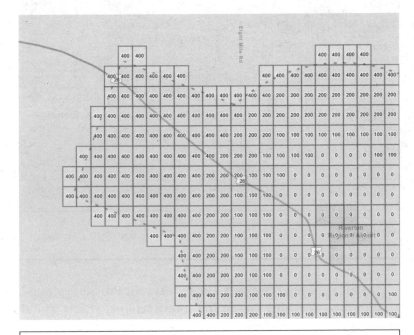

2.7 / UAS Facility Maps are available for hundreds of airports across the country and indicate the altitude to which a drone or model airplane may be flown with permission from ATC via the LAANC system.

Unlike crewed aviators, you will not obtain this permission by talking to ATC on the radio. Instead, you will use a system called the *Low-Altitude Authorization and Notification Capability* (*LAANC*; pronounced like "lance"). I warned you about how pilots love acronyms, didn't I?

You can access LAANC through several private, third-party providers, but ironically, not through B4UFly, even though it is the official FAA drone app. These come and go and change names every so often, so I'll leave it to you to find the one that suits you best. There is a full list of them on the FAA's website. You will need to register with your email address and password and provide your cell phone number. Once you sign up and input the details of your flight, you will get a text message back after just a few seconds informing you that your operation has been approved and providing a confirmation number. It's your call, but I always record these confirmation numbers in my logbook, just in case.

If, for some reason, you want to fly in a grid square marked with a zero, you can contact the FAA through the DroneZone and request an airspace authorization. This will require you to present a written safety case to the agency and wait several weeks, or longer, for a response, which may well include a request for even more information. As a professional drone operator, this authorization is part of the job. As a recreational operator, you are also entitled to avail yourself of this option, but why? There are plenty of other places to go flying with none of the hassle.

THAT WAS EASY

Whew! So how about that? In just a few short pages we've figured out everything we *need* to know about airspace. I mean, there is more we *could* know, but we know enough to pass TRUST and avoid flying dangerously close to airports. I mean, it's not like *20,000 airports are hiding out there* that barely show up on B4UFly and don't show up at all on LAANC because that would be insane! No competent civil aeronautics authority with safety as its top priority staffed by 35,000 highly trained professionals could possibly allow such a bizarre set of circumstances to occur, right? *Right!?*

Well, yeah, about that…I didn't want to scare you too badly right off the bat, so I left out this one minor detail. More airports are located in uncontrolled airspace—Class G—than in all of the other categories combined (about 20,000, in total). To understand how this can possibly be true, we need to understand a little bit more about what separates controlled airports from uncontrolled airports. The short answer is a control tower. No control tower, no controlled airspace.

So, these airports located in uncontrolled airspace are typically very small—private airstrips, helipads, crop-dusting bases, and so forth. Traffic is generally light enough that crewed aviators can coordinate and deconflict their operations among themselves over the radio using a *Common Traffic Advisory Frequency* (*CTAF*) (Figure 2.8).

2.8 / Professional remote pilots will use hand-held aviation radios to listen in on the radio chatter of crewed aircraft operating in their vicinity, to improve their overall situational awareness (SA).

As remote pilots, we are forbidden from interfering with crewed air traffic, so it is incumbent upon us to be aware of the location of *all* airports in the vicinity of our operations (not just the ones in controlled airspace) and take appropriate precautions. This will mean doing a little extra research if you intend to fly beyond established facilities, like AMA fields, but it's a small price to pay for safety.

EXIGENT CIRCUMSTANCES

In a world where nothing ever changes, we could end this chapter right here. However, in our world things do change, and as remote pilots, we need to be prepared to adapt to those changes. For our purposes here, these changes fall broadly into two categories: airspace and weather.

The airspace system as we've discussed so far does change, albeit very slowly. An airport is upgraded or downgraded from one class of airspace to another, enters service or is shut down, and so on. Sometimes change can happen in an instant: A wildfire breaks out, the police have to respond to a hostage situation, the local big-league team is playing a home game, or the president comes to town. Under these sorts of circumstances, the FAA will issue a *Temporary Flight Restriction (TFR)*. A TFR prohibits all non-participating aircraft—crewed and uncrewed alike—from entering the affected area without permission from the entity that requested the FAA establish the TFR in the first place.

> "The reality is that regulation often lags behind innovation."
>
> – Bill Maris,
> American Entrepreneur
> and Venture Capitalist

As an example, imagine a major wildfire. The response is likely to include lots of aircraft: air tankers, smokejumper drops, flying command posts, reconnaissance airplanes, and even drones, large and small. It would be dangerous for everyone involved, including the intruding aircraft, if some random Cessna 172 suddenly appeared in the midst of all this activity. So, emergency managers will request, and the FAA will grant, a TFR covering the area. This tells everyone else to keep clear until the emergency is over—and that includes you.

2.9 / It's perfectly legal to fly around stadiums or other major public venues (provided that the airspace is accessible) until there is an event that brings out the crowds. When that happens, the FAA will most likely issue a Temporary Flight Restriction (TFR) prohibiting non-participating aircraft from operating in the vicinity.

Under other circumstances, like a presidential visit or a major league sporting event, a TFR is established as a security measure. As we all learned to our collective horror on September 11, 2001, aircraft can become terrible weapons of destruction in the hands of fanatics. And, of course, the development of drones has even removed the requirement for self-sacrifice from the equation. So, to help guard against this type of attack, a TFR is used to limit access to the surrounding airspace so that any intruding aircraft can be assessed as a potential threat that much sooner (Figure 2.9).

As a remote pilot, it is your responsibility to be aware if any TFRs have been posted that will affect your operation. Helpfully, these will be displayed in B4UFly and LAANC authorization apps, but if you're simply heading out to fly at your favorite nearby park, you may not think to check in with them. Of course, you could make verifying airspace availability one of your pre-flight procedures.

Alternatively, you could check for *NOTAMs* in your local area. An acronym for *Notices to Air Missions*, NOTAMs are bulletins published by the FAA regarding a wide variety of aeronautical circumstances and events. These can range from a taxiway being closed at a local airport, to a tall crane being erected along an approach corridor, to a TFR being declared. If you join the AMA and provide them with a cell number, they will send you a text message when a TFR goes up in your area. Membership has its benefits.

A second external factor that can change quite quickly is the weather, and aircraft are obviously even more vulnerable to rough weather than a ship at sea because the sky is their sea. The good news is that you're a recreational pilot, so you get to choose where and when you fly. Sometimes, circumstances demand that a professional drone pilot working for a public safety agency must fly at night through blowing snow in subzero temperatures, but that's because lives are a stake.

You do this for fun. Flying at night through blowing snow in subzero temperatures isn't fun. Go home and drink some hot cocoa, for goodness' sake. I promise the weather will get better soon enough, and you can go flying then.

2.10 / Fortunately, this severe buildup of ice on the leading edge of a rotor blade occurred inside a NASA wind tunnel at Glenn Research Center in Cleveland, Ohio. Out in the real world, structural icing poses a lethal threat to crewed aircraft and can affect uncrewed systems, as well.

Two weather-related issues that the FAA is particularly keen on you understanding, because they are highlighted in TRUST, are *wind* and a phenomenon called ***structural icing***. Wind is pretty straight forward: It will push your aircraft around and cause it to perform unpredictably. If the wind is blowing hard enough, such that it exceeds your aircraft's top speed, your aircraft will be carried away from you and there is nothing you can do except land as soon as possible.

Structural icing (Figure 2.10) is a lethal threat to crewed aviation, which may be why concern about it crossed over into the recreational remote piloting rules. Ice that builds up on the structure of the aircraft wreaks all kinds of havoc: It increases the aircraft's weight and drag (both enemies of flight as we'll learn in Chapter 4), and it can disable critical instruments, such as the altimeter and airspeed indicator. It really, truly is bad news.

However, for icing to occur, the air temperature must be below freezing, and water must be present in a liquid form, like rain. On the surface, that combination of factors is commonly referred to as an *ice storm*. Ice storms are not readily compatible with outdoor recreation, like flying drones and model airplanes for fun. You know the drill: stay inside, dress warmly and drink your cocoa.

3

The Many Different Types of Aircraft

Aircraft, it will not surprise you to learn, have been built in many different types and sizes over the past 250 years. The largest ever made was over 800 feet long: That's equivalent to two football fields and most of a third. The smallest one—available to the general public, at least—is less than three inches across and can be purchased on Amazon.

As a pilot, it's important that you be able to distinguish between different types of aircraft and how they fly. The key to understanding such an immense variety of specimens is to divide them into categories based on their defining characteristics, and then further divide each of those categories into ever-smaller subcategories until we accurately describe each type of flying machine in a just a few words, which will nevertheless tell us everything we need to know about how it operates (Figure 3.1).

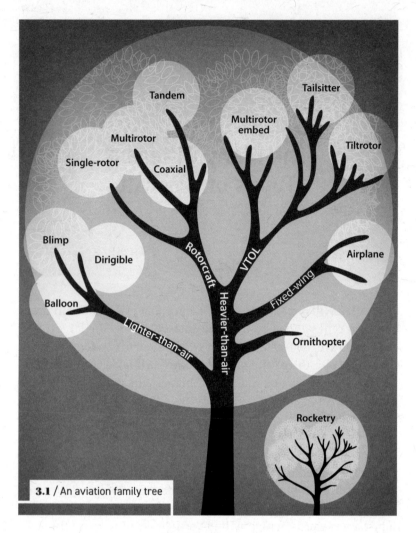

3.1 / An aviation family tree

FLOAT OR FLY?

As everyone knows, the history of aviation begins with an industrious pair of brothers, hard at work in the family business, which had nothing to do with aeronautics, while living in a small, provincial town. I refer of course to the Montgolfier brothers, Joseph-Michel and Jacques-Étienne, who in 1783 became the first to build and fly a machine capable of carrying human beings aloft: the hot air balloon.

It would be almost exactly 120 years before another pair of brothers, those upstart bicycle mechanics from Dayton, Ohio, Orville and Wilbur Wright, would themselves make history by flying the first airplane on the lonely, windswept beaches of Kitty Hawk, North Carolina. The difference between the creations of these two pairs of brothers represents the first fundamental distinction between two broad categories of aircraft: *lighter-than-air* and *heavier-than-air*.

There are three basic types of lighter-than-air flying machines:

- Balloons
- Blimps
- Dirigibles (Airships)

All three of these types stay aloft using buoyancy. This is the same principle that allows a steel ship weighing 100,000 tons to float on the surface of the ocean: The water that it displaces weighs even more than the ship itself.

> **"To propel a dirigible balloon through the air is like pushing a candle through a brick wall."**
>
> – Alberto Santos-Dumont, Brazilian Aeronaut

While a sheet of plate steel is far denser than seawater and will happily sink to the bottom, the hull of a ship encloses, among other things, lots of air, which is far less dense than seawater. Determine the average density of a ship, accounting for both the steel and the air, and you'll find it's less than the water, or, if you're on a submarine, it's the same.

The secret to achieving buoyancy in the air is to find a gas that is less dense than the surrounding atmosphere and capture it inside a lightweight container—essentially a giant bag, politely referred to as the *envelope*.

Just like modern day balloonists, the Montgolfier brothers heated ordinary air, thereby reducing its density until the envelope displaced enough of the colder air surrounding it to pull the balloon up into the sky. Atmospheric density decreases with elevation (which anyone who has ever visited Telluride, Colorado, can tell you, once they catch their breath), so the balloon will continue ascending until it reaches an altitude where the pressure differential is just sufficient to off-set the weight of the aircraft and its crew (Figure 3.2).

3.2 / Flying in a balloon means not having much control over where you're going or when you'll get there, but at least you'll look good doing it!

BALLOONS, BLIMPS, DIRIGIBLES—WHAT'S THE DIFFERENCE? AND WHY CAN'T I FLY ONE BY REMOTE CONTROL?

Balloons are distinguished from other types of lighter-than-air flying machines by the fact that the pilot has no direct means of controlling the direction of flight. With no engine or other propulsion system, the balloon floats wherever the wind carries it. Consequently, balloon pilots—also known by the romantic appellation *aeronauts*—need to wait for favorable winds before launching their aircraft.

Once aloft, it is possible to exercise some limited control over the direction of travel by ascending or descending in the hopes of finding winds at a different altitude blowing in another direction. However, all these vagaries make it impossible for balloons to ever represent a practical form of transportation and likewise prohibit the creation of a remote-control balloon, in the style of a drone or a model airplane.

Unlike balloons, the pilots of blimps and dirigibles can control their movements through the air using externally mounted motors with small propellers attached, called *thrusters*, as well as movable surfaces on the tail fins that act like the rudder of a ship at sea. They are slow compared to most other types of flying machines and cannot operate safely in high winds.

The difference between a blimp and a dirigible is that the envelope of a blimp maintains its shape only because it is inflated with gas. After you land, you can drain the helium, fold up the envelope and put it in a very large suitcase, if you are so inclined. The envelope of a dirigible, however, is supported by a rigid internal frame made of a lightweight aluminum alloy.

Note that the performance characteristics of blimps and dirigibles make it possible to operate one by remote control, and they have been used occasionally for professional applications that require long endurance, such as persistent surveillance or linear infrastructure inspection. A few recreational blimps have been introduced to the market over the years, as well. However, it can cost many hundreds of dollars, sometimes upwards of a thousand, to fill the envelope with helium, which only allows for one day of flying before the gas starts seeping through the material of the envelope. So, while it's possible to fly a remote-controlled blimp, it's not especially practical.

As the science of lighter-than-air flight advanced over the next two centuries, new gases were found that provided even greater buoyancy without the need for a constant supply of hot air. Hydrogen was first among these, and while its unique status as the lightest element on the periodic table provided it with a distinct advantage in terms of buoyancy, it has the alarming characteristic of reacting violently in the presence of oxygen, which comprises 21 percent of Earth's atmosphere, more or less.

The era of hydrogen-filled envelopes ended in abruptly at 7:25 p.m. on May 6, 1937, at Naval Air Station Lakehurst in New Jersey, when the 804-foot German dirigible Hindenburg caught fire while attempting to dock and was consumed by flames in mere seconds. Given the apocalyptic scene that unfolded in full view of the news cameras, it seems astonishing that almost two thirds of the people on board survived, including 36 of the 49 passengers (Figure 3.3).

3.3 / The horrifying destruction of the Hindenberg put an end to the use of hydrogen as a lifting gas in airships.

Ever since, helium has ruled the skies as the lifting gas of choice for blimps and dirigibles. While it doesn't provide quite as much buoyancy as hydrogen and is rare—and therefore much more expensive—the fact that helium is completely inert, and therefore incapable of catching fire or exploding, proved to be a decisive advantage. Helium is also used to lift uncrewed balloons carrying scientific instruments high up into the atmosphere. While much closer to the surface of the Earth, crewed balloons continue to fly using the method pioneered by the Montgolfier brothers more than two centuries ago.

Unfortunately, given their stately elegance and grace in the air and their ability to fly for many, many hours without refueling, balloons, blimps, and dirigibles are largely impractical as remote-control aircraft—certainly for a recreational pilot who is just getting started, and even for the vast majority of commercial operators. So, this is where we will part company with lighter-than-air flight, both in this chapter and for the rest of the book and focus our attention on where virtually all the action is in both crewed and uncrewed aviation: heavier-than-air flying machines.

THE WRIGHT WAY

Just like their lighter-than-air counterparts, heavier-than-air flying machines can be divided into a number of categories. These are:

- Airplanes
- Rotorcraft
- Powered lift (VTOLs)
- Ornithopters

Of these four types, airplanes—also described as **fixed-wing aircraft**—are the most common and the most familiar, and they have a number of key advantages as flying machines. First, they are relatively energy efficient compared to the other types and able to carry a heavier payload farther using less fuel or electrical power. The principal disadvantage of airplanes is that they must maintain a certain minimum airspeed to stay airborne. So, like a shark, they must always keep moving forward or die—which for us means crash, but you get the idea. (More on why this is true in Chapter 4.) As a result, airplanes require specialized assets on the ground to facilitate takeoff and landing, such as a *runway* or a *launch catapult* and *arresting gear*.

Rotorcraft, which include helicopters and drones, are nearly the opposite of airplanes. They are much more energy intensive to operate and typically are capable of carrying much smaller payloads than an equivalent fixed-wing platform. The principal advantage of rotorcraft is that they can take off and land almost anywhere. Find a flat, clear patch of ground large enough to accommodate the span of their rotors, and you're good to go.

Powered lift aircraft, also commonly called *VTOL* (an acronym for *vertical takeoff and landing*), initially sounds like another way to say helicopters, because they take off and land vertically, don't they? Well, yes, that's true, but the phrase "vertical takeoff and landing" only refers to how these machines get into the air, not what they do once they're up there.

Essentially, a VTOL is a hybrid design that attempts to capture the efficiencies and advantages of both a fixed-wing and a rotorcraft. It can take off and land like a helicopter—from a small, unprepared patch of ground—but once airborne, the VTOL transitions into fixed-wing flight, thereby taking advantage of the efficiency inherent in the design of an airplane. Of course, this necessarily requires compromises between these two disparate types of aircraft, such that VTOLs never enjoy the maximum advantage of either one.

Ornithopters (Figure 3.4) are machines that fly by flapping their wings like birds. Whimsical, hard to control, and almost completely impractical, ornithopters have occasionally appeared over the years as remote-control novelty products and for use in scientific research. Experiments with crewed ornithopters began at the dawn of heavier-than-air flight alongside more conventional designs and continue to the present day. However, none has ever managed to fly for more than a few seconds. Except to mention that they exist and that they can be a quirky and occasionally frustrating alternative to a more conventional remote piloting experience, we will not discuss them further.

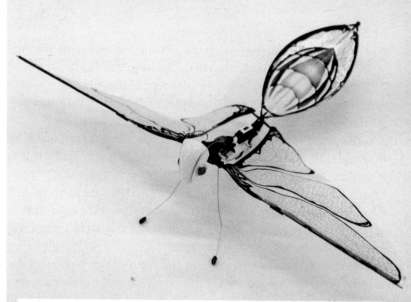

3.4 / Practical designs and applications for ornithopters, like the MetaFly from Bionic Bird, remain largely elusive even after more than a century of heavier-than-air flight.

Now that we understand the broad categories of heavier-than-air flying machines, we can further divide each of the three main types into additional sub-categories based on their specific characteristics. That's what we'll be exploring next, starting with fixed-wing aircraft.

AIRPLANES: FROM THE GROUND UP

When aircraft must move around on the ground under their own power, a process called *taxiing*, they rely on systems commonly referred to as *landing gear*, but which the cool kids call the *undercarriage*. The undercarriage of an aircraft can be configured in many ways, but we'll begin by discussing those that incorporate wheels.

While there are exceptions, most wheeled aircraft have three wheels (or three sets of wheels), which ensure stability during ground handling by relying on the same physics as a photographer's tripod. Within this category, there are two basic configurations with two large wheels mounted at or near the wings, which are intended to absorb the primary shock of landing, and a smaller wheel used for steering—with the distinction between the two types indicated by the location of the smaller wheel.

If the small wheel is located at the rear of the aircraft, a nearly universal configuration for fighter planes during World War I and World War II, that aircraft is referred to as a *taildragger* (Figure 3.5). The reason is that with the tail of the aircraft supported by that one tiny wheel, it appears to drag along the ground while it is taxiing. Indeed, some World War I airplanes had a skid, rather than a wheel, at the rear of the aircraft, making them literal tail draggers. This is occasionally referred to as the *standard* undercarriage configuration, which is ironic since it hasn't been the standard for the better part of a century.

If the small wheel is located at the front of the aircraft, as is seen in virtually all modern airplanes, it is said to have a *tricycle* (Figure 3.6) undercarriage, for its general resemblance to the peddle-powered conveyance for children. In crewed aviation, the tricycle configuration offers a big advantage for pilots: It provides them with a clear view of the surface ahead during taxi, takeoff, and landing. When it is on the ground, the nose of a tail dragger obstructs the pilot's forward view until the moment the aircraft actually starts flying (though since you will be operating your aircraft from the outside, this is merely a point of trivia you can use to impress your fellow remote pilots).

Another key distinction between different undercarriage configurations is whether they are *fixed* or *retractable* (Figure 3.7).

3.5 / Like virtually all fighter aircraft that flew in World War II, this model of the Messerschmitt Bf 109 features a tail-dragger undercarriage configuration.

As the name suggests, a fixed undercarriage always remains in the same position, even while the airplane is flying. The advantage of this configuration is reliability and mechanical simplicity—because the undercarriage never moves, it's always where you need it to be. The disadvantage is that having pylons and wheels hanging off the bottom of your aircraft tends to degrade its aerodynamic performance by inducing additional *drag*.

3.6 / This model of the de Havilland Twin Otter incorporates a tricycle-type undercarriage.

3.7 / A retractable undercarriage, called "retracts" for short, provides improved aerodynamic performance in flight.

A retractable undercarriage offers the exact opposite when it comes to advantages and disadvantages. Aerodynamic performance is improved, but once retracted, the wheels may not be where they need to be when it's time to land, either because of a mechanical failure or pilot error.

On model airplanes, a retractable undercarriage is only found on larger and more expensive models intended for experienced pilots. Additional hardware is required on board, meaning more weight, and the pilot must have the skill to manage the change in aircraft performance when the undercarriage is raised and lowered.

If you want to land on something other than a flat, solid surface (like water, for example) wheels probably aren't your best choice. Pontoons, also referred to as *floats*, will allow an airplane to safely make a water landing. As a practical matter, floats are virtually always fixed, and because of their size and weight, they have an even greater impact on the aerodynamic performance of an aircraft than a wheeled, fixed undercarriage. Steering during a water taxi is accomplished by means of rudders located at the rear of the floats. An aircraft equipped with floats is referred to as a *floatplane* (Figure 3.8).

3.8 / If you're planning on making a water landing, wheels probably aren't your best option for an undercarriage.

Although it is definitely a specialty, a number of model float-planes are available for remote pilots. Like their crewed counter-parts, several airframes are available from manufacturers that can mount either wheels or floats, and you can even change back and forth with a few minutes' work at your bench. If you choose to fly floatplanes once you gain some experience with remote piloting, always make sure you've got a plan to get your machine back to shore in the event it can't make it under its own power.

The final major option when it comes to the undercarriage is not to have one at all. For obvious reasons this isn't a popular choice in crewed aviation, but it can be an effective approach with model airplanes—especially smaller models and those intended for new pilots. Landing an aircraft without an undercarriage is referred to as a **belly landing** (Figure 3.9).

The advantages of this type of aircraft include improved aero-dynamic performance and more forgiving landings, since the pilot doesn't have to set the machine down precisely on the **main gear** (the pair of big wheels mounted near the wings). The disadvantag-es include zero ground-handling capability, meaning it is simply unable to taxi. Also, a hand launch, that is, tossing the model into the air with one hand while holding the controller in the other, is necessary to get it aloft.

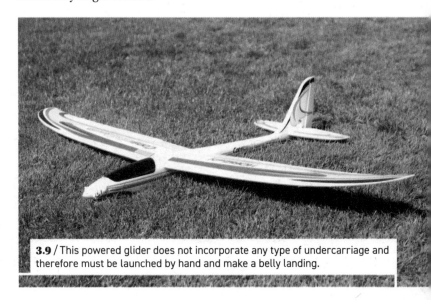

3.9 / This powered glider does not incorporate any type of undercarriage and therefore must be launched by hand and make a belly landing.

If you're going to start out by flying an airplane that makes belly landings, and that's a good choice for a new pilot, you'll want to find something other than concrete or asphalt for your landing surface. Almost all these beginner aircraft are made from foam, which has the potential to get torn up by a rough surface. Much better to land on grass or something else soft. Also, if your belly-landing airplane has any sensitive components, like a camera or other sensors, you'll need to take this into account.

Bonus content: An airplane designed to make a belly landing on water is called a *flying boat*.

WINGING IT

There are myriad possible configurations for the wings of an airplane, but we will only consider the most basic variations here:

- High-wing
- Low-wing
- Multi-wing
- Swept-wing

The first thing to be aware of when examining the design and placement of an airplane's wings is that they mostly involve considerations only relevant to crewed aircraft: the ease of loading cargo, the visibility afforded the pilot from the flight deck, the space available in the cabin, and the function of the fuel system, just to name a few. None of these matter at all to us as model airplane pilots. However, since many model airplanes are, in fact, models of specific crewed aircraft, they will reflect the configuration of their full-sized counterparts.

3.10 / The Turbo Timber employs a high-wing design to maximize stability in flight.

When it comes to their wings, airplanes are described based on where the wings are placed. If the wings are attached to the top of the fuselage, the aircraft is said to have a *high-wing* design (Figure 3.10). Unsurprisingly, if the wings are attached to the bottom of the fuselage, it's a *low-wing* design (Figure 3.11). All things being equal, which they usually are not, a high-wing airplane will be more intrinsically stable than a low-wing airplane, due to the relationship between the *center of gravity* (CG) and the *center of pressure* (CP) inherent in their design. That's way more aeronautical science than you need to bite off and chew at this point in your career, so we'll just leave it at that.

3.11 / This model of a T-28 Trojan Navy trainer incorporates a low-wing design.

Low-wing aircraft can, and frequently do, make up for this deficiency in stability by introducing a *dihedral* angle to their wings (Figure 3.12). That's a fancy way of saying that the wings slant upward as they extend away from the body of the airplane. Again, as a beginner, don't worry about the science behind it, just cement in your mind the idea that "dihedral = stability." Given this fact, you won't be surprised to learn that many trainers both in model and crewed aviation incorporate a high-wing, dihedral design—doubling-down on stability.

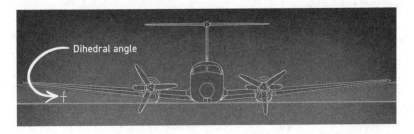

3.12 / Introducing a dihedral angle to the design of a low-wing airplane will compensate for the relative loss of stability from an equivalent high-wing design.

Another option when it comes to wing configuration is to choose "all of the above" and put a wing on the top and the bottom of the fuselage. The result is a ***multi-wing*** design, the most common being the ***biplane*** (Figure 3.13). Like virtually all other early airplanes, the original 1903 Wright Flyer was a biplane.

From the perspective of those early aeronautical engineers, the main advantage of the biplane was that it allows the same total wing area using shorter individual wings, which meant they could be more rigid and lightweight in their construction. As engines grew more powerful and aluminum replaced wood and fabric as

3.13 / This immaculate model biplane re-creates the Boeing PT-17 Stearman. Introduced in 1934, both the Army and the Navy employed the PT-17 as a trainer in the years leading up to World War II.

Getting Started With Drones and Model Airplanes

the preferred material of choice for building airplane wings, these structural considerations become irrelevant, and the ***monoplane***, an airplane with one wing, has ruled the skies ever since.

The monoplane's biggest advantage over biplanes and other multi-wing designs is speed. They can fly significantly faster than multi-wing airplanes, and fast is typically the name of the game when you're flying. Biplanes, however, have the advantage when it comes to maneuverability, which explains why the few modern biplanes being flown today by crewed aviators are used almost exclusively in aerobatic demonstrations. Model airplane manufacturers occasionally release both modern and historic biplane designs, so you'll have the opportunity to try one out for yourself.

Swept-wings (Figure 3.14) are one final type to be aware of as you begin your career as a remote pilot and are distinguished from the ***straight-wing*** design of most propeller-driven airplanes (and therefore, most model airplanes, as well). Swept wings are angled backward from the point where they are attached to the fuselage, creating a distinctive V shape when viewed from above or below. The main advantage of swept wings is that they produce less turbulence as they pass through the air, and turbulence increases with speed.

3.14 / This model of the Cessna Citation business jet incorporates the swept-wing configuration of its crewed progenitor, but will never achieve anything approaching the 500 mph required for this design to be practical, but it sure looks cool.

Therefore, it makes perfect sense that swept-wing designs appeared on the first crewed jet-powered airplanes, because only jets can fly fast enough for this increasing turbulence to be a problem. On the other hand, aircraft with straight wings perform better at lower speeds. Now, you may be thinking that it's unlikely for any model airplane to ever fly fast enough to actually require swept wings, and you're thinking that because you're a smart person.

> **"The airplane stays up because it doesn't have the time to fall."**
>
> – Orville Wright,
> Pioneering American Aviator

The only time swept wings will ever show up on a model airplane is when that model is attempting to recreate the appearance of a much faster airplane, like a fighter jet or a commercial airliner. And, since you'll never achieve the speeds required to gain any advantage from those swept wings, you're paying a price in terms of performance and stability for the sake of good looks alone. (Hmmm... There's a nugget of wisdom in there somewhere for a middle-aged man like me—I'm sure of it!)

MOVING FORWARD

In crewed aviation, there are two fundamental types of power systems for moving an airplane forward: propellers and jets. Propellers spin, typically driven by a piston engine, like the one in a gasoline-powered automobile. Jets combine compressed air with fuel in a combustion chamber, creating a powerful, well, jet of hot exhaust gasses that push the engine and the airplane it's attached to in the opposite direction.

A few exotic variations are out there, like turboprops, which turn a propeller using a turbine like the one inside a conventional jet engine, as well as ramjets, scramjets, and pulse jets, but those lie well beyond what you need to know as a beginning remote pilot. This is true not least because these types are applicable to crewed aircraft, and your goal in reading this book is, presumably, to fly uncrewed aircraft.

To propel fixed-wing model airplanes, there are three basic systems available:

- Propellers;
- Electric-ducted fans (EDFs); and, yes,
- Jets

The idea of using a real-life, miniature jet engine to fly a model airplane for the sole purpose of recreation absolutely terrifies me personally, and it's not something you're likely try any time soon, so we'll acknowledge they exist and leave it at that. Propellers you're already familiar with because, at a minimum, you've seen small, crewed aircraft, or at least a desk fan, during your time here on planet Earth.

That leaves us with the *electric-ducted fans (EDF)*, which raises the question: What is an EDF? (Figure 3.15) Like the swept-wing model airplanes we discussed above, an EDF is a means of accomplishing something that probably shouldn't be accomplished in the first place—putting form ahead of function. Some people, and perhaps you will be among them (just like me, if I'm being honest), enjoy flying model airplanes that look like sleek jet fighters. And, of course, sleek jet fighters don't have propellers, so putting one on your model would ruin the whole effect.

3.15 / This model of a private jet uses a pair of electric-ducted fans (EDFs) to maintain the appearance of the original, full-sized aircraft without employing actual jet engines.

So, being the crafty sort they are, model airplane designers put a propeller inside a tube and that tube inside the body of the aircraft. Now, in this context, the propeller is called a "fan," and the tube is called a "duct," and the whole thing is powered by an electric battery—EDF is making a lot more sense now, huh? Thanks to this innovation, you get to live out your "Top Gun" fantasies without the danger an expense of spinning up an actual jet turbine, and rest assured, it is plenty dangerous and expensive.

As is always the case in aviation, you need to understand some important trade-offs. First, EDFs are significantly less efficient than a conventional, propeller-driven design, which is why there are no crewed EDF aircraft—it's all for show. Consequently,

SO, YOU WANT TO FLY A MODEL WITH A REAL JET ENGINE— ARE YOU SURE? REALLY? REALLY!?

The first thing to say about putting a miniature, working jet engine on a model airplane is that it is expensive and dangerous—*really* expensive and *really* dangerous—when compared to the alternatives. This is not something you should imagine yourself doing in the next few years as a fun addition to your hobby of flying drones and model airplanes. If it happens at all, it will be the crowning achievement of a career built across decades in the craft of model aviation.

Why? First, let's talk price. A jet turbine will set you back a minimum of around $2,000, and a suitable airframe to support it will cost at least that much. Furthermore, after a given maintenance interval—something on the order of 25 hours of operation—the turbine must be returned to the manufacturer for service, which isn't cheap. In addition, you'll need to purchase specialized firefighting gear and have it ready every time you go flying.

Now, let's talk safety. A turbine-powered model airplane can fly upwards of 200 miles per hour while loaded with flammable jet fuel. Some people would consider that a missile, and there is no doubt that it could be used as one. Imagine the nightmare of an airplane like that getting away from you, either because of a mistake or a control failure. It's going to crash somewhere—maybe a kindergarten?

the aircraft is less powerful and more unforgiving to fly, which goes double because it has likely been styled like a swept-wing jet despite the fact it will never achieve anything approaching the speed where that could be at all useful from an aerodynamic perspective.

Second, EDFs emit an ear-splitting whine while in flight. Take my word for it; they are *loud* and *obnoxious*. If you try flying one in a location where other people might reasonably expect some peace and quiet, like a public park or school grounds on a weekend, you are liable to catch a lot of justified side-eye from those folks. So, please be considerate about when and where you choose to go flying with an EDF.

To prove you can do this safely and earn a turbine waiver from the Academy of Model Aeronautics (AMA), you'll need to log a minimum 20 hours of flight time alongside an experienced turbine pilot and take a check ride to demonstrate your ability to perform basic and advanced maneuvers while flying upwards of 100 MPH. You'll also need to demonstrate competence across a range of other skills, such as fueling, emergency procedures and field maintenance.

No doubt this could be a thrilling and personally rewarding adventure, but make sure you go into it with clear eyes, expert skills and a thick wallet.

A model airplane with a working jet turbine engine is a possibility, just make sure you are prepared for the associated expense and the dangers.

By now, you will likely believe we have considered every conceivable variation of fixed-wing aircraft. Well, before we move on, there is one more distinction you should be aware of: Is the propeller at the front of the airplane or the back of the airplane? To be sure, the front of the airplane is far and away the most common location. This is referred to as a ***tractor***, because the propeller pulls the aircraft through the air.

However, it is also possible to mount the propeller behind the wings, making it a ***pusher***—because it pushes the airplane through the air. By now, you probably know the song well enough that you can sing along: There are advantages and disadvantages to each of these configurations.

From the perspective of a remote pilot, pushers are both less efficient and make more noise than an equivalent tractor configuration. On the plus side, your propeller and your motor won't be the first thing to hit the ground in the event of a crash, which might improve the chances that the aircraft will fly again afterward.

ROTORCRAFT: COUNT THE PROPELLERS

The principle means of distinguishing between different types of rotorcrafts lies in the number and placement of their propellers. Until the early 2000s, the word "rotorcraft" was basically synonymous with "helicopter," because they were the only type that anybody ever saw. However, that changed in the 2010s with the advent and eventual widespread adoption of drones. As always, there are quirky exceptions, but generally rotorcraft can be divided into four subcategories:

- Single-rotor helicopters
- Tandem-rotor helicopters
- Coaxial-rotor helicopters
- Multirotors

Single rotor (Figure 3.16) is a term that drone pilots will use to describe an aircraft with a conventional helicopter design—otherwise known as a "helicopter." This is ironic because all "single-rotor" helicopters actually have two rotors: a big one on top that is responsible for lifting it into the air and a smaller one at the end of a boom located at the rear of the aircraft that helps it maneuver, as we'll see in Chapter 4.

"Helicopters don't fly, they vibrate so badly that the ground rejects them."

– Tom Clancy,
American Novelist

3.16 / The Yamaha R-MAX as an uncrewed aircraft of that employs a conventional "single-rotor" helicopter design. Weighing more than 200 lbs. at takeoff, it was originally developed for precision crop dusting on small plots of Japanese farmland.

3.17 / While the tandem-rotor helicopter is extremely uncommon as either a drone or model aircraft, crewed versions are deployed when the mission requires moving large or heavy payloads, like this CH-46 Sea Knight in service with the U.S. Marine Corps.

Tandem-rotor helicopters (Figure 3.17) have two main rotors overhead and no tail rotor. They are used almost exclusively in crewed aviation when the ability to lift heavy payloads is a key mission parameter, as is often the case for the armed services.

Coaxial helicopters (Figure 3.18) mount two separate propellers on a single shaft. While crewed coaxial designs that have flown over the decades, the type has gained its greatest fame over the past few years thanks to *Ingenuity*, the Mars helicopter that stowed away with the *Perseverance* rover and made its first flight on the Red Planet in 2021 (Figure 3.19).

Coaxial helicopters are more intrinsically stable than other common rotorcraft designs, while simultaneously allowing for a compact airframe, both no doubt critical factors in NASA having selected the configuration for the first heavier-than-air flight on another world. For these reasons, coaxial designs are also a popular configuration for inexpensive remote-control helicopters intended for new pilots.

Drones introduced the concept of *multirotors* (Figure 3.20) to society at large. Indeed, the words have sometimes been used synonymously, as in, "Hey, that's a cool multirotor! Where'd you get it?" Multirotors are distinguished by having an even number of small propellers mounted on limbs that extend away from the body of the aircraft. By far, the most common configuration has four propellers, making it a "quadcopter." However, there are also versions with six propellers, a "hexacopter," as well as eight, the "octocopter," and so on.

3.18 / Their intrinsic stability makes coaxial helicopters a good choice for beginning rotorcraft pilots.

3.19 / Seen here in a NASA rendering, the Mars helicopter *Ingenuity* employs a coaxial propeller configuration to maximize stability while reducing the overall size of the aircraft.

3.20 / The multirotor has emerged as the preferred configuration for small, civilian drones due to its mechanical simplicity and the ability to take off and land vertically, hover, and fly in any direction.

Other identifying characteristics, such as the configuration of the undercarriage and the type of propulsion—so crucial in distinguishing between different types of fixed-wing aircraft—are generally not accorded the same level of attention when it comes to rotorcraft. Now, if you're a pilot flying a crewed helicopter, you obviously need to know whether its power source is a turbine or a piston-driven engine, but from the outside looking in, all that matters is that it can fly up and down, forward and backward, left and right (just like a hummingbird).

MULTIROTORS: NOT A NEW THING

The only multirotor that most people have ever seen is a drone or perhaps an all-electric air taxi. This, quite naturally, causes the general public to assume that they are something entirely new. However, as a student of aviation, you know better—or at least you will 30 seconds from now, if you keep reading.

Multirotors were actually among the earliest flying machines and even beat conventional, single-rotor helicopters into the air. In 1924, a multirotor in France set the first-ever distance record by a rotorcraft at 1,180 feet. In the United States, Dr. George de Bothezat, who had fled his native Russia in 1918 during the Bolshevik revolution and settled in Dayton, Ohio, contracted with the Army Air Service to develop the quadcopter nicknamed the "Flying Octopus" by those who saw it in action.

Unfortunately for de Bothezat and the other pioneers, the multirotor was an idea whose time had not yet come. They were plagued by problems with reliability, and the pilot had his hands full simply keeping the machine in the air. Hovering and a few simple maneuvers, like flying in a straight line, were as far as they got.

However, about 90 years later, the combination of reliable brushless electric motors, microprocessors, and miniaturized accelerometers and gyroscopes transformed the multirotor from a forgotten dream into a remarkably capable flying machine that now appears poised to significantly alter the fabric of our society. Just don't let anybody tell you it's new.

The de Bothezat helicopter was among a number of early crewed flying machines in the 1920s that used a multirotor configuration to achieve vertical flight.

VTOLS: LIKE A BAR BET GONE WRONG

It has been said that "a camel is a horse designed by committee." In other words, it combines disparate features that should make it even more versatile and capable than the original, but somehow, it never quite manages to achieve its full potential. Also, if I'm being honest, it's kind of ugly (Figure 3.21).

Furthermore, from an aeronautical science perspective, managing the transition from vertical to horizontal flight and back again is a fraught proposition. The idea was first given serious consideration in the late 1920s and 1930s, with patents being awarded to famed inventor

3.21 / The VTOL is neither as beautiful or elegant as the alternatives, but it will get the job done when nothing else can.

Nikola Tesla, among others. It wasn't until the 1950s that experimental prototypes were developed and the 1970s when the first operational platforms were deployed.

The advent of powerful flight control systems and sensors, which also allowed the drone revolution to occur (we'll examine this further in Chapter 5), made it much easier to manage the strange aerodynamic forces at work when an aircraft transitions from hovering to flying and back again. Thus, today a $100 model can perform maneuvers with ease that would have astonished the developer of a multimillion-dollar prototype in the 1950s.

Leaving all that aside, the three basic types of VTOL platforms, with more than the usual number of caveats about sundry outliers and oddballs, are:

- Tiltrotors
- Tailsitters
- Multirotor embeds

If any type of VTOL is familiar to the general public, it would be the *tiltrotor*. This design is exemplified by the V-22 Osprey, developed for the Marine Corps and in active service today (Figure 3.22). It uses a pair of main rotors to take off and land like a helicopter and then, once airborne, tilts those same rotors forward and flies like an airplane.

The tiltrotor has two cousins worth mentioning. The first is the *tiltwing*, which is the exact same idea, except that the entire wing tilts from vertical to horizontal and back again, and the propellers, which are attached to the wing, go along for the ride. The second is the *thrust-vectoring* aircraft, which incorporates a jet engine. Rather than tilt the entire engine, or the entire wing, this type of aircraft uses nozzles to redirect the propulsive force of the jet horizontally and vertically, as needed. Although it is largely a footnote from the Cold War at this point, thrust-vectoring aircraft took hold in the popular imagination with the deployment of the Harrier "jump jet," developed in the UK.

3.22 / The V-22 Osprey is a tiltrotor VTOL developed for the Marine Corps. Due to their relative technical and aerodynamic complexity, tiltrotor designs are not common among small UAS.

3.23 / This tailsitter, the X-VERT from Horizon Hobby, is one of the relatively rare examples of a VTOL manufactured for recreational remote pilots.

3.24 / The Convair XFY-1 Pogo is an example of a tailsitter VTOL. The last time someone thought this was a good idea for a crewed platform, Eisenhower was in the White House.

With *tailsitters* (Figure 3.23), the name pretty much says it all. Like a rocket ship, the tailsitter VTOL takes off and lands with its nose pointing straight up into the sky and its tail on the ground. As an approach to crewed aircraft, the tailsitter was abandoned by the end of the 1950s (Figure 3.24). However, the type has seen a resurgence in interest with the development of uncrewed aircraft. While only furtively made available for hobbyists by model airplane manufacturers, the tailsitter is growing in popularity with commercial drone pilots for delivering on much of the inherent potential in the VTOL concept while looking only slightly absurd.

3.25 / The Lynx VTOL was developed for U.S. special forces and employs a multirotor embed design. While not the most efficient VTOL configuration, it is simple and avoids much of the aerodynamic complexity associated with transitioning from vertical to forward flight.

The *multirotor embed* (Figure 3.25) is essentially two separate aircraft sharing the same airframe. The design most frequently pairs a quadcopter with a conventional, propeller-driven fixed-wing airplane. The operation is similarly straight forward: to take off, the aircraft spins up the multirotor propellers and rises to altitude. Then, the main propeller starts turning, moving the aircraft forward. As soon as the wings are generating enough lift to maintain its altitude, the multirotor spins down, and it flies like a conventional airplane until it's time to land, at which point the whole process happens in reverse.

Multirotor embeds are a straight-forward design with one big drawback: They aren't very efficient. When they are operating in one flight mode—either horizontal or vertical—they are hauling along with them all the components that are required to sustain the other flight mode, and very few of them are shared in common. Historically, the multirotor embed has never been considered as a design for a crewed aircraft, nor are they widely available for recreational remote pilots. However, their simplicity and robust design have created a market for them among commercial operators and military users.

WHAT ABOUT ROCKETS?

It may have occurred to you that one type of vehicle that travels through the atmosphere—the rocket—is conspicuously absent from our catalog of flying machines. This is a deliberate choice, as rockets are generally regarded as belonging in a category entirely separate from the aircraft we have examined at length in this chapter. However, if you look closely, you'll find the boundaries that separate rockets from other flying machines are a little fuzzier and more permeable than they might at first appear.

One argument frequently made in favor of separation is that other flying machines are beholden to the laws of aerodynamics—they rely on lift generated by wings and rotors, or buoyancy, to fly—while rockets get the job done by pure thrust. But, of course, a rotorcraft flies by pure thrust until the moment it makes a lateral maneuver, so the difference is…what, exactly?

Another argument is that other heavier-than-air flying machines are **air-breathers**: that is, they rely on the oxygen in Earth's atmosphere to achieve combustion. Rockets, however, carry their own oxidizers with them, which is why they can fly in space where there is no atmosphere. With that said, rocket engines have been used in several specialized instances to power fixed-wing aircraft, so again the distinction is rather more muddled than it might at first appear.

The most honest answer might be that we've always done it this way, and we're not going to change now. This sidebar represents the sum total of our examination of rockets in this book. That said, they can be a lot of fun—and I grew up flying model rockets rather than model airplanes. If you're interested in getting into rockets as a hobby, check out the **National Association of Rocketry (NAR)**. Their mission is to do for model rockets what the Academy of Model Aeronautics (AMA) does for drones and model airplanes.

Model rocketry is another pastime with nearly unlimited potential to entertain and educate.

YEAH, BUT *HOW* DO THEY FLY?

By now, it may have occurred to you that we have spent the preceding 6,000 words describing the various types of aircraft that have flown over the past two and a half centuries while giving scant attention to how flight is actually achieved, especially in regards to heavier-than-air flying machines, which are, after all, allegedly the subject of this book. That all changes in the next chapter as we turn our attention to the science of *aerodynamics*.

4

Aerodynamics: A Dangerously Incomplete Education

Like every other material object in the universe as we understand it, aircraft obey the laws of physics. That portion of physics that specifically that describes the performance of flying machines is known as *aerodynamics*. Needless to say, it is an incredibly complicated subject upon which weighty tomes have been written, replete with intricate mathematical formulae that describe the action and interaction of innumerable factors that act upon and within a body in flight.

This is not one of those tomes. The goal of this chapter is to make you conversant in the fundamental forces that make heavier-than-air flight possible, as well as the tools we use to control them, and the words we use to describe

> **"There's no such thing as a routine flight."**
>
> – Chesley B. Sullenberger, American Aviator

them. This is important both to allow you to understand what your flying machine is doing and why it is doing it, and so that you can correctly interpret manuals and other materials you may subsequently encounter as well as engaging constructively with your fellow remote pilots.

THE FOUR FORCES OF FLIGHT

Every new pilot's journey begins with an introduction to the *four forces of flight* (Figure 4.1). Congratulations, now you're one of them. These are the fundamental factors that sustain a flying machine in the air and determine whether it ascends or descends, speeds up or slows down. They are *thrust*, *lift*, *drag*, and *weight*. As we will see, they come in pairs that tend to balance each other out. For simplicity's sake, we'll consider these first in the context of fixed-wing flight.

- Thrust is the force that moves an aircraft forward through the air. In the case of a conventional airplane, thrust is created by a spinning propeller or the action of a jet engine. Acting against and balancing out the effect of thrust is drag.
- Lift is the force that pulls an aircraft up into the sky. It is generated by the wings of an airplane as they pass through the air. Weight acts against lift.
- Drag is a result of the friction created when the body of the aircraft passes through the air. It resists and balances out the effects of thrust.
- Weight is the force caused by gravity that pulls the aircraft down toward the surface of the Earth. Lift acts against the effects of weight.

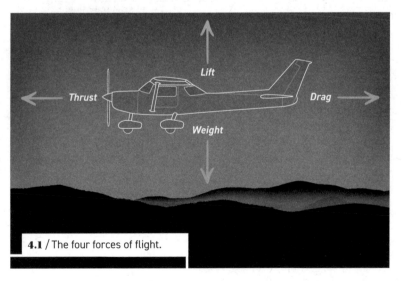

4.1 / The four forces of flight.

By now you have realized that describing "weight" as one of the four forces of flight is, at best, a misstatement of the facts or, at worst, actively misleading. As a learned individual, you recognize that weight is merely a measure of mass, used to define its interaction with a gravitational field. Therefore, shouldn't this force be more properly described as "mass," or better still, "gravity"?

Well, yes, it should be...Congratulations, you're very smart. However, generations of aviators have grown up calling this force "weight" and whatever the truth may be, it's simply too late to change it now. So just go with it, okay?

When all four forces are in balance, an aircraft will fly at a constant speed, neither gaining or losing altitude. When thrust exceeds drag, the airplane accelerates. When drag exceeds thrust, the airplane decelerates. When lift exceeds weight, it ascends. When weight exceeds lift, it descends.

Of course, these same four forces are at work in the case of a drone or other rotorcraft, although they can be obscured by all of those moving parts. Drag and weight work exactly the same way they do with fixed-wing aircraft. Lift is generated by the propeller(s) that rotate parallel to the ground. These substitute their own rotation for the forward movement that causes a fixed wing to generate lift. To generate thrust, a rotorcraft redirects some of the lift generated by its propeller(s) horizontally, thereby pushing it in the opposite direction.

As a denizen of planet Earth, three of these four forces—thrust, drag, and weight—are intuitively obvious. You have encountered each of these phenomena often enough in your daily life to understand how they work. In case you need a quick refresher: To experience thrust, stand in front of a fan; to experience drag, stick your hand out the window of a moving car; to experience weight, jump up and down. Lift, however, is a bit more mysterious, and since it is the one that is responsible for flight happening in the first place, it deserves a little more attention.

UNDERSTANDING LIFT

Along with "What makes the sky blue?" and "What happens if I swallow a watermelon seed?" a question that young children often ask is, "How do airplanes fly?" For the most part, adults give up on asking this question and simply hope that their flight won't be delayed and maybe they can swing a last-minute upgrade to Economy+ seating. However, as a pilot, that's not good enough. You need to understand how the wings of an airplane generate lift—and why sometimes they don't.

It all comes down to the distinctive shape of a wing, called an *airfoil* (Figure 4.2). An airfoil is any surface designed to obtain a useful reaction, or lift, from air passing over it. At its most basic level, an airfoil is flat on the bottom and curved on top. By the way, propellers share this same fundamental shape, meaning that they, too, are airfoils, so the same science that explains lift also explains thrust. That assumes, of course, we aren't talking about jets, which we most emphatically are not. If you want to learn how a jet engine works, you're reading the wrong book.

> **"Takeoffs are optional. Landings are mandatory."**
>
> – Aviation Aphorism

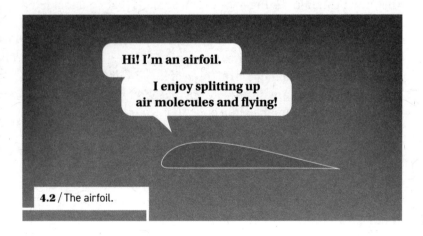

4.2 / The airfoil.

When an airfoil passes through the air, either because it is attached to the side of an airplane or spinning atop a rotorcraft, that distinctive shape presents each oncoming air molecule with a choice: It can either take the short road, along its smooth bottom side; or it can take the long road, up and over its curved top side (Figure 4.3). It turns out that this choice makes all the difference in the world.

While it sounds paradoxical and very complicated at first, as the speed of a gas *increases*, the pressure it exerts on its surroundings *decreases*. Thus, the air molecules taking the long road over the top of the wing exert less pressure on its surface than the air molecules taking the short road over the bottom of the wing, because they have farther to travel in the same amount of time. This creates a pressure differential between the two surfaces, and the wing is drawn up into the pocket of low pressure that forms above its top surface. Much the same way a dust bunny is pulled to its doom by a household vacuum cleaner.

The faster the airfoil moves, the greater the pressure differential becomes and the more lift it generates, and the beauty of flight begins. Suddenly, those long runways at airports make a whole lot more sense, don't they?

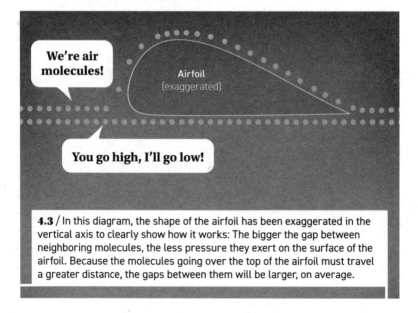

4.3 / In this diagram, the shape of the airfoil has been exaggerated in the vertical axis to clearly show how it works: The bigger the gap between neighboring molecules, the less pressure they exert on the surface of the airfoil. Because the molecules going over the top of the airfoil must travel a greater distance, the gaps between them will be larger, on average.

If you've ever stood in front of a household fan, then the idea that fast-moving air somehow exerts *less* pressure than slow-moving air seems absurd, which makes the whole idea about how airfoils work suspect, to be sure. So, why should we believe it? Two reasons: First, because a really smart guy who lived hundreds of years ago figured it out and wrote it down for us. Second, because you can conduct an experiment in 10 seconds with nothing more than a slip of paper and your own mouth that will prove it's true.

In this case, the smart guy was named Daniel Bernoulli, and he lived in Switzerland in the eighteenth century. Bernoulli hailed from a family of famous mathematicians, and happily for the rest of us, he went into the family business. He made many discoveries, but the one for which he is best remembered is called the ***Bernoulli Principle***.

This principle states that as the speed of a fluid increases, the pressure that fluid exerts on the surrounding environment decreases. We don't commonly think of the air we breathe as a "fluid," but according to those rarefied minds who contemplate the immutable rules which govern our universe, that's the correct category for any substance that conforms to the shape of its container.

To understand why the Bernoulli Principle works, it helps to understand what creates pressure in the first place. It turns out that, like distant relatives staying together in a rented condo over a long holiday weekend, molecules in a fluid don't especially enjoy being near one another. Indeed, they would just as soon be as far apart as possible. This reaches its ultimate expression in the void of space, where you might find one single—presumably very happy—hydrogen molecule floating around in a dozen cubic feet of nothingness.

Those molecules trapped within Earth's gravitational field aren't nearly so lucky: They are packed together so closely that their combined weight on each square inch of the planet's surface is about the same as a bowling ball—14.7 pounds, give or take. Still, they retain that perpetual yearning to spread out from one another, and from one instant to the next, that creates the phenomenon we know as pressure.

When those molecules start moving, like air flowing over a wing, they have less time available to manifest their desire to escape. Therefore, the pressure they exert is reduced when compared to air that is moving more slowly or not moving at all. Of course, as a clear-eyed pilot, you're not going to take the word of some guy who has been dead for 250 years that any of this is true. You need to see it for yourself. So, go find a scrap of paper, hold it below your lower lip, and blow across it. It will flutter and rise as your exhaled breath sets the molecules above it in motion, reducing the pressure of the air above it.

Why didn't I just lead with that and spare you the preceding essay on an eighteenth century scientist from Switzerland? Because it's lovely to realize that once upon a time a family could be famous for being mathematicians instead of Kardashians. It seems like we could use more of that today.

Not only was Daniel Bernoulli an exemplar of 18th century sartorial refinement (and check out that coiffure!), he also laid the groundwork for heavier-than-air flight with his mathematical insights.

THE LIMITS OF LIFT

As powerful as lift is, it does have a couple limitations, and, as a pilot, it's critical that you understand them, because lift is the only thing that distinguishes "flying" from "falling." The first of these is that an airfoil must be traveling at a certain minimum speed before it can overcome the weight of the aircraft it is attached to and pull it up into the air. This speed varies with different aircraft and is based on a vast number of variables, such as the size and shape of the wing, the weight of the aircraft, the density of the surrounding atmosphere, and so on.

This minimum speed is called the "stall speed," because it is the speed at which an *aerodynamic stall* will occur. To be clear, this is nothing like what happens when your car stalls: The propeller keeps turning, and all of the electronic and mechanical systems continue to function normally. There just isn't enough air passing over the airfoil to create the lift required to maintain flight.

The good news is that stalls are generally, at least to some degree, self-correcting. Any competently designed fixed-wing aircraft will, upon experiencing an aerodynamic stall, fall nose-first toward the ground. In the process, it will pick up speed, more air will start flowing over the wings and it will resume flying. If the plane is two feet off the ground when this happens, that's a problem. At altitude, this process will give the pilot an opportunity to advance the throttle—providing more thrust and thus more speed to avoid stalling again—and then restore the aircraft to straight and level flight.

The second key limit on lift starts out not so much as a limit but rather as a way of dramatically increasing lift. It involves the angle at which the wing meets the oncoming air and is referred to as the *angle of attack* (Figure 4.4). While this has nothing to do with actually attacking anybody, a deeper understanding requires the comprehension of additional concepts, like *chord lines* and *relative wind*, which, while interesting, aren't crucial for you to understand as a novice remote pilot.

What you do need to know is that as a wing's angle of attack increases, the lift it generates increases, as well. Essentially, increasing the angle of attack forces the air molecules going over the top of the wing to take an even longer path than before,

Getting Started With Drones and Model Airplanes

further reducing the air pressure over the wing. That's great, and it explains airplanes lift their noses to gain altitude, but it turns out that there can be too much of a good thing.

When an airfoil reaches its ***critical angle of attack*** (Figure 4.5)—which, like stall speed, varies between aircraft and is determined by a bunch of different variables—the smooth flow of air over the upper surface of the wing collapses and, once again, the aircraft will experience an aerodynamic stall. The process of recovering is the same, so you want to be sure to avoid this happening at low altitude.

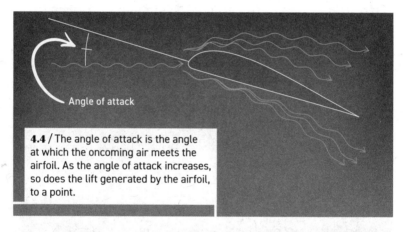

Angle of attack

4.4 / The angle of attack is the angle at which the oncoming air meets the airfoil. As the angle of attack increases, so does the lift generated by the airfoil, to a point.

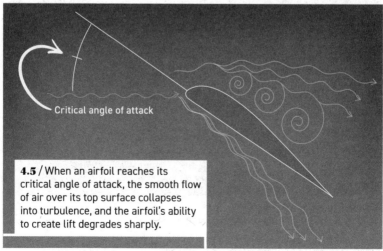

Critical angle of attack

4.5 / When an airfoil reaches its critical angle of attack, the smooth flow of air over its top surface collapses into turbulence, and the airfoil's ability to create lift degrades sharply.

LIFT AND ROTORCRAFT

No doubt you've noticed that the foregoing discussion focused entirely on fixed-wing aircraft. Because rotorcraft generate lift by spinning their rotor blades (airfoils), rather than relying on the forward movement of the aircraft to do it, they are functionally immune to aerodynamic stalls that are related to the speed and attitude of the aircraft, thus allowing their ability to hover, fly backwards, and so forth.

This is not to say that rotorcraft are somehow unbound from the rules of aerodynamics, but the relationship is much more complicated and not as easily understood (Figure 4.6). If you intend to fly drones, the good news is that the on-board *flight control system* (FCS) will manage all these details for you. These systems simply will not allow you to put your machine anywhere near a flight condition that might cause a catastrophic problem for you.

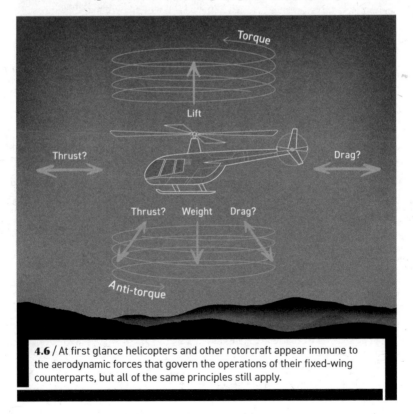

4.6 / At first glance helicopters and other rotorcraft appear immune to the aerodynamic forces that govern the operations of their fixed-wing counterparts, but all of the same principles still apply.

The same is largely true of palm-sized models that you might choose to start out with if your ambition is to fly helicopters or that you might fly alongside a drone to refine your piloting skills. However, as you start flying larger-model helicopters, it will become ever more incumbent on you to understand these complex forces and how to recognize and manage their effects on your machine. Providing you with that knowledge goes beyond the scope of this book, but here is a free sample, just to get you started: let's examine the *vortex ring state*.

Although it sounds like something that might imperil the starship *Enterprise* while investigating a black hole, vortex ring state can occur when a helicopter is making a relatively rapid vertical descent. A donut-shaped vortex forms around the perimeter of the disk defined by its spinning rotors. Consequently, the aircraft's own downwash is pulled back up into the rotor disk.

The result is a loss of lift as the rotor blades stall, just like an airplane's wings at its stall speed. The helicopter will then begin a rapid and uncontrolled descent, and the most intuitive solution, increasing power, will *not* arrest this loss of altitude. Instead, helicopter pilots are trained to transition forward or laterally—fancy pilot talk for flying straight ahead or off to one side—to escape the vortex and restore lift.

This is just one hazard among many associated with helicopter operations. Before you ever go anywhere near a machine with a rotor diameter that approaches your inseam measurement, you had better know them all and be prepared to handle each one. Don't expect that flying an uncrewed helicopter is going to be anything like flying a drone. Yes, they are both rotorcraft, but that's where the similarities end.

FIND YOUR CENTER

Another fundamental concept that you must understand before you can call yourself a pilot is *center of gravity,* called *CG* for short. This concept has applications that go well beyond aerodynamics, such as structural engineering. The CG of any given object is that single point at which the total mass of that object is said to act.

Let's put it another way: If you take a model airplane up to the International Space Station, be sure to bring me along. Once we get there, we'll give it a whirl and let it spin in the free air. The CG is the point around which the model will rotate (Figure 4.7). To be clear, the CG is not a fixed part of the structure or even a physical object. It's entirely possible that the CG could be located in a hollow space within the aircraft fuselage.

> **"An aircraft with a center of gravity that is too far forward flies poorly. An aircraft with a center of gravity that is too far aft flies once."**
>
> – Aviation Aphorism

This generally isn't true of aircraft, but it's even possible for the CG of an object to be found outside the object itself. As an example, imagine a bridge supported by two heavy stone piers, with a road deck spanning the space between them. Given the mass of the piers, its entirely plausible that the CG of that structure might lie at a point below the deck, equidistant between them, with nothing but the open air to call its home (Figure 4.8).

With buildings and bridges, if the CG ever wanders beyond its base of support, that is, the structure that anchors it to the Earth, it will topple over. That's why it is such a crucial factor in structural engineering and why structural engineers cling so urgently to their slide rules. CG is a critical factor in aerodynamics as well.

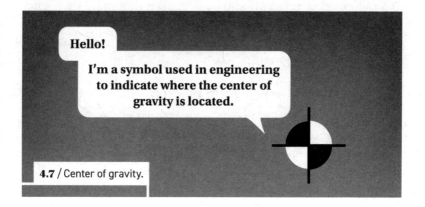

Hello!

I'm a symbol used in engineering to indicate where the center of gravity is located.

4.7 / Center of gravity.

4.8 / One of the most important things to understand about the center of gravity is that it is not a material object: It can exist in the middle of thin air, as in this bridge.

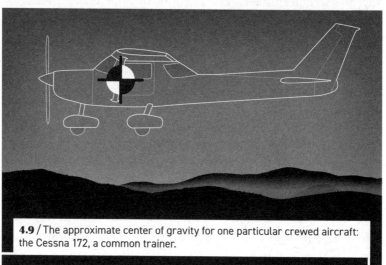

4.9 / The approximate center of gravity for one particular crewed aircraft: the Cessna 172, a common trainer.

All aircraft, to include remotely piloted aircraft, are designed to fly with their CG in a narrowly defined zone (Figure 4.9). In a model airplane, for example, that space might be one cubic inch, or even less, depending on the size of the model. Obviously, an aircraft won't topple over like a building if the CG is misplaced, but it can make it difficult, or impossible, to fly.

As an example, consider the case of a fixed-wing airplane with a CG that is too far to the rear. While it is flying, this airplane stalls. However, instead of its nose dropping and regaining speed to escape the stall, it starts settling tail-first toward the ground. The stall quickly becomes unrecoverable, and at that point a crash is inevitable.

Getting the CG right in a crewed aircraft is an essential part of the pilot's job. The process is called **weight and balance** and involves using a table created by the aircraft manufacturer to determine how the position of passengers and cargo within the airframe impacts the CG. If it drifts too far out of position, the results could be fatal.

As a remote pilot, the stakes generally won't be that high, but you should still take all possible measures to ensure the CG is correct before you go flying. Reputable model airplane manufacturers will include a diagram indicating where the CG should be located and how to determine it. This is primarily affected by the weight and placement of the battery within the fuselage, and the same is true for model helicopters. Put the battery where it is supposed to go, and you should be fine.

Since virtually all drones you are likely to fly as a novice pilot are closed systems, designed to be flown using only batteries and other accessories from the manufacturer, you can generally take the position of the CG for granted. However, if you do need to attach something external to the aircraft, try to place it as near to the center as possible. Then, do a series of short-range, low-altitude test flights before going any farther.

WATCH YOUR ATTITUDE

In our everyday vernacular, the word "attitude" is used almost exclusively to refer to a person's emotional disposition, as in "He's had a bad attitude ever since he wrecked his expensive model airplane. Too bad he didn't take the time to read *Getting Started with Drones and Model Airplanes* by Patrick Sherman. He could have saved himself a lot of grief—and money." However, this being aviation, we must inevitably grab hold of that common word and assign it a completely different meaning.

In aviation, "attitude" is used to describe the relationship between different parts of the aircraft and the horizon. So, for example, if the nose of an aircraft is below the horizon, that aircraft is said to have a nose-low attitude, and so forth. However, this can quickly become unwieldy as we try to characterize a "left-wing high" attitude and think about what that would mean.

So, instead, we define the movement of aircraft using three axes of rotation. And, just to be clear, that's got nothing to do with the kind of axe you use to chop wood—it's the plural of axis. All aircraft, and all material objects in this universe for that matter, have three axes of rotation: pitch, roll, and yaw. The exact same terms are used with drones and other rotorcraft, but we'll begin by explaining the concept using a fixed-wing airplane (Figure 4.10).

- **Pitch** defines the relationship between the front of the aircraft and the horizon. An aircraft can either pitch up or pitch down, as when it is ascending or descending.
- **Roll** defines the relationship between the wings of the aircraft and the horizon. An aircraft can either roll left or roll right.
- **Yaw** defines the position of the front of the aircraft on the horizon—essentially steering in the conventional sense. An aircraft can either yaw left or yaw right.

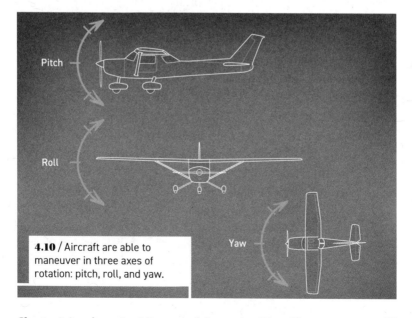

4.10 / Aircraft are able to maneuver in three axes of rotation: pitch, roll, and yaw.

No doubt you've noticed that we have two different ways of going "left" and "right" in an airplane, roll *and* yaw, which points to the need for this specialized language in the first place. Unless you are already a pilot (in which case, why are you reading this book!?) every vehicle you have ever guided in your entire life is only capable of one of these three types of maneuvers: yaw.

Imagine driving a car around an empty parking lot. You can steer in any direction you would like, which is to say toward any particular point on the horizon and, using the steering wheel, you can change directions at will. In this example, you are controlling your car's yaw. The same is true for a motorboat in the middle of a lake.

Now, ground vehicles and watercraft do pitch and roll as well, but these movements are quite limited and are not under the direct control of the person at the wheel. If a boat rolls too far, it capsizes, for example—an outcome sailors generally seek to avoid.

So, with this newfound understanding of pitch, roll and yaw, our next task is to understand how we, as pilots, control them and what impact they have on the performance of our aircraft. As usual, the same general concepts apply to fixed-wing and rotorcraft, but their application is completely different, so we'll consider them separately, starting with conventional airplanes.

FIXED-WING MANEUVERING

To allow the pilot to control pitch, roll, and yaw, airplanes have movable panels attached to the trailing edges of their wings and stabilizers. These are known collectively as ***control surfaces*** (Figure 4.11) and include elevators, ailerons, and the rudder.

- **Elevators** are located at the back of the airplane, on the horizontal stabilizer. They move up and down together and allow the pilot to control the pitch of the aircraft.
- **Ailerons** are located on the wings and move opposite to one another: When one goes up, the other one goes down. They allow the pilot to control the roll of the aircraft.
- The **rudder** is located on the vertical stabilizer and moves left and right, like the rudder of a ship. It allows the pilot to control the yaw of the aircraft.

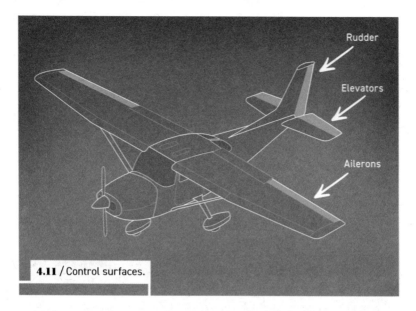

4.11 / Control surfaces.

Now, as ever, there are countless variations to this basic configuration. Sometimes, the whole horizontal stabilizer moves like a giant elevator, a configuration known as a "stabilator." Or, the elevators and the rudder can be combined to create a "ruddervator." On flying wings, like the stealth bomber, the elevators and ailerons are conjoined in a control surface known as the "elevon." The list, I can assure you, goes on and on and on...

As a new pilot, you don't need to worry about these exotic configurations, with one possible exception. Some training aircraft designed specifically for beginners omit the ailerons entirely, relying on the rudder to do double-duty: controlling both roll and yaw. Even this isn't something you should spend too much time worrying about. Trust the aircraft designers to have done their job correctly—and with your needs in mind—and focus on keeping the machine in the air. More on that in Chapter 8.

So, now that we understand the location and function of the basic control surfaces, what happens to the airplane when we *actuate* (a fancy word for "move") them? If you use the elevators to pitch the nose up, the aircraft ascends due to the increased angle of attack causing the wings to generate more lift. Pitch down and the opposite happens: The aircraft descends.

Things start getting a little tricky when we get to the ailerons and aircraft roll. Yes, as expected, aileron input causes one wing to drop below the horizon and the other to rise above it. However, you'll notice that this results in some of the wing's lifting force being directed "sideways," and as a result, the aircraft will start to turn. This is referred to as a ***banked turn*** (Figure 4.12), because the aircraft accomplishes it by banking (i.e., rolling).

Now, even across the time and space that separate us, I can sense your dismay: "You said that 'turning'—which you just insisted that I refer to properly as 'yawing'—is controlled by the rudder, like on a boat! So how is it that we're now making a turn using the ailerons to roll!? Clearly, Patrick, you can't be trusted. I want my money back!"

FLAP YOUR WINGS!

As I mentioned in the main text, there are numerous other types of control surfaces, and combinations of control surfaces, that exist beyond the three basics: elevators, ailerons, and rudders. There is one more type you should know about, because it is nearly ubiquitous on crewed airplanes and can be found on many more complex models as well: *flaps*.

The flaps are found on the trailing edge of the wings, inboard from the ailerons. Unlike the ailerons, they work together, moving in the same direction at the same time. Also, flaps are generally only used during takeoff and landing, and spend the rest of the time tucked in nice and snug behind the wing.

In essence, extending the flaps changes the shape of the wing, exaggerating the airfoil and causing it to generate more lift at a given speed, allowing it to fly more slowly without experiencing an aerodynamic stall. During takeoff, that means the plane doesn't have to travel as fast before becoming airborne, so it can use a shorter runway. On landing, the plane can fly more slowly, again requiring less runway, as well as reducing the force on the ***undercarriage*** when it makes initial contact with the ground.

If flaps are so wonderful, you may be thinking to yourself, why not just leave them extended all the time? The problem is that flaps limit the top speed of the aircraft, which would significantly degrade its performance under most flying conditions. Also, on crewed aircraft, there is a maximum speed beyond which the flaps cannot be safely extended lest they cause dangerous and unpredictable maneuvers or even tear off the wing entirely.

Getting Started With Drones and Model Airplanes

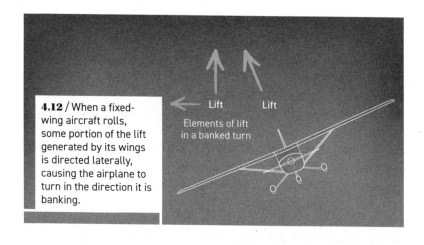

4.12 / When a fixed-wing aircraft rolls, some portion of the lift generated by its wings is directed laterally, causing the airplane to turn in the direction it is banking.

Lift   Lift

Elements of lift in a banked turn

Plenty of model airplanes do not have flaps, including virtually every trainer made and sold for new pilots, so this won't be something you'll need to think about for a while. When that time arrives, exercise caution and give yourself plenty of altitude to recover if you don't get what you were expecting when you extend the flaps.

And, yes, in the best tradition of amalgamating different types of control surfaces and assigning that pairing a funny name, flaps and ailerons can be combined to create the "flaperon."

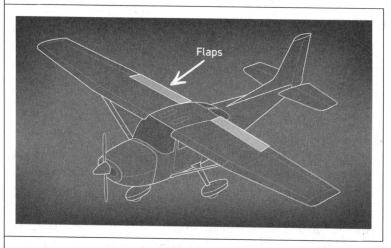

Flaps

The flaps are typically located inboard from the ailerons on fixed-wing aircraft.

All I can say is, "If it was easy, you wouldn't have had to read this book."

The truth is that almost every time an airplane makes a turn, and this goes for crewed aviation as well, banking—otherwise known as rolling—is involved. In fact, those beginner models I described earlier that dispense with the ailerons entirely? They fly by treating the rudder as if it were the ailerons. In other words, most of the time you can fly just fine without touching the rudder control.

So, what's the point of the rudder then? You'll figure that out as you gain more experience, but as an example, the rudder allows you to accomplish what is called a **coordinated turn**. Remember that when an airplane banks, some of the lift from its wings is siphoned off to make the turn. Well, guess what, that portion of the wing's lift is no longer available to maintain the airplane's altitude, so it will descend.

You can counteract this effect using the rudder, making a turn that maintains all the forces on the aircraft in perfect balance without ever touching the throttle. Also, your passengers—if you had any—would be more comfortable and less prone to air sickness if you execute coordinated turns. Aerodynamic perfection *and* less vomit to clean up after you land!? Who wouldn't want that?

ROTORCRAFT MANEUVERING

Just like their fixed-wing brethren, rotorcraft can pitch, roll, and yaw, but how they accomplish it and the impact each type of maneuver has on their performance is completely different. To begin with, let's expand on an idea we touched on briefly earlier: the **rotor disk** (Figure 4.13).

Obviously, the propeller(s) on a helicopter or drone have individual blades, most often two, but sometimes more. As the propeller(s) turn, their airfoil-shaped blades pass through the air, generating lift from an intricate series of aerodynamic forces that are far too complex for us to even begin to contemplate here. Instead, we'll treat this entire spinning system as if it were a single, lift-generating component: the rotor disk. Now, the rotor disk doesn't exist as a material object, it is defined by those individual propeller blades turning hundreds or thousands of times per minute.

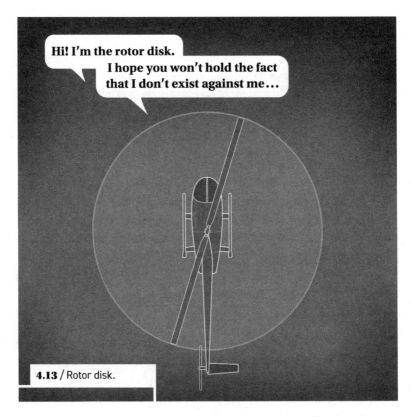

4.13 / Rotor disk.

For our purposes here, we can pretend that it is simply a lift-producing body, not unlike an airplane's wing, albeit with very different characteristics. And of course, single-rotor and multi-rotor platforms achieve pitch, roll, and yaw using techniques that are distinct from one another, so we'll need to account for that, as well.

To begin with, let's consider pitch and roll in the context of a rotorcraft. If you think about it for a minute, they are actually the exact same maneuver, the only difference being the direction in which the aircraft moves. Pitch forward, that is, nose down, and the aircraft moves forward. Pitch back, nose up, and the aircraft moves backward. Roll left and the aircraft moves left. Roll right and the aircraft moves right.

In this case, the cause is exactly the same as a fixed-wing airplane making a roll maneuver; some portion of the lift generated by the rotor disk(s) is transformed into thrust that moves the aircraft in the direction of the maneuver. This, of course, results in a decline in the amount of lift available to maintain its altitude.

With their sophisticated *flight control systems* (FCS) and suites of high-tech sensors, virtually all modern drones will make up the difference for you, adding just enough lift to maintain a constant altitude.

Helicopters—not so much. Model helicopters will require you to add throttle when you pitch or roll if you want to maintain a constant altitude. It's all part of the fun.

But how does an aircraft with zero control surfaces pitch and roll? Great question—I'm glad you asked. In the case of a conventional helicopter, it distorts the shape of its own rotor disk, so that one side generates more lift than the other. The aircraft then pitches, or rolls, in the opposite direction. In the instance of a drone with four rotors, the two propellers on one side of the aircraft speed up, again generating more lift, and pitching or rolling the aircraft in the other direction.

FEELING TORQUED OFF?

Rotorcraft yaw requires that you begin by understanding a specific instance of Newton's Third Law, called the *torque reaction*. In case it's been a while since you took high school physics, I'll catch you up. Sir Isaac Newton taught us, among a great many other things, that "for every action there is an equal and opposite reaction."

As a thought experiment, imagine a conventional helicopter that weighs 100 pounds supported by a main rotor that weighs 10 pounds. According to Newton's Third Law, every time the main rotor turns 10 times in a counterclockwise direction, the body of the aircraft must rotate once in a clockwise direction (Figure 4.14). Of course, spinning 'round and 'round isn't a practical design for a flying machine, which is why helicopters have tail rotors, the small propeller at the rear of the aircraft and at the end of a boom.

The tail rotor, which is also called an *antitorque rotor* by smart people (a category that now includes you, by the way), generates lateral thrust that cancels out the torque reaction from the main rotor, which is why helicopters can fly straight in one direction in spite of Newton's Third Law, and why many people believe that

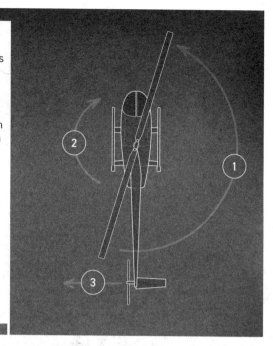

4.14 / As the main rotor of a "single rotor" helicopter spins counterclockwise (**arrow 1**) Newton's Third Law tells us that the body of the aircraft must rotate in the opposite direction (**arrow 2**) at a rate which is proportional to the relative mass of these two bodies. The anti-torque rotor at the rear of the aircraft counteracts the torque reaction (**arrow 3**) allowing the helicopter to fly in a straight line and maneuver in the yaw axis.

helicopters can somehow defy the laws of physics. Furthermore, if the antitorque rotor creates more thrust beyond that which is necessary to maintain its direction of travel, the helicopter will yaw in the same direction as the main rotor's spin. Conversely, if it creates less thrust, the torque from the main rotor will cause the helicopter to yaw in the opposite direction.

Drones are also able to yaw because of the torque reaction, although the lack of an antitorque rotor should be a big hint that they do it differently. If you look closely at a typical drone with four rotors, you will notice that two of the rotors turn clockwise and the other two turn counterclockwise. As you have probably guessed by now, that isn't a fluke.

To yaw in a clockwise direction, the drone's two counterclockwise propellers start spinning faster and the resulting torque reaction pulls the front of the aircraft around. Yawing in the other direction involves doing the exact opposite. Of course, spinning propellers faster means doing more than generating excess torque: It also means creating more lift.

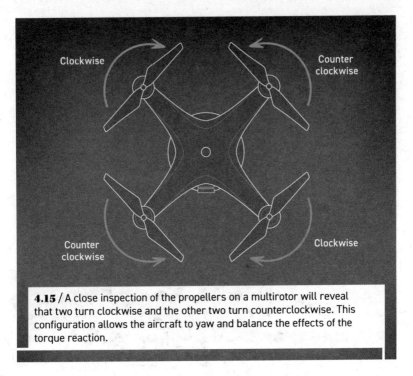

4.15 / A close inspection of the propellers on a multirotor will reveal that two turn clockwise and the other two turn counterclockwise. This configuration allows the aircraft to yaw and balance the effects of the torque reaction.

For the aircraft to maintain a constant altitude during a yaw maneuver, the two rotors turning in the same direction as its airframe must slow down a little bit so that the net lift generated by all four rotors remains constant. In the way-back time, maybe 15 years ago, this could lead to a distinctive and unsettling wobble during yaw maneuvers. However, once again, the advances in flight control algorithms and sensors have banished this issue from any drone you are likely to ever find yourself flying.

MISSION ACCOMPLISHED?

Congratulations! If you've been reading closely and maybe scribbled a few notes in the margins, you now possess a rudimentary understanding of aerodynamics. There is far, far more that you could still learn than what you have learned already, like every other subject we cover in this book—but this goes double for aerodynamics. People get doctorates in this stuff with plenty of math and physics involved, more than even I would ever choose to contemplate, let alone try to understand.

My goal here was never to provide you with all the answers but rather to prepare you to ask the right questions. If your model airplane isn't flying the way you expect, you now understand that its CG might be the source of the problem, and you know what heading to look for in the flight manual. You know the difference between an elevator and an aileron, so you can ask another pilot about it without having to say, "You know, the thingy at the back that makes it go up and down."

So, here ends the lesson—and now the real learning can begin.

5

Bits and Pieces:
What's on the Inside?

Some clever joker once offered the opinion—most likely without being asked—that an airplane is just a collection of spare parts flying in close formation. Regardless of your take on that particular bit of received wisdom, it's important that you, as a pilot, understand how the individual parts of your aircraft actually work—and work together to make flight possible (Figure 5.1).

Having said that, you already understand what an aileron is, along with an elevator, a rudder and a propeller, and how each of them works from having closely read Chapter 4, right? Do you really, truly need to understand all the individual components that make them move, especially as a new pilot anxious to spread or spin your wings?

Well, maybe not. If you want to skip ahead to Chapter 6 and start flying, I won't think any less of you. Do me the favor of revisiting this chapter after you've got some flight hours in your logbook. You'll definitely need to understand these details to achieve your full potential as a remote pilot.

THE BRAINS OF THE OUTFIT

Any uncrewed aircraft you are likely to pick up today will contain, at its heart, a miniature computer that manages its operations. Drones are literally unable to fly without one, and they offer over-

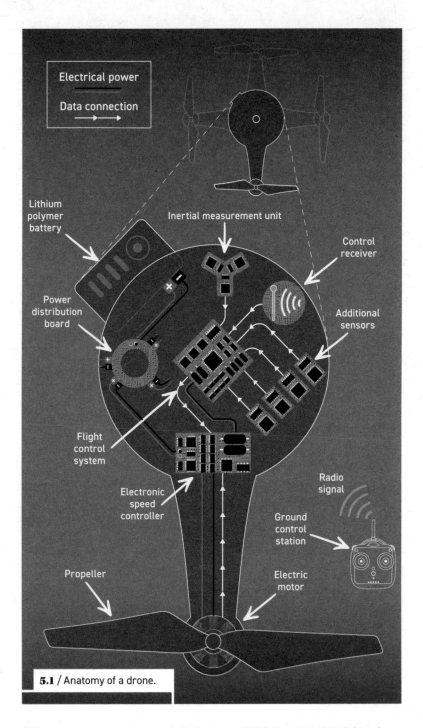

Electrical power

Data connection →

Lithium polymer battery

Inertial measurement unit

Control receiver

Power distribution board

Additional sensors

Flight control system

Electronic speed controller

Radio signal

Ground control station

Propeller

Electric motor

5.1 / Anatomy of a drone.

whelming advantages for model airplanes and helicopters, as well, which has made them nearly ubiquitous among remotely piloted aircraft today. This computer is called the *flight control system* or FCS, for short (Figure 5.2). Many modern crewed aircraft incorporating *fly-by-wire* technology use this same type of system, albeit far more complicated and robust. These are sometimes also referred to as a *flight management system (FMS)*.

The FCS runs in a continuous loop. Hundreds of times per second, it assesses the attitude of the aircraft, the control inputs from the pilot and the action of external forces such as wind and turbulence. It then combines all this information, adjusts the speed of its electric motors and the position of its control surfaces to keep the aircraft stable, and implements the commands given to it by the pilot.

Put another way: You don't actually fly a modern uncrewed aircraft—the FCS flies it, and you just tell the FCS what you want it to do. As mentioned in a previous chapter, under certain circumstances the FCS will even ignore you. Don't let your feelings get hurt, however. This is usually for the best.

Of course, this ability is entirely contingent on the FCS knowing something about the aircraft's *attitude*, at the very least. To accomplish this crucial task, it receives input from a variety of sensors; the most fundamental and crucial among these being

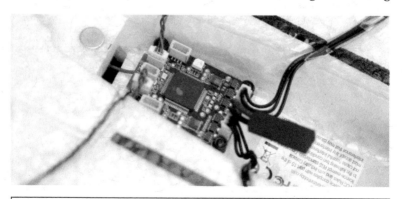

5.2 / The Flight Control System (FCS) included in all modern drones and model airplanes has benefited from huge advances is microprocessing and microelectromechanical systems (MEMS) technology over the past two decades.

gyroscopes and *accelerometers*. There will, at a minimum, be three of each—one for each axis of rotation that we learned about in Chapter 4: pitch, roll, and yaw.

The gyroscopes determine the aircraft's relationship to the horizon in each axis. Which way is the aircraft pitching or rolling, or is it flying straight and level? The accelerometers determine how quickly the relationship between that part of the aircraft and the horizon is changing. Is it steady, as when flying straight and level, or at any other constant attitude, like a gradual descent or a banked turn? Or is it changing quickly, like when the aircraft is making aggressive maneuvers? Don't tear your drone apart looking for a traditional gyroscope, it's all part of the microprocessor now, like the one in your iPhone that tells it at what orientation you are holding the phone, so the image is always upright.

This combination of gyroscopes and accelerometers is known as the *inertial measurement unit*, or IMU. These days, the IMU is

MEMS SENSORS

If you've ever seen a gyroscope, then the notion that one of them—let alone three—would somehow fit inside a drone or model airplane seems absurd. That they should all somehow fit on a circuit board seems like absurdity squared. This miracle of physics has nevertheless been accomplished by the development of what are called **MEMS sensors**.

MEMS is an acronym, which stands for **microelectromechanical systems**. These systems are created using the same techniques used to create conventional integrated circuit chips made from silicon, resulting in precise and reliable sensors that can be only two percent of the width of a human hair, which makes them fit, and integrate, quite easily on a small circuit board.

As noted in the main text, drones would be essentially impossible to fly without the gyroscopes and accelerometers made possible by MEMS technology. It is therefore fortunate indeed that Steve Jobs decided that the original iPhone, released in 2001, be able to sense and respond to users twisting and turning the device.

This led to the MEMS being produced at scale, driving the price down to the point that they could be incorporated into these flying machines, ultimately facilitating their production at prices everyday consumers could afford, and thereby ushering in the drone revolution.

almost always integrated directly into the FCS, such that you will seldom see it listed as a separate component anymore, but it's in there, working as hard as ever to ensure stable, predictable flight performance.

An integrated FCS allows even model airplanes costing less than $150 to limit the maneuvers the pilot can make. While this may initially seem like an intrusion on the pilot's authority, it can be a big help—especially for new pilots. By only allowing the plane to pitch, or roll, so far and no farther, the FCS can prevent the airplane from entering what could be a very disorienting attitude, like flying upside down or straight at the ground.

One example of this type of system is the *Sensor-Assisted Flight Envelope (SAFE)*, which is incorporated in many aircraft manufactured by Horizon Hobby. We'll look more at these types of systems in Chapter 6.

Drones and model airplanes do not rely on conventional gyroscopes to provide feedback for their flight control systems (FCS), because they never would have gotten off the ground.

For drones, the FCS-IMU pairing is only the beginning. The platforms sold by top-tier manufacturers incorporate suites of sensors that provide the FCS with a wealth of data and allow them to function as true flying robots, capable of carrying out complex missions while operating autonomously.

SENSOR SMORGASBORD

Of all the sensors typically incorporated into drones, the single most consequential and ubiquitous is the *GPS receiver*. Picking up radio transmissions from a constellation of *Global Positioning System (GPS)* satellites in orbit 12,000-ish miles overhead, a GPS receiver can fix its position on the surface of the Earth with astonishing precision. This is precisely the same technology that allows your smartphone to provide you with turn-by-turn directions while driving.

GPS is a remarkably powerful tool, allowing drones to find their way home without pilot input or fly complicated, waypoint-driven missions autonomously. GPS also allows a drone to hover in place despite the action of outside forces, like the wind. This is referred to as a *stationkeeping* maneuver and would otherwise require considerable skill and effort on the pilot's behalf (Figure 5.3). In the olden days, we had to do this all by ourselves. We also had to walk to school in the snow—up hill in both directions, no less!

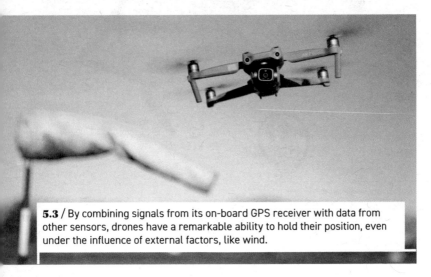

5.3 / By combining signals from its on-board GPS receiver with data from other sensors, drones have a remarkable ability to hold their position, even under the influence of external factors, like wind.

Although it began as a U.S. Air Force project to benefit military users, **Global Positioning System (GPS)** technology has become ubiquitous in modern life. However, as usual, if you scratch beneath the surface, you'll find the situation is more complicated than you've been led to believe. First, GPS is the brand name for the U.S. system. These types of systems are known more generally as **global navigation satellite systems**, or **GNSS** for short.

The very fact that there is a generic term for this type of system must mean there is more than one of them, right? You guessed it! Each of them is referred to as a **constellation** of satellites. GPS is the most robust system at present, with 31 operational satellites and another three in reserve. The Soviet Union built a comparable system during the Cold War that is still maintained by Russia. Its full name is **Global'naya Navigatsionnaya Sputnikovaya Sistema**, which is more than a mouthful, so people use the acronym GLONASS, instead. At present, this system has 23 operational satellites in orbit.

Other countries are building their own systems, as well. China began launching its **BeiDou Navigation Satellite System** in 2000 and currently has 30 satellites in orbit. The European Union has a constellation of 23 functional **Galileo** satellites and both Japan and India maintain their own regional networks: **QZSS (Quasi-Zenith Satellite System)** and **NavIC (Navigation with Indian Constellation)**, respectively.

Because the main driver of GNSS accuracy is how many satellites the receiver can "see" overhead from any particular location, most drones—and other "GPS" systems, for that matter—have been designed to detect and reference signals from multiple constellations.

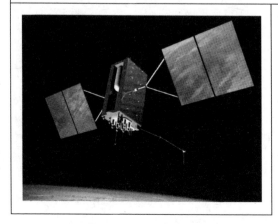

Since the United States launched its first Global Positioning System (GPS) satellite in 1978, other countries have been hard at work putting their own hardware into orbit, a benefit to all users, because more satellites mean better, more accurate service for everybody.

For all its capabilities, GPS also comes with some important limitations. First, when a GPS receiver is powered up, especially in a new location, it needs time to acquire the faint radio signals coming down from the satellites and establish an accurate fix. Until that happens, the receiver may yield a location, but you shouldn't trust it. Second, the satellites are scattered across the sky, and the more the receiver can "see," the better. So, if the receiver's "view" of the sky is blocked by tall buildings or other obstacles, it may not be able to detect the signals, or even worse, those obstacles may reflect or distort the signals, resulting in an incorrect fix.

So, when you power up your drone, make sure that you give it enough time to acquire an accurate GPS lock and that it has a clear view of the sky. Otherwise, you may find it behaves in unpredictable ways, and in aviation, unpredictable is never good.

The GPS receiver's partner in navigation is the *magnetic compass*. Used for centuries by explorers and others who wander but are not lost, a compass is an instrument that senses the Earth's magnetic field and always indicates which direction is north, and by extension, which direction is south, east, and west, to boot. This process is not nearly as simple as it sounds, because not only does magnetic north vary significantly from true north, the degree of variation changes from one geographic location to another, and even from year to year. Consequently, it is necessary to calibrate your drone's compass periodically, with some people recommending that you do it any time you fly more than a mile from your previous location. There is certainly debate on this subject, which I attribute to the quality of the sensors getting better every year.

Another core sensor that virtually all drones include is a barometric altimeter. This instrument determines the altitude of your aircraft by measuring changes in atmospheric pressure. As mentioned in Chapters 3 and 4, atmospheric pressure decreases as altitude increases, and the altimeter can detect that change and attach a value to it, in terms of the aircraft's altitude *above ground level (AGL)*. This is different from crewed aviation, where the altimeter is calibrated to indicate its altitude above *mean sea level (MSL)*.

Most drones will notify you when you need to calibrate the compass, and often will prevent you from flying until you do so. Fortunately, it's a straight-forward process, and the app on your smart device will walk you through it step-by-step.

The process begins by finding an open, outdoor space away from metal objects, like cars and fences, for example. Also, be cautious of potential underground sources of magnetic interference, such as water mains and steel-reinforced concrete structures. A utility hole cover in your immediate vicinity is never a good sign. Also, overhead electrical lines can cause problems. Finally, best practice would have you remove metal objects from your person—to include a watch, key ring, coins, and so forth.

Once you are ready, follow the prompts in the app, which will most often tell you to turn your drone through each axis of rotation: pitch, roll, and yaw. As you will likely be standing at least several feet away from your cell phone owing to its potential for magnetic interference, it helps to have a friend call out the steps for you.

Old-timey drone pilots refer to this process as the "compass dance." Obviously, you should perform this ritual whenever your drone requests it and it's a good idea to do it at least once a year or if you've traveled more than 500 miles with your drone, to account for the natural variations in the Earth's magnetic field.

If your compass is not calibrated correctly, you may be treated to a spectacle known as the *TBE*, the **toilet bowl effect**. Your drone will swirl around and around in the air like it is headed down the—well, never mind, you get the idea. As soon as you are able, land safely recalibrate your compass.

If your compass is not calibrated correctly, you may be treated to the aerial spectacle known to remote pilots as the "toilet-bowl effect" (TBE). If your drone appears to be circling the drain, land and re-calibrate your compass.

At first, an altimeter might seem redundant with the GPS receiver, which can be used to determine the aircraft's position, so why not its altitude as well? The answer involves too much mathematics to be worth explaining here but suffice it to say that GPS generally does a poor job of fixing the elevation of an object, relative to its position. The difference is such that the altimeter will generally deliver a measurement that is correct within plus or minus three feet, but with a GPS receiver, it would be more like plus or minus 60 feet. Still, this makes a crucial point: All altitude measurements provided by your aircraft are necessarily estimates, so always err on the side of safety and caution.

One other point about the altimeter: Remember that in Chapter 4 we touched on the fact that a drone will turn all its propellers just a little bit faster while pitching or rolling to maintain a constant altitude? It's the input from the altimeter that allows the FCS to accomplish this.

Generally, the compass and the altimeter live inside the same box, or on the same circuit board, as the FCS and IMU, having become marvels of microminiaturization. For the rest of the sensors that make modern drones so easy to fly, we'll need to look elsewhere.

OUTSIDE THE BOX

Of all the sensors that you can see on the external surface of a drone, probably the most technologically advanced is the *collision avoidance system*. Look closely at a modern drone, and you'll see what look like small cameras, in pairs, facing forward, behind, and likely in other directions as well (Figure 5.4). They look like cameras because that's precisely what they are—and they come in pairs because, just like your own Mark 1 human eyeballs, they use the images from two separate optical inputs to build a 3D model of the surroundings.

Thus, they can estimate the distance between the drone and an object in the environment that you might prefer not to hit, like a tree or a brick wall. As you get closer to an obstacle, the FCS will send you a series of increasingly urgent warnings until it ultimately refuses to continue moving forward or in whatever direction

5.4 / Just like human eyes, the collision avoidance systems incorporated into most drones sold today use a pair of cameras to build a 3D model of the surrounding environment to identify and avoid obstacles.

the obstacle might lie. This is one of those instances I referred to earlier where the FCS will actively ignore you—and you will more than likely be glad for it.

While they are a remarkable technological achievement in what is commonly referred to as *machine vision*, collision avoidance systems are far from foolproof. First of all, they have a limited range: typically, something on the order of about 15 feet. A side effect of this fact is that if your drone is flying fast, it may not have time to stop after detecting an obstacle, so always exercise special care when flying at or near your aircraft's maximum speed.

Also, small objects, like utility wires and bare tree limbs, will often escape their notice—creating the possibility of a collision with these sorts of obstacles. And, of course, because they work like your eyes, there must be enough light for the system to be able to detect an obstacle in the first place, so it's not going to do you any good at night. Your drone also may think that the glare from a sunrise or sunset is an obstacle, causing you to cease movement midair, seemingly for no reason.

Finally, you can opt to *manually disable* the collision avoidance system. As a novice flying for fun, there probably isn't any reason you would ever want to do this. With that said, professional remote pilots occasionally confront circumstances where the collision avoidance system actively inhibits them from accomplishing their mission—thus the option to switch it off. However, if you do disable it, make darn sure that you re-enable it before you count on it working again. That's an exceedingly silly way to crash a drone. Don't ask me how I know.

Another type of machine vision system that is quite common on modern drones is the *optical flow sensor* (Figure 5.5). This works in precisely the same way as an optical computer mouse. A camera on the belly of the aircraft is constantly capturing images of the ground below and comparing the most recent with the ones that preceded it, looking for any change between them. When features on the ground move in one direction, the optical flow sensor concludes that the aircraft must be moving in the opposite direction and shares its opinion with the FCS.

If this movement is the result of input from the pilot, then everything is hunky-dory. However, if not, then the FCS concludes that some outside force—like a gust of wind—must be acting on the aircraft, and it implements a maneuver to maintain the aircraft in its current position. It should be noted that this essentially duplicates the function of the GPS receiver in regard to stationkeeping,

5.5 / Located on the underside of many drones, the optical flow cameras identify shapes and patterns on the ground below in order to enhance the aircraft's stationkeeping abilities at low altitude.

and the FCS considers input from both the GPS and the optical flow sensor to enhance stability.

Optical flow sensors do have some important limitations. First, they only work when the drone is relatively close to the ground—at an altitude no greater than 10 to 15 feet. Second, in order to function, they rely on the surface they are flying above being static. If you're flying over a flowing stream or leaves blowing in the wind, for example, it will not provide any useful data. However, the FCS is generally good at disregarding these types of bad input thanks to the data provided by the GPS receiver.

The final type of sensor you should be aware of sends out active pulses into the environment and listens—or watches—for their echo. These are **ultrasonic** and **infrared rangefinders**. They are used to measure the altitude of the aircraft above the ground and, like the optical flow sensor, they only function at low altitude. Their primary contribution is to enhance aircraft stability during takeoff and landing.

The ultrasonic variety (Figure 5.6) emits a sound at such a high frequency that it is inaudible to humans, as well as our canine companions, in this case. It then listens for that burst to bounce off the ground and return to the aircraft. Take the elapsed time, multiply it by the speed of sound and then divide by two, and you get a relatively accurate estimate of the drone's altitude. The infrared variety (Figure 5.7) uses precisely the same approach but using invisible light—like the remote control for a television.

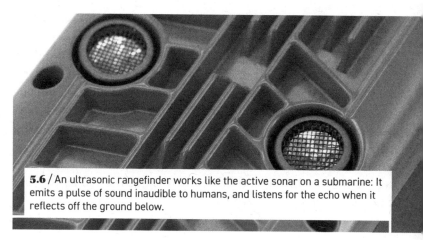

5.6 / An ultrasonic rangefinder works like the active sonar on a submarine: It emits a pulse of sound inaudible to humans, and listens for the echo when it reflects off the ground below.

5.7 / Infrared rangefinders work in a manner identical to their ultrasonic counterparts, albeit using a pulse of invisible light rather than inaudible sound.

MAKING A MOVE

So now the FCS is marinating in data that allows it to understand the position and movement of the aircraft relative to the ground and the horizon. Next up, it must be able to do something with all of that data. As we learned in Chapters 3 and 4, virtually all remotely piloted aircraft rely on spinning propellers to make that happen. Fixed-wing platforms rely on them for thrust, and rotorcraft rely on them for everything.

This means that there must be something that makes the propeller spin: an *electric motor* (Figure 5.8). Electric motors rely on a combination of *permanent magnets* and *electromagnets* to function. Permanent magnets are full-time magnets: like the sort you might use to post your shopping list on the door of your refrigerator. Electromagnets, on the other hand, just work part time. They are only magnetic when an electric current is flowing through them. Otherwise, they are inert. You might find this variety mounted on a crane at a junkyard being used to haul around wrecked cars—lifting and dropping them as needed by turning the electromagnet on and off.

5.8 / Electrically powered uncrewed aircraft, including most model airplanes and virtually all drones, rely on electric motors like this one to transform stored power into torque, permitting them to fly.

Inside an electric motor, the permanent magnets are arrayed around the outside of the motor's housing, which is also the part that spins. Several terms are associated with this component and its configuration. The spinning outer housing constitutes the motor's *rotor* (Figure 5.9)—that is, the part that rotates—as opposed to the *stator* (Figure 5.10), which doesn't move. More on that in a minute. Also, this rotor has nothing to do with the rotor blades that make up the aircraft's propeller, although the two are physically connected.

5.9 / The inside of an electric motor's rotor has permanent magnets affixed to it, so that each magnet has a polarity which is the opposite of both its neighbors.

Perhaps you noticed that I have consistently referred to the source of rotational power on board model airplanes, helicopters, and drones as "motors." In everyday conversation, we tend to use the words "motor" and "engine" interchangeably—you might say, "My car has a problem with its motor, so I dropped it off at the mechanic."

However, there is in fact a technical distinction between the two: Motors generate torque using electrical power, while engines generate torque through combustion, the burning of gasoline or other fuels. Thus, unless it's all electric, your car would more properly be said to have an engine, not a motor.

While the overwhelming majority of uncrewed aircraft that you are likely to encounter in your career as a remote pilot do, in fact, use motors, the early pioneers of remote, fixed-wing flight used small gas engines as their power source. Though rare at this point, a few die-hards still enjoy the smell of burning fuel in the morning—or any other time of day, I suppose.

If that sounds like fun to you, by all means look into it further once you've gained some experience. Be advised that gas-burning engines make quite a racket—imagine piloting an un-muffled leaf blower—and require specialized fuel-oil mixtures and regular maintenance, as well. Oh, and they also cost more than electric motors, so you can see why this has become a niche activity within model aviation.

Before the advent of energy-dense LiPo batteries, small gasoline engines were the only means of achieving powered, remote-control flight.

"The engine is the heart of an airplane, but the pilot is its soul."

– Aviation Aphorism

5.10 / The stator, the portion of an electric motor that is stationary, incorporates electromagnets that constantly shift polarity, drawing the permanent magnets inside the rotor toward them and causing the motor to spin.

In addition, this component is also referred to as the **bell housing** because it kind of looks like a bell. Finally, because the outside of the motor spins, this type of motor is called an **outrunner**. Inside the bell housing, each magnet is aligned so that its polarity is the opposite of its neighbors. These magnets are separated by the tiniest of spaces—called the **air gap**—from the **stator**. The stator consists of a ring of electromagnets and is fixed to the body of the aircraft, transmitting the propeller's thrust to the aircraft, allowing it to fly. While in operation, the electromagnets inside the stator change polarity thousands of times per second, first pulling one magnet within the rotor toward them, and then the other. As a result, the propeller spins, and the aircraft flies.

This, of course, raises the next question: What provides the power that makes the motor spin? That component is known as an *electronic speed controller* or *ESC* for short (Figure 5.11). The ESC regulates how fast the motor turns, speeding it up or slowing it down by controlling how quickly—or slowly—the electromagnets inside the motor change polarity.

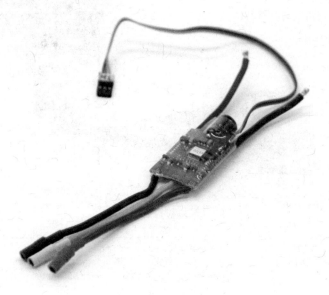

5.11 / The electronic speed controller (ESC) receives control inputs from the flight control system (FCS) and supplies the electrical current required to turn the motor at an appropriate speed to maintain aircraft stability and complete the maneuvers commanded by the pilot.

The FCS sends a signal to the ESC to turn the motor at the speed required, based on the pilot's input and the need to maintain flight stability. In a fixed-wing aircraft, this is pretty straight-forward. The pilot sets the amount of throttle and the FCS, the ESC, and the motor deliver the required performance.

Helicopters use a different approach. The ESC maintains a constant rate of rotation—called the helicopter's *head speed*—and maneuvers are performed by changing the pitch of its rotor blades. This includes both the main rotor and the anti-torque rotor. This is comparable to how a fixed-wing aircraft moves its control surfaces, as we'll see in the section below.

Controlling the speed of a drone's motors requires the constant and active engagement of the FCS. If you read Chapter 3 closely, you'll recall that multirotors were among the earliest flying machines, but they were abandoned for decades because the workload demands on the pilot made it impossible to accomplish anything more than hovering or making extremely simple maneuvers.

Multirotors create extremely complex aerodynamic forces, which are essentially impossible for a human pilot to manage. Therefore, drones give over the problem of aircraft stability entirely to the FCS, which makes hundreds of changes per second to the speed of each of the motors to keep the aircraft stable, even before the pilot gives it any control inputs. Furthermore, each electric motor requires a dedicated ESC, so a quadcopter will have four, a hexacopter will have six, and so on.

> ## "It's much like playing jazz, flying. It's multitasking in real time. You have a number of instruments that alone won't tell you exactly what the airplane is doing, but together give you a picture of everything that's going on."
>
> – Aaron Diehl, American Jazz Musician

BRUSHLESS VS. BRUSHED MOTORS

So, all those details about how electric motors work? Well, like pretty much everything else I've told you in this book, it's true most of the time. To provide just a little more context, what I was specifically describing are brushless electric motors. They are the nearly universal standard for remotely piloted aircraft, with the only exceptions typically being extremely small and inexpensive models. Of course, the very fact I described them as brushless motors tells you that there must be another variety, most likely called brushed electric motors. And, as usual, you would be right.

So, what's the difference? And why are brushless motors the favorite for drones and model airplanes? First, the drawbacks: Brushless motors are more expensive than their brushed counterparts and require an ESC (electronic speed controller)—or something like it—to function, which drives the total cost for the whole system even higher. The main advantages of brushless motors are that they are extremely efficient and can run for years without maintenance.

Brushed motors, on the other hand, cost less and can operate without an ESC. However, they also include parts—the brushes and the commutator—that must be in physical contact with one another for the motor to function. This creates friction and additional heat, making brushed motors less efficient. Also, these parts wear down over time, meaning that brushed motors will inevitably fail and must be replaced or overhauled.

Given that the few brushed motors remaining in service on drones and model airplanes cost just a few dollars each and could balance on the tip of your finger, replacement is the only realistic option.

Seen here along with a dime to provide a sense of scale, brushed motors are no longer used in remotely piloted aircraft, except in the smallest and least-expensive models.

BEING PUSHY

When it comes to fixed-wing aircraft, a propeller, a motor, and an ESC are not enough to make flight happen—well, not controlled flight, anyway. As you'll recall from Chapter 4, maneuvering requires movable panels called *control surfaces*: the *elevator*, the *ailerons*, and the *rudder*, among others. On crewed aircraft, the pilot can manipulate these directly using control cables or hydraulic systems. However, on model airplanes, these movements are controlled using mechanisms called *servos*. A servo is an electrically powered device which can rotate a gear precisely within a fairly narrow range of movement. A limb, called a servo horn (Figure 5.12), is attached to this gear and provides mechanical advantage in the form of leverage. This is then connected to a *push rod*, which actuates the control surface using a *control horn* (Figure 5.13).

So, for example, if a fixed-wing pilot gives the FCS an input to pitch the nose of the airplane up, it will send a signal to the pitch servo. The gear on the servo will rotate, moving the push rod such that the elevator tilts upward, causing the nose to rise.

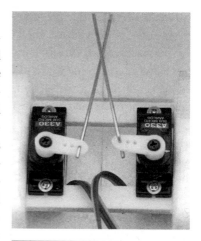

5.12 / Seen here within the fueselage of a model airplane are a pair of servos used to control the elevators and the rudder. The servos themselves are the small black boxes with orange highlights, connected to the flight control system (FCS) by the orange and brown wires. The servo horns, made of white plastic, are fastened to the servos using a Phillips-head screw. The metal push rods move with the servo horn, actuating the control surfaces.

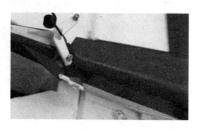

5.13 / Here, the metal push rod emerges from the aircraft's fueselage in the lower-right corner of the image. It is connected to the rudder by the red plastic control horn.

The yaw servo works in precisely the same way, with a control rod connected to the rudder. The ailerons are almost always controlled by two separate servos because they are located at opposite ends of the wing and must tilt in different directions.

Making pitch and roll maneuvers with a helicopter requires manipulating its *swash plate* (Figure 5.14), which is also controlled by a pair of servos. The swash plate operates in two modes: *collective* and *cyclic*. In collective mode, the swash plate changes the pitch of the blades throughout the entire rotor disk. This allows the helicopter to ascend and descend vertically. In cyclic mode, the swash plate only changes the pitch of the blades through one portion of the rotor disk, creating more lift on one side of the aircraft than the others so that it can maneuver in the pitch and roll axes.

5.14 / Helicopters are able to maneuver due to their ability to deform the shape of their rotor disks, a feat made possible by the intricate control linkages within the swash plate.

In truth, the main rotor can respond simultaneously to both collective and cyclic inputs, so that a helicopter can ascend vertically while pitching forward to move in that direction at the same time. The *antitorque rotor* (Figure 5.15) at the rear of the aircraft can also change the pitch of its blade to increase or decrease the thrust it generates. However, smaller model helicopters will simply speed up or slow down the motor driving the antitorque rotor to achieve the same change in thrust, allowing for greater mechanical simplicity.

5.15 / Rather than rely on a variable-pitch antitorque propeller like a crewed helicopter, small model helicopters use a fixed-pitch propeller and generate more or less thrust as needed by varying its speed.

As we learned in Chapter 4, drones pitch, roll, and yaw by altering the speed of their motors relative to one another. This is why once the problem of stability was solved, multirotors became such a popular type of flying machine. With only four moving parts, all of them proven reliable electric motors, it can fly like a helicopter but without the need for the complex mechanical control linkages that allow the swash plate to function. Consequently, drones deliver the same general capabilities as helicopters, but with far fewer maintenance requirements, and that's enough to make this once-obscure aircraft type into a pretty big deal.

LOUD AND CLEAR

The pilot of a crewed airplane can trace a direct, physical connection between the yoke and pedals on the flight deck to the control surfaces they actuate, be they cables or hydraulic lines. As a remote pilot, there is nothing but empty air between the controller in your hands and your aircraft. Since your ability to control your aircraft and maintain the safety of flight is contingent on something as insubstantial as a moon beam, this is a topic that deserves further consideration.

Of course, the answer is right there in the name: the "RC" in "RC Airplane" stands for *radio-controlled* (Figure 5.16). Radio transmissions are integral to modern life: Whether they are carrying music to our cars via AM or FM signals, streaming media to our computers via Wi-Fi, or sending conversations with friends and family through the cellular network, we all interact with radio technology every single day. At its most fundamental level, a functioning radio

5.16 / A conventional controller used in model aviation relies on two primary joysticks to adjust aircraft pitch, roll, and yaw, as well as throttle. Additional knobs and switches can be used for other aircraft functions, like raising or lowering the flaps or undercarriage.

system must have two basic parts: a *transmitter* and a *receiver*, referred to by the cool kids as the *TX* and the *RX*, respectively.

The transmitter takes information—in the form of music, video, voice, or data—and transforms it into a radio wave, which is transmitted on a specific frequency through an antenna. If a radio receiver is tuned to that same specific frequency, its antenna absorbs that signal and transforms it back into its original form: music, video, voice, or data.

A vast number of discrete radio frequencies are available, which is why the FM receiver in your car can bring you rock, golden oldies, hip hop, classical, and country music. Adjust the frequency it's tuned to, and you receive a different transmission, separate and distinct from all of the other transmissions that permeate the space around us.

Radio is a natural phenomenon—it exists in the universe whether or not we are there to enjoy it. It is one part of the *electromagnetic spectrum*, which also includes visible light, which we perceive with our own eyes, without the need for further instrumentation. Consequently, radio doesn't include any intrinsic divisions between AM and FM, for example, those are artificial constructs we have created to impose order on the chaos.

In the United States, the *Federal Communications Commission (FCC)* defines how each frequency can be used and who can use it, organizing neighboring frequencies used for the same purpose into radio *bands*. Bands are set aside for all sorts of different applications: commercial radio, broadcast television, cellular communication, aviation and maritime operations, satellite communications, amateur (ham) radio, and so forth—as well as the systems we use in our homes, such as: Wi-Fi, Bluetooth, cordless telephones, baby monitors, and garage door openers, to name just a few.

These regulations are required because each frequency can only carry one signal at a time. Put two signals on the same frequency, and all you'll get is a garbled, unintelligible mess. If you think all of this sounds like a daunting means of controlling an aircraft in flight, you're not wrong.

In the early days of radio-controlled flight, pilots would use discrete frequencies to send control inputs to their aircraft. A pilot might use "Channel 37," for example, and woe be it unto that person if someone else in the vicinity powered up a controller tuned to that same frequency. Suddenly, that aircraft would be receiving multiple, contradictory control inputs. Needless to say, that usually didn't end well. Consequently, those early model airplane enthusiasts had to develop and scrupulously adhere to a set of procedures designed to keep that from happening.

Fortunately, we live in the future, and these are the concerns of a bygone era. This is true because of the development of *frequency-hopping spread spectrum (FHSS)* radio technology. Essentially, rather than all the control signals being transmitted from a given controller to a given aircraft on one discrete frequency, that signal is chopped up into thousands of little signals and sent on multiple, separate frequencies selected at random within the radio-control band. This happens at a rate of 200 times per second.

So, even if two signals happen to collide for a tiny fraction of a second, it's overwhelmingly likely that the next one will get through, and the occasional loss of an individual five millisecond signal is negligible for the performance of the aircraft. Thus, today hundreds of remote pilots can gather and fly together without any concerns regarding interference. Indeed, variations on this same basic approach are employed in Wi-Fi, Bluetooth, and many other types of consumer technology that rely on radio transmissions. That's why everyone living in an apartment building can use Wi-Fi and they can all watch different shows on Netflix at the same time.

Of course, your aircraft must know which of these myriad signals it should be listening to, which requires *binding* it to your controller. This is essentially the same thing as pairing a Bluetooth accessory with a smart phone. The exact procedures vary between manufacturers, but these should be straight-forward and clearly explained in the manual. Just make sure that your controller and the receiver inside your model are compatible.

Spend any time at all looking at controllers for model airplanes and you will conclude that the most crucial distinction between them is the number of "channels" each one has, so it seems reasonable to ask: What do they do and how many do I need?

A channel is a discrete conduit within the overall transmission your controller sends to your aircraft, capable of controlling one of its on-board systems. Thus, one channel is dedicated to the aircraft's motor and another one to the elevators, the ailerons, and the rudder, for example. As we learned in Chapter 4, those are the four essential controls for a fixed-wing airplane, and they have their analogs among rotorcraft, as well—so a four-channel controller is the bare minimum that you will require.

Why would you ever need more? Well, let's say that as your skills improve you decide you want to fly a model with flaps and retractable landing gear, that's two more channels. Maybe you want to drop an inert bomb from your warbird or turn the running lights on and off, that's another two channels.

The key point is that increasingly sophisticated models will have additional functions and features that will require additional channels for you to be able to control them. Also, as a general rule, controllers with more channels offer additional benefits, like high-resolution color screens and the ability to store more models in their internal memory. They are, of course, also more expensive—potentially much more expensive.

Since you're brand new to remote piloting, you probably don't want to over-invest right at the start, but it's nice to have some flexibility so that your controller can grow with you up to a certain point. I find that an eight-channel controller tends to hit the sweet spot in terms of capabilities, features, and price. Your mileage may vary.

Also, if you're flying drones, none of this is even slightly relevant to you. Your drone came with a controller perfectly suited to its operational requirements, and you will most likely never use it to control another aircraft. So, there is nothing to see here. Go about your business.

One final note: Most often, model airplane pilots will have one controller with the built-in capacity to bind with multiple aircraft. If you want to change over from your glider to your replica World War II fighter plane, you just select it on the menu. Drones, on the other hand, typically arrive from the manufacturer with a controller that is intended to be used with that one aircraft. If you end up owning a lot of drones, you'll end up with quite an impressive collection of controllers as well (Figure 5.17).

5.17 / Each drone comes from the manufacturer with its own controller, so owning multiple drones will mean owning—and growing accustomed to using—different types.

BACK AT YA

While sending control inputs to an aircraft is the minimum requirement for remote piloting, the advent of drones has created a fundamentally new paradigm—one in which the aircraft sends information back to you. While this could include almost anything, most of this data falls into one of two categories: *telemetry* and *imaging*.

5.18 / With the arrival of small, civilian drones, the concept of receiving real-time feedback from an aircraft in flight in the form of video and telemetry became possible.

"Telemetry" sounds like a very fancy word—the sort you might hear people throwing around at NASA's mission control center in Houston. However, it has a simple meaning: measurement ("-metry") at a distance ("tele-"). This is information about the performance of the aircraft and is analogous to what aeronautical instruments provide for the pilot of a crewed aircraft: airspeed, altitude, heading, and so forth.

As a remote pilot, this information is an immense benefit: alerting you when the aircraft battery is low or when you are approaching the maximum altitude allowed by the regulations, for example. These alerts contribute to what professional pilots refer to as *situational awareness (SA)*, which means maintaining an accurate mental picture of your aircraft and the flying environment. Loss of situational awareness is often the precursor to a *bad thing* happening, so you should take advantage of every tool at your disposal to maintain it, like telemetry.

In the context of recreational remote piloting, drones were the first type of aircraft to offer robust telemetry. However, model airplanes have largely closed this gap over the past decade. Regardless of what you are flying, you should have detailed, real-time information regarding your aircraft's performance available—use it!

The other main category of information provided to you by your aircraft is imaging: primarily live video. This was the initial breakthrough application that drove, and continues to drive, interest around drone technology—the ability to see the world like a bird does and share that perspective with others by capturing aerial video of the environment.

Like telemetry, imaging would seem to have the potential to enhance your situational awareness as a remote pilot, but in keeping with the sage tactical insight of Admiral Akbar, "It's a trap!" The video feed provided by drones is far too limited to contribute to overall situational awareness, but it's great at lulling you into a false sense of security.

There are several reasons for this: First, the video only shows what is ahead of the aircraft. An eagle could be swooping down from behind you, intent on carrying off your machine in a misguided attempt to feed its chicks at home in the nest, and you would never know it was there. Second, the cameras on board drones generally have a wide field of view—meaning that objects in the distance appear smaller than they would to your own human eyes, if they were somehow suspended 300 feet above the ground. Thus, the Cessna 172 coming up fast on your position would be all but invisible until the last possible second, when it could be too late to get out of the way.

Finally, there is always the possibility that you could lose the video feed, leaving you lost and blind if you were relying on it to maintain some semblance of situational awareness. Video requires much greater bandwidth than sending either control inputs or telemetry, so it is far and away the most likely of the three types of signals to be disrupted during flight.

To be sure, aerial video has many potent applications—from vicariously enjoying the freedom of flight to capturing the beauty of the world around us in a way that is impossible by any other means—but it is not, and should not be regarded as, a means of piloting your aircraft. This is why, as we learned in Chapter 2, it is important to always maintain a direct, visual line of sight with your aircraft, so you can see what's happening all around it.

EMI AND RFI

While current drones and model airplanes are effectively immune to the sort of interference that bedeviled earlier generations of aeromodeller, they are still reliant on radio signals to receive control inputs, and there is always the possibility that those signals will be overpowered by another source. These other sources, generally speaking, fall into two categories: electromagnetic interference (EMI) and radio frequency interference (RFI).

EMI is created by sources that emit radio waves as a byproduct of their primary function. Examples of these include high-tension power lines and electrical substations. Nobody tunes into either one of these on purpose. However, whenever electricity flows through a wire, it creates electromagnetic waves. The more electric current, the more powerful the wave—to the point that it can blot out signals from other nearby sources, like your controller.

RFI is caused by devices that intentionally transmit radio waves. Of course, being regulated by the Federal Communications Commission (FCC), any such device will transmit signals in a narrow and precisely defined band, so there are a relative few that could potentially interfere with your operations as a remote pilot. Any system that you will be using as a beginner will use the 2.4 GHz band, which is also used by many other types of consumer electronics, such as Wi-Fi systems.

Just like your controller, these employ spread spectrum technology, so a massive concentration of such systems would be needed before a problem would occur. It's unlikely, but not impossible.

Professional drone pilots will occasionally use a tool called a spectrum analyzer to check for possible sources of interference. It's not something you'll need to spend too much time worrying about, but always be aware of potential sources of EMI and RFI in your environment.

ASSAULTIN' BATTERY

There is only one essential component of all remotely piloted aircraft we have yet to discuss: its power source. However, don't let the fact that I've saved it for last or its prosaic purpose put you off guard. There are hundreds of different types of failure, human and mechanical, that could destroy your aircraft, but only one component of your aircraft that could destroy your home—its battery.

Lithium-polymer batteries, called *LiPos*, are far more volatile than any other type of electrical storage device in widespread use today. If they are charged incorrectly, discharged incorrectly, physically damaged, or simply get too hot—among other provocations—they can experience **thermal runaway** and burst into flames. These flames cannot be extinguished by ordinary means, such as water or a household fire extinguisher and, by the way, the smoke that they give off is poisonous. So, that's fun.

> "I'm sad that my childhood came just slightly before the lithium-ion-battery boom, because I would've killed for the cheap radio-controlled helicopters they have now."
>
> – Randall Munroe, American Cartoonist

Honestly, it's best to assume that *your aircraft batteries hate you and their sole ambition in life is to burn your house down* (Figure 5.19). With that attitude you'll never be caught unaware—otherwise, you might be.

I know several remote pilots, each of them competent professionals exercising reasonable safeguards, who have experienced LiPo fires, one of which destroyed an outbuilding containing all his models and a good deal of property belonging to his flying club.

After the firefighters arrived, they asked him what was inside the shed. When he said, "LiPo batteries," they decided it was best to let it burn, limiting themselves to making sure the fire didn't spread to adjacent structures. They are really, truly that bad, and the moment you forget that fact, you are courting disaster. If you take only one lesson from this whole book, I hope that this is it.

5.19 / Okay, so your LiPo batteries might not actually hold rallies while your back is turned, cheering the destruction of your home in the style of a nighmare version of Pixar's *Toy Story*—but it's probably best for your sake that you act as if they do.

So, if LiPos are so absurdly dangerous, you may be asking why we would ever choose to use them in the first place. The answer is because there is no other choice available. Electrically powered flight would be impossible without lithium-polymer batteries. Here's why: Batteries (and other sources of power, for that matter) can be measured in terms of their ***energy density***. That is, how much power they can deliver, given their mass and volume. Almost every other type of battery chemistry we use, like lead-acid and nickel-cadmium, are really, truly awful on this score. They are heavy and they don't store that much power—certainly not enough to sustain flight.

FLYING WITH LIPOS

If you're going to travel by air with remotely piloted aircraft—like taking a drone with you on vacation, for example—you'll need to bring along some LiPos if you actually want to fly it. Needless to say, having cargo on-board airplanes capable of runaway combustion makes both the Federal Aviation Administration (FAA) and air carriers very nervous. Since you now understand the destructive power of LiPos, it should make you nervous, too.

You are allowed to transport LiPos on commercial airline flights, but there are rules. Most importantly, you must pack them in your carry-on baggage that goes with you in the cabin rather than beneath your feet in the cargo hold. Yes, the idea of a fire in the passenger cabin emitting poisonous smoke is very unappealing, but at least there you and the flight crew have a chance to deal with it. Since the alternative is that same fire burning uncontrolled in the cargo bay, alongside the airplane's fuel tanks, well, I'm sure you can see the logic.

To help reduce the risk involved in bringing LiPos on a flight, make sure they are discharged to about 50 percent of capacity before boarding and store them in a fireproof container. Better yet, store each battery in an individual fireproof container, if possible, to reduce the risk that one burning battery will ignite the others.

Personally, I always travel with one eye on the overhead bins, even when I'm not carrying batteries. You never know what other yahoo on the plane did not follow proper procedures. The good news is that most commercial air crews have been trained to deal with an in-flight LiPo battery fire.

As it happens, liquid fuels, like gasoline, offer terrific energy density, far exceeding even LiPo batteries. However, then you're stuck dealing with the noise, expense, mechanical complexity, and the general unpleasantness of using a combustion engine to release that stored energy. Not to mention that storing a can of gasoline in your garage probably isn't high on the list of safety tips you're likely to get from your local fire department, either.

So, since our ability to fly is contingent on our use of LiPo batteries, how can we do it safely? Obviously, this is a question that experts have given a lot of thought and distilled into the following basic precautions:

- Only use batteries from reputable, high-quality manufacturers.
- Inspect each battery before use. Remove from service and dispose of it safely if there is visible wear, damage, or swelling.
- Keep batteries away from high temperatures, including cars on sunny days.
- Do not keep a battery connected to the charger once the charging cycle is complete.
- Always stay in the vicinity when batteries are charging—never leave a charging battery unattended.
- Use only the charger that came with the battery, or a charger approved by the battery's manufacturer.
- Charge and store batteries in a fire-proof container.
- Do not store fully charged LiPo batteries any longer than necessary. If they are not used as planned, make sure they are discharged to about 50 percent of capacity.
- LiPo batteries are the enemy of all that is decent and good. They are only too happy to burn the hand that charges them and the home where the person attached to that hand lives. Give no quarter and expect none in return.

Okay, so I may have ad-libbed a little bit on that last one, but only in the service of making you understand that you should never take them, nor their potential to cause havoc, for granted. Finally, your management of LiPo batteries is made just a bit more complex because we find ourselves at a moment of transition with regards to how they are designed.

SMART VS. DUMB

Virtually all drones use what are called *smart batteries* (Figure 5.20). These are charged by connecting them to a streamlined charger that doesn't look too much different from what you would use for video camera or other piece of consumer electronics with removable batteries. Follow the manufacturer's instructions, take reasonable precautions, and you should be fine.

The big advantage of smart batteries is that if you don't use them within a couple of days, they will begin to discharge themselves to about 50 percent of their maximum capacity, also known as a *storage charge*. This is where LiPo batteries are happiest—or maybe it would be more accurate to say "least vicious"—and it is where they should be maintained for long-term storage.

5.20 / Drone batteries appear so innocuous and refined that it's easy to forget the fact that there is a fire-breathing monster at the heart of each one. Don't!

With model airplanes, it can be a little (or a lot) trickier. Model airplanes are moving toward the use of smart batteries. However, an awful lot of, well, dumb batteries are still out there, so you need to keep an eye out for them at the very least (Figure 5.21). Dumb batteries do not self-discharge, so you need to do it yourself, either by flying—cruel, I know—or by using a discharger.

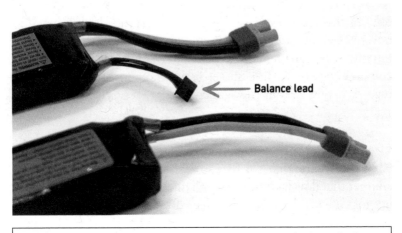

Balance lead

5.21 / Dumb batteries can always be disguinished from smart batteries by the addition of a balance lead (blue arrow), along with the main connector that will power your aircraft (top). Smart batteries will only have the one connector (bottom).

5.22 / This is a typical example of a LiPo battery charger that model aviation enthusiasts have been using for decades.

The real challenge when it comes to dumb batteries is that they require not one, but two connectors between the charger and the battery. One delivers the juice, and the other one manages the individual cells within the battery to make sure they are all charged to the same level. If the cells are not kept balanced, you know what happens next: thermal runaway, fire, mayhem, grief, and then a visit from the insurance adjusters.

Using dumb batteries means that you need a smart charger (Figure 5.22). The problem is that almost all chargers designed for the model aviation community will only communicate with you through tiny, LCD screens capable of displaying just a few numbers and letters that might as well be written in Sanskrit for all the sense they will make to you unless you already understand how to use them.

These charges can do a lot more than just charge batteries. They can discharge batteries down to a storage charge; they can charge them up to a storage charge if you've just returned from using them but don't anticipate flying again in the next few days; they can balance the cells without fundamentally affecting the overall charge level of the battery; and so forth.

There are so many variations between manufacturers that I can't possibly explain them all here. Instead, I'll leave you with this advice. Use smart batteries whenever possible. If circumstances require you to use dumb batteries, sit down with a living, breathing human being who knows what they are doing and have them teach you how to use the charger, how to charge safely, and how to store them when not in use. If the person you choose tells you not to worry or that it's easy, ask someone else. This is the time you want to consult your most safety-oriented friends.

Maybe this person is a new friend you met out at the flying field, as we'll discuss in Chapter 6. Or maybe it's the nice person behind the counter at your local hobby shop, which you should be supporting whenever possible, anyway. As with everything else in aviation, it's important that you learn to do this right—because the penalty for doing it wrong is severe.

6

How to Learn How to Fly

Over the previous chapters, we've given due consideration to how it is even possible to fly and do it safely and within the regulations that are placed upon remote pilots by the *Federal Aviation Administration (FAA)*. Next, we'll turn our attention to the actual process by which you will become a remote pilot: Learning how to fly.

Even this is not as straight-forward as it may seem. You can take multiple paths to becoming a skilled pilot, and not all of them involve going out straight away to buy an aircraft and starting its propellers turning. Indeed, I would argue that approach could easily be the most expensive and frustrating option available to you.

> **"Experience is a hard teacher because she gives the test first, and the lesson after."**
>
> – Vernon Law, American Baseball Player

Fortunately, there are alternatives. You can recruit a copilot, human or electronic, or get started in a simulator that will help you master the fundamentals without ever putting a real aircraft at risk. To help you find the best path, let's consider a fundamental question: What is all of this going to cost you?

CRASH COURSE

Let's acknowledge one fact right up front: As a new remote pilot, it is nearly inevitable that you are going to crash—most likely more than once—before you achieve a degree of competence. If you accept this assertion as true (and take it from me as a person who insisted on doing it the hard way, it is), then the only real question that remains to be answered is how much will each crash cost you?

First, let's consider model airplanes. If you start out with a small, lightweight foam airplane that costs $99, then the absolute maximum cost of a crash is $99. Well, unless you manage to hit somebody or a vulnerable piece of property—then the costs could escalate dramatically, as we've discussed previously.

Furthermore, since these small models tend to be pretty resilient, they will likely be able to shrug off quite a few crashes before you finally succeed in wrecking one for good. If we make the not-unreasonable assumption that such an airplane will survive nine crashes before meeting its inevitable doom on the tenth, then your cost per crash is $9.99.

That's more than a good cup of coffee, but it's not likely to be prohibitive if you can afford to take up remote piloting in the first place. On the other hand, if you start out with a larger, scale model of a real-world airplane (those World War II fighters sure look cool, don't they?) the cost of a catastrophic loss goes up substantially, as does the risk it will happen. Big airplanes don't survive crashes nearly as well as little ones, so now the average cost per crash goes up to maybe $150. If that isn't enough to start your heart beating just a little bit faster, then you and I live in different tax brackets.

Now, let's take a look at drones. Generally speaking, even the least expensive drone, with a camera and a live video downlink, is going to cost about the same as a scale airplane—and likely it won't be any more crashworthy. So, let's assume your cost per crash is probably about the same: $150-ish. Instead of the budget option, let's say you start out with a drone from a top-tier manufacturer. The price will likely approach $1,000 or more, and while all the integrated safety systems and sensors reduce the risk of crashing, it's still not zero. Experience a total loss while you're flying one of those, and suddenly you're hiding your credit card statements from your spouse.

I'm not trying to put you off flying altogether—quite the opposite—but I am hoping you'll think carefully about the total cost of becoming a proficient pilot, so that you're able to stick with it for the long term. I've seen the careers of far too many eager, new remote pilots cut short by making a single bad purchasing decision up front. Losing or wrecking an aircraft never gets any less painful no matter how many times you do it. Trust me, I know. However, if it's your very first time flying, a setback like that—especially with a significant price tag attached—may be enough to put you off flying permanently.

Assuming that you take me at my word, then no doubt you will be thrilled to learn that there is one method of learning to fly where the price-per-crash is $0. That knowledge alone would be more than enough to off-set the cover price of a book about getting started with drones and model airplanes, right?

SIM IT TO WIN IT

Flight simulators have grown up alongside aviation almost from the beginning. Today, they are used extensively by military and civilian pilots to hone their skills. Why? They allow pilots to develop basic proficiency and practice hazardous maneuvers without having to face the brutal consequences of a real-world failure. As wonderful as it is not wrecking a $500 model airplane, imagine how much *more* wonderful it is not flying a commercial jetliner into the side of a mountain, killing yourself, your co-workers, and 200 paying customers. Now *that's* a bad day at the office.

Short version: Simulators work—so why not take advantage of that fact by beginning your journey as a pilot in the virtual sky? It's an option you should definitely consider and one that will likely reduce the overall cost and frustration associated with learning to fly. And just so we are clear on this one

> **"Let's take flight simulation as an example. If you're trying to train a pilot, you can simulate almost the whole course. You don't have to get in an airplane until late in the process."**
>
> – Roy Romer, American Politician and Educator

point, we're talking about a radio-control (RC) flying simulator, not to be confused with flight simulators that put you inside the virtual airplane.

SIMULATORS IN AVIATION

Starting out your flying career with a simulator, even as a remote pilot, may seem like a bit of a letdown. That's not the way *real* pilots get their start, is it? As it happens, simulators have a long and honorable history in aviation, going back much farther than you might think.

For example, while it wasn't exactly a "simulator," during World War I, the French air corps introduced new pilots to the fundamentals using the "penguin" method—named after a bird that doesn't fly, get it?

The trainees would take the controls of an airplane with foreshortened wings, preventing it from doing anything more than hopping a couple of feet off the ground before settling right back down again, thereby letting pilots get the feeling for how the machine responded to their inputs without putting them in (too much) danger.

Between the wars, a man named Ed Link developed a fully enclosed flight simulator using air-powered bellows and other components borrowed from his father's pipe organ factory. The Link Trainer pitched and rolled in response to the pilot's inputs and included a complete set of working instruments, such as an altimeter, air speed indicator, and compass. In total, more than 500,000 pilots were trained to fly using the "Blue Box" in the United States and allied nations from the 1930s to 1950s.

Surprisingly, the first flight simulators to let the pilot see outside the cockpit preceded the advent of computer graphics by several decades. Beginning in the late 1950s and into the 1960s, simulators were built that moved a video camera over a three-dimensional replica of the terrain beneath the aircraft, called a "model board." The resulting image would be projected on a television screen inside the simulated flight deck. The camera's movements would respond in real time to the pilot's input, creating the illusion of flying over the landscape.

In the late 1960s, the first flight simulator to rely on computer-generated imagery (CGI) was created by General Electric to train the Apollo astronauts, and the technology was adopted by the military beginning in 1972. Of course, computing power has grown exponentially since then and today professional aviators ranging from airline transport pilots to the Blue Angels rely on simulators to train and maintain their skills.

So, if it's good enough for the Blue Angels it's probably good enough for you. Besides, this way you can boast that you train like an astronaut, because you are one serious pilot!

To be sure, you can learn an awful lot about aviation from a high-quality sim like Microsoft Flight Simulator or X-Plane, but how to fly an aircraft with your feet planted firmly on the ground isn't very high on that list. Fortunately, there are dedicated RC simulators available, both for laptop and desktop computers, as well as mobile platforms, like smartphones and tablets. Prices range from free up to about $100. Even a cheap simulator can make you a better pilot, provided you are willing to put in the effort.

A friend of mine who trains new drone pilots using a fleet of dozens of drones worth millions of dollars always starts them out on simulators. Why? Because those simulated drones are repaired with the click of a button. Furthermore, my friend reports that the simulators are actually harder to fly than the real thing, so when these pilots head out into the "real world" for the first time, they find it is actually easier than their simulator training. Overall, I concur with his assessment.

When selecting a simulator, there can be a temptation to purchase the most expensive, feature-rich package with the absolute best graphics—and, indeed, that's what I did—but it probably isn't necessary for a beginning pilot. At least when you are starting out, you don't need a hyper-realistic flight model that accounts for every micro-Newton of energy imparted to each surface of your model by a transient gust of wind.

What you need is the opportunity to move the control sticks and see how your model reacts at the most fundamental level. To be sure, you will be awkward and deliberate at first, and you'll fly enough models into the dirt that you'll be grateful the debris gets automatically swept away between each flight, lest your virtual environment comes to resemble the ocean floor beneath the Bermuda Triangle. However, after 10 hours of practice—or 20, or 30, or more—your inputs will become smoother and more intuitive, to the point you stop thinking about moving the sticks and start thinking about moving the aircraft. When that happens, it's time to contemplate flying a machine in the real world.

The key to making the most of your simulator time is to take it seriously. Although you might derive some perverse satisfaction from flying aircraft at full speed into the ground just to watch the pieces scatter—not that I've ever done this myself, mind you—this is not going to do much for your piloting skills. In fact, it might even make them worse.

> **"Judgment comes from experience. Experience comes from poor judgment."**
>
> – Aviation Aphorism

Contrary to the popular aphorism, practice does *not* make perfect. Practice only makes *permanent*. Practice crashing machines in the simulator, and guess what skill you will have mastered when you arrive in the field? Yup—crashing machines. Only *perfect practice* makes perfect, so that is what you should strive to achieve.

Also, the more closely your simulated flying resembles the real thing, the more beneficial it will be. This makes it imperative to use a two-stick controller during your visits to the virtual field, because it is only by using the same physical inputs in the simulator that you will meaningfully train your mind and your muscles to perform correctly in real life.

The ubiquitous, two-stick controller familiar to console gamers right around the world is sufficient to the task, but I would urge you to upgrade to something that resembles an actual RC controller. There are models that incorporate a USB cable instead of an antenna, allowing you to plug them directly into a laptop or a desktop.

Alternatively, there are receivers—about the same size and shape as a thumb drive—that allow you to use a real RC transmitter to control your virtual aircraft. If you already own a controller, this approach will allow you to achieve the ultimate fidelity to the real-world environment while saving money at the same time.

Of course, no simulator is going to perfectly re-create every nuance of actually flying—and that isn't the point. Our goal is simply to give you the chance to master the basics while keeping the breakage to an absolute minimum. However, if you aspire to be something more than a gamer, it's going to be necessary to head out and throw some money—in the form of a flying machine—into the wind.

ELECTRONIC COPILOTS

Any remotely piloted aircraft that you purchase today—be it a model airplane or a drone—is likely to include some features that will enhance its stability in the air, prevent you from pushing it past certain predefined limits, or even take over control of the aircraft from you entirely to complete a maneuver all on its own. While these can be valuable, and even necessary, for pilots of any skill level, they are obviously a huge advantage when you are learning how to fly.

Model airplanes tend to be less sophisticated in this regard. Even with all these systems engaged, you don't have to try very hard to crash one. Drones, especially the top-end models from major manufacturers, can be remarkably capable while operating autonomously. There aren't many circumstances where you would do this for fun—that is, as a recreational pilot—but professional drone operators will often fly entire missions without touching the sticks to manually control their aircraft.

Let's begin by looking at the systems that have been incorporated in model airplanes. The most aggressive of these uses a combination of on-board sensors, like accelerometers and gyroscopes, to limit how far the aircraft will bank and roll. One example of this type of system is known by the acronym *SAFE*, which stands for *Sensor-Assisted Flight Envelope*, and is incorporated into many of the model airplanes produced by Horizon Hobby.

With such a system engaged, for example, it is literally impossible to fly the airplane upside down—it won't let you. Give it a full-stick roll input, for example, and it will roll 30 degrees but no further. Also, when you release the control stick and it returns to center on your controller, the aircraft will return to level flight all on its own (Figure 6.1).

> "As a new pilot, you start with a bag full of luck and an empty bag of experience. The trick is to fill the bag of experience before you empty the bag of luck."
>
> – Aviation Aphorism

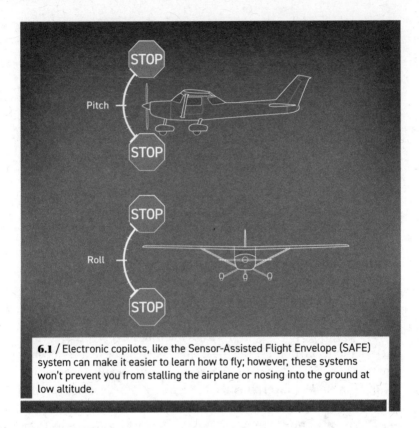

6.1 / Electronic copilots, like the Sensor-Assisted Flight Envelope (SAFE) system can make it easier to learn how to fly; however, these systems won't prevent you from stalling the airplane or nosing into the ground at low altitude.

This should help keep you out of trouble, but it's hardly a panacea. Limiting an airplane to 30 degrees of down pitch means it can't go inverted, but it can still hit the ground and do a lot of damage while flying at that angle. However, if you understand how a system like SAFE works, as well as its limitations, and you pay careful attention to the aircraft and the flying environment, it can be a big help in learning how to fly.

In addition, these systems can typically be engaged or disengaged using a toggle switch on your controller, meaning you can take off and climb to altitude with it working, then turn it off and practice more complex or challenging maneuvers, then turn it back on when it's time to land. If the aircraft starts to get away from you at any point, just flip the switch and the system will bring it back to straight and level flight.

In addition to systems like SAFE, model airplane manufacturers have used the same underlying technology to enhance the stability of their aircraft. These go by names like AS3X and ORX. By default, these systems are typically engaged every time you go flying, and depending on the manufacturer, it may or may not be possible to turn them off.

Unlike SAFE, they do not exist to limit the effects of your control inputs. If you want to fly upside-down, backwards, or do anything else the laws of aerodynamics will allow a system like AS3X will not stand in your way. Bear in mind that this could be a good thing or a bad thing: It's not going to save you from yourself, either.

What these systems do is smooth out the performance of your aircraft, making it less susceptible to a transient gust of wind, for example, along with minor changes to its center of gravity and esoteric aeronautical phenomena like tip stalls. Most likely you'll never even know that it's there, working quietly in the background to make sure your airplane does what you want it to do, or at least what you tell it to do.

This may—or may not—be enough to save you from crashing if you make a mistake while flying at low altitude, and the only way to know for sure is to experiment with it at an altitude where you can be sure it will have enough time to work its magic. Time in the simulator and experience in the field are the only way to figure this out.

Sophisticated drones, on the other hand, are quite good at preventing you from crashing them. Not only do they incorporate accelerometers and gyroscopes like modern model airplanes, but they also include a whole suite of other sensors, including barometric altimeters, ultrasonic or infrared rangefinders, GPS receivers, and even machine-vision systems that can detect obstacles and override your control inputs if you attempt to fly into the ground.

If you take your thumbs off the control sticks of a drone, it will simply stop moving and hover in one place, and unless you do something, it will stay there until the battery runs low, at which point it will fly itself home and land all on its own. If you try to fly it into the side of a building, it will start beeping at you and display warnings across your video downlink. If you keep pushing, it will simply refuse to move farther. If all of this sounds like it would make drones almost foolproof for starting pilots, you're not too far wrong, and yet somehow, we all manage to crash one when we start. I hope this book and the time you are investing by reading it will prevent you from making my mistakes.

Two things you should know, however: First, less-expensive drones possess fewer of these capabilities, so be darn sure you know what yours will—and won't—do before you start playing chicken with brick walls. Second, "almost foolproof" is not the same thing as "foolproof." Rookie pilots still manage to crash plenty of drones: They just need a little more dedication and creativity to get the job done. As ever, start slowly and take the time to really understand your machine.

BUDDY UP

To be sure, some of the best resources you can draw on to become a competent remote pilot are knowledgeable friends. They can provide you with insight and feedback, help you understand what you are seeing and introduce you to the etiquette of flying in your local environment. On the flight line, they can be invaluable as an extra set of eyes and hands as well as a resource for good judgment tempered by experience.

If your goal is fly model airplanes or helicopters, a ready supply of friends you haven't met yet is likely not too far from where you are sitting right now—and better still, they are easy to find. There are more than 2,000 flying fields chartered by the *Academy of Model Aeronautics* (AMA) all over the United States, and the AMA's website (modelaircraft.org) provides a simple tool that will allow you to identify ones that are located nearby. There are new friends to meet, people like you, enthusiastic about aviation, and very likely they are the type of person who will help another pilot. To fly at an AMA field will require that you are an AMA member (Figure 6.2). As a new pilot, one of the biggest advantages of having seasoned pilots as friends is that they can help you learn how to fly, and not just by giving advice and coaching. Virtually all hobby controllers allow you to "buddy box" with another pilot. Using this system, your controller will be linked, either wirelessly or with an old-fashioned cable, to a controller in the hands of another, more

6.2 / There is no better resource in all the world to help you learn a new skill than a fellow human being who has already mastered that same skill.

experienced pilot. This setup allows you to fly a real aircraft in the real sky but gives your buddy the ability to instantaneously assume control of the aircraft if you get into trouble, or you need help with one phase of flight, like taking off or landing. Sometimes, just having this assistance available is enough of a confidence booster that you can take on new maneuvers all by yourself that you might not have been willing to try on your own.

If your goal is to become a drone pilot, your path to finding friends to help you on your way won't be quite as smooth. Despite a few brave attempts over the years, there is no national organization parallel to the AMA that caters specifically to drones. Drones, and their pilots, are welcome at some AMA fields but not others. Contact a couple of nearby fields to figure out where you would be most welcome.

In addition, you may well find local groups that do not fall underneath the AMA umbrella that are dedicated specifically to drones, through general internet searches, social media, and community forums. It may take you a little more effort to find your tribe, but it will be well worth it in the end.

One fact to be aware of is that buddy boxes aren't a "thing" with drones—the requisite capabilities simply have not been incorporated into their ground control stations. That doesn't mean there aren't big advantages to having a skilled friend standing within arm's reach while you are learning to fly. Any drone worthy of the name will have the ability to hold its position based on GPS signals and data from other sensors. If you simply stop touching the sticks, you can generally expect that the aircraft will stop moving and hover in place until you start moving it again. You can take advantage of this built-in capability to simply hand off the controller to your buddy, so that they can assist you as needed.

GROWING AND MAINTAINING YOUR SKILLS

Initially, whether in a simulator or the real world, simply keeping a machine in the air will qualify as a triumph, and you should be legitimately proud at having achieved it. However, as you log additional flight time and your skills grow, you should begin to demand more of yourself. When I was just starting out as a remote pilot and the dreary winter weather in my home state of Oregon kept me indoors, I purchased a tiny helicopter that fit in the palm of my hand so I could practice flying around my family room.

In addition to the dual consequences of provoking my dog and annoying my wife, this new flying environment meant that I had to achieve a greater degree of control than I had previously. After all, the great outdoors doesn't have ceilings and walls to hit. Eventually, I was able to keep my machine airborne for its entire 6-minute battery life without hitting anything. This, I prematurely concluded, meant that I had essentially mastered the art of remote piloting.

I discovered that was pretty far from the truth when I decided to test myself by taking off from the coffee table, flying over to the breakfast bar, then landing before taking off again and returning to the coffee table. This exercise proved to me immediately that I still had a long way to go in terms of precision and control. I later experienced a similar revelation when I discovered I could reliably execute beautiful clockwise circles with the helicopter but would inevitably spin out of control while attempting the same maneuver in a counterclockwise direction.

Growing your skills as a remote pilot means stretching them—taking on new, more complicated maneuvers while performing old ones with ever-increasing confidence. As you do this, remember how you learned how to fly in the first place. You should preferably attempt these new skills for the first time in the simulator, or with a small, durable aircraft. A $500 aircraft still costs $500 to replace, regardless of what you were attempting to do or how many hours you have in your logbook when it hits the ground.

> **"A superior pilot uses his superior judgment to avoid situations which would require the use of his superior flying skills."**
>
> – Frank Borman,
> American Astronaut

Now, let's fast-forward a decade or two: You have become a legitimately talented remote pilot with hundreds of flight hours in your logbook. Surely at this point, you think to yourself, I can be confident in my skills and trust my judgment from this moment until I set down my transmitter for the very last time—right? If this was an audio book, I would have just blasted you with a game-show buzzer, because the answer to that question is a categorical no.

Unfortunately, like any intensive activity that combines both mental and physical components—including marksmanship, surgery, and athletics, to name a few—remote piloting is a perishable skill. It isn't like reading or riding a bicycle. Every day that you spend *not* remote piloting, your skills degrade just a little bit. This effect is negligible over the span of a week or two but becomes noticeable after a few months' time.

So, for example, if the climate in your home region obliges you to stop flying outdoors during the winter months, you had better plan on flying indoors or spending some quality time on the simulator and/or anticipate that you will need time to sharpen your skills when the spring thaw comes before you can once again do your best. The most important lesson is that there are always more lessons to learn. The moment you think you know everything, the countdown timer to your next crash starts ticking. Can you hear it?

KEEP A LOGBOOK

Like simulators, the pilot's logbook has been a fixture in the aviation community almost from its outset. Orville and sWilbur Wright, the first to achieve sustained, heavier-than-air flight, kept detailed records of their flights, but this was done first and foremost with the intent of documenting and improving upon their experimental flying machines.

In 1912, less than a decade after the Wright brothers made history at Kitty Hawk, the UK's Royal Flying Corps instituted a rule that required its pilots to maintain a log, and the first pre-printed logbooks were published the following year based on the ledgers used in the shipping industry. In 1926, the Air Commerce Act set down in law the expectation that pilots would record their flight hours and other details of their activities.

Traditionally, model airplane pilots have not maintained logbooks, and following their example, the early pioneers in the use of small, civilian drones didn't either. At present, there is an expectation—albeit no requirement—for professional remote pilots to log their hours, although the practice remains largely unknown among recreational drone and model airplane pilots.

Obviously, if you intend to become a professional remote pilot, I urge you to start logging your hours immediately. Hours in your logbook are like dollars in your bank account: The more you have, the better. However, even if you plan to restrict yourself exclusively to recreational flying, I still recommend you keep a log for two reasons.

First, your logbook can be a valuable learning tool. Through it, you can see patterns emerging in your own development as a pilot, you can keep track of when and where you had different experiences and, over several years, you can even learn to estimate how much "rust" there will be on your skills after time away from flying.

Second, you never know what the future will bring. At this moment in your life, the notion of working as a professional remote pilot may seem as unlikely as Beatles reunion, but there might come a time when either your interests or your opportunities—or both—change, and those logged hours will be invaluable.

7
Spaces and Places: Choosing Where to Fly

Your choice of flying sites will be driven by two key considerations: first and foremost, safety, and second, what you hope to accomplish by flying. The first point is non-negotiable, but the second offers as many possibilities as there are combinations of remote pilots and aircraft—and that's a lot of possibilities. Since we can't conceivably cover all of them, we'll look at the general characteristics of different types of flying sites and explore procedures that will allow us to operate safely at each of them.

Two steps must be taken before flying in any location—verifying the airspace and assessing the environment.

FIRST THINGS FIRST

We looked extensively at the question of airspace in Chapter 2, but by way of a quick review—or in case you're jumping around in the book like I would—the two kinds of airspace are *controlled* and *uncontrolled*. You can use the FAA's *B4UFly app* to figure out which one you're in, and either answer requires some additional work. If you're in controlled airspace, you'll need authorization before you can fly from the *Low-Altitude Authorization and Notification Capability (LAANC)* system. If you're in uncontrolled airspace, you'll need to verify that no airports are in the vicinity that could cause crewed aircraft to be operating at low altitude.

Hopefully, all that sounds familiar—if not, go back and read (or re-read) Chapter 2. You really need to know this stuff—especially airspace—or you're just asking for trouble. With this kind of trouble, the best-case scenario is an unpleasant interaction with representatives of the law enforcement community or the Federal Aviation Administration (FAA). The worst-case scenario is that you cause an incident, or worse yet, you hurt somebody, which will result in an *even more* unpleasant interaction with law enforcement or the FAA.

Next up, you need to assess the local environment before every flight. This basically means looking around and noticing anything that could pose a threat to your aircraft or that your aircraft could harm. Bear in mind that your aircraft will be spending most of its time in the sky, so you definitely need to look up, and maybe in a way that you never have before in your entire life.

Notice the location of tall trees, overhead utilities or other obstacles that might pose a collision risk for your aircraft (Figure 7.1). You also need to ensure that there is sufficient space for your aircraft to take off and, most especially, to *land*. Remember the old-timey wisdom from our friends in crewed aviation: Takeoffs are optional, landings are mandatory.

There have been a few instances where I have forgotten this all-important rule while flying drones. Their remarkable stability and collision-avoidance capabilities have allowed me to launch from a narrow patch of ground where it was impossible for me to safely

7.1 / Once you take flight, tall trees, utility lines, and other obstacles could bring your aerial adventure to an abrupt end.

set the aircraft back down again. A few mad scrambles to identify an alternative landing site with my machine's battery running low broke me of that habit. Hopefully this is a lesson you can learn from my experience, rather than your own.

With fixed-wing aircraft, this is perhaps an even more important consideration. Especially as a new pilot, you are likely going to need far more open space to set up an approach and land than you will require to take off in the first place. The sky is infinite—it's really hard to miss once you are in the air. Space on the ground is finite. Even a football field can suddenly look small when you're trying to corral an aircraft and get it back on the ground in one piece.

Of greater importance is to study your prospective flying site for things that your aircraft could harm. Again, as we've discussed previously, you should always assume that your aircraft may stop working at any moment. All electrical and mechanical systems will fail, it's only a matter of when. Rotorcraft will most likely drop straight down to the ground at their present location, although they could spiral off in some random direction depending on the exact nature of the malfunction. Fixed-wing aircraft will most likely continue in their current direction of travel and begin descending with increasing speed. However, if the control surfaces get stuck in the middle of a maneuver, it could pitch, roll, or stall into the ground. And, of course, if the propeller(s) are still turning, the risk of severe lacerations is added on top of getting whacked by a two-pound object falling from 400 feet.

> **"Prepare for the unknown, the unexpected, and inconceivable… After 50 years of flying, I'm still learning every time I fly."**
>
> – Gene Cernan, American Astronaut

So, the key to finding a safe place to fly is to find somewhere that nothing—people, vulnerable property, or moving vehicles—will ever be underneath your aircraft that could suffer harm if it comes down out-of-control. Hitting dirt is fine. Hitting grass is fine. Hitting pavement is fine. Hitting a group of second graders on a field trip is *not* fine.

Something else to think about while you are considering a prospective flying site is how your operations will affect not only the physical safety of others but also their enjoyment of the outdoor space. If someone is sitting cross-legged like the Buddha, waiting in silence to greet the rising sun, the buzzing sound of your propellers is likely not going to enhance their inner calm.

It's not against any rule to fly under these circumstances, but it is extremely rude. You should always consider the impact your operations will have on other people—to include whether it will disturb or annoy them. Not only is this simply polite, but being a good neighbor reduces the likelihood that the locals will take up a petition to ban flying in the area. Remember, every time you go flying, you are representing not only yourself—but also me and millions of other remote pilots. Enlightened self-interest is a real thing.

Another part of your environmental assessment is to anticipate what may change in the future. Just because it's an empty field right now doesn't mean that it will still be an empty field half an hour from now. Are there soccer goals at either end of the field? Maybe a team will show up to practice or to play a game. Are there walking paths and signs reminding dog owners to clean up after their pets? Your quiet field could soon be overrun by dogs who are just going to *love* chasing your flying machine. That makes for a tricky landing—believe me!

Assessing the weather is another key factor you should keep in mind while surveying an environment before flying. Hopefully you did this before you left home, either by checking the local weather forecast or just looking out the window. This assessment should continue once you arrive at the field. In particular, look at the tops of any trees in the vicinity. Their movement, or lack of movement, can give you a hint about the wind you are likely to encounter once your machine is aloft. Also, keep in mind that the weather can change during a day of flying. Dark clouds on the horizon may indicate that it's time to cut your expedition short.

Finally, you should also be alert for any potential sources of ***electromagnetic interference (EMI)*** or ***radio frequency*** *interference (RFI)* in your vicinity. As we learned in Chapter 5, these can be generated by sources like electrical substations or high-tension power lines and unusual concentrations of radio transmissions occurring on the same frequencies used by your aircraft's controller. These are relatively rare, but it only takes one to ruin your whole day (Figure 7.2).

7.2 / If you see this in your flying environment, find somewhere else to fly. The Electro-Magnetic Interference (EMI) generated by electrical substations may interfere with your controller signals.

FIXED-WING FIELDS

If you're flying fixed-wing, most likely your only goal is to success-fully guide your machine through the air—as opposed to flying a drone, which could involve capturing interesting photos or video of something other than an open field. For this reason, selecting a fixed-wing flying site is a pretty straight-forward process: You need a large, open space with few obstacles and no people around. The less experience you have, the more space you will need.

Fortunately, 2,500 such sites already exist across the country that have been prepared for this specific purpose—flying fields affiliated with the *Academy of Model Aeronautics (AMA)* (Figure 7.3). Use the "Club Finder" on its website to locate one near you. These will have prepared runways, shelters, and other specialized facilities and, most important of all, they are inhabited by people who are acutely aware of the hazards involved in flying model airplanes. Indeed, as a new pilot, you will likely find that they are a terrific source of help and advice, as we discussed in Chapter 6 (Figure 7.4).

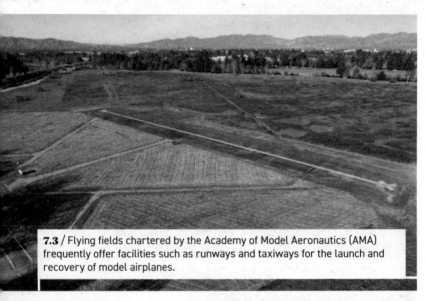

7.3 / Flying fields chartered by the Academy of Model Aeronautics (AMA) frequently offer facilities such as runways and taxiways for the launch and recovery of model airplanes.

7.4 / AMA fields also offer shelters, restrooms, and electricity for re-charging your batteries between flights, along with plenty of experienced and friendly remote pilots.

If a local AMA field isn't an option, you'll need to find a space that provides as many of the same amenities as possible: lots of open ground where people are scarce, at a minimum. Athletic fields—while not in use, of course—can be a good choice. One of my personal favorites, located only about 10 minutes from my home, is a large community park with two vast fields, each large enough to host three soccer matches simultaneously. Dogs are prohibited on the fields, and because there are beautiful, well-maintained trails that meander through the trees all around, the fields themselves aren't especially popular with the walkers and joggers. Also, it's located in uncontrolled airspace, and there are no airports in the vicinity (Figure 7.5). A quick internet search may also yield flying fields within your local area that may or may not be associated with AMA.

7.5 / A public park almost ideally suited for remote piloting operations is located just a few miles from my house, and I couldn't ask for better. Maybe I'll see you out there some time.

The park near my home is about as good a place as you could hope to find for flying fixed-wing aircraft apart from an actual AMA flying field or other local model aircraft club, and I'm far from alone in using it for that purpose. I've made several friends among the remote pilots and onlookers I've met while flying there.

Of course, all that space is put to good use by plenty of other people as well. Over the spring and summer months, soccer and baseball players appear with increasing frequency, first to practice and then to play in tournaments that can bring out hundreds of spectators.

These are first and foremost athletic fields, not flying fields, so my fellow remote pilots and I cede them to their intended users and seek out alternative venues during these days, although none offer the same nearly ideal combination of attributes (including proximity to my very own front door, *sigh*). Still, it's the price of being a good neighbor, and I'm glad to pay it.

Maybe you are not fortunate enough to have a public park nearly ideal for model aircraft operations nearby. If you live in a rural area, unused farm fields can offer some of the most forgiving geography available anywhere—just be sure to get the farmer's permission.

THE FAA ISN'T THE ONLY ONE WITH A RULE BOOK

While the FAA has exclusive domain over the **National Airspace System** (NAS), that won't prevent local authorities from regulating the use of drones and model airplanes. For example, your local community might prohibit drones and model airplanes in local parks, or limit them to only certain parks, or certain times of day, and so forth.

Before you go flying in a public space, you should do some research to find out if any limitations or restrictions are in place. Even if you don't find any, you should still be prepared in case you are approached by law enforcement or park personnel with some bad news. Explain that you'll need a few minutes to safely land your machine and that you'll be happy to speak with them once that is accomplished.

Technically, only the FAA actually has the legal authority to prohibit flight operations. Once your machine is one foot off the ground, it's within the agency's sole domain. So, well-crafted local ordinances will prohibit taking off or landing, rather than flying. However, this is a technicality and will be of precisely zero value in arguing your case with the cop who takes you aside for a chat.

If you're arrested after attempting to make this point a bit too emphatically with local authorities, *do not* call me looking for bail money. You have been warned.

DRONING ON

If you're flying a drone, my advice is to log your initial flight hours at a location suitable for fixed-wing operations. More open space means fewer opportunities to get yourself into trouble. Eventually you will want to use that amazing, three-axis gimbal-stabilized 4K video camera on the snout of your aircraft to do something other than capture imagery of unadorned fields. There's an entire world out there, just waiting to be seen from above (Figure 7.6).

The first thing to realize is that absolutely nothing changes in terms of assessing your flying environment just because your goal is aerial photography—indeed, those requirements can be even more stringent. As a fixed-wing pilot, you'll likely have a few favorite flying sites that you return to regularly, and while it's appropriate and necessary to look at them with fresh eyes every time you arrive, you will become increasingly aware of their hazards and challenges through experience

7.6 / New environments that provide the opportunity to capture dramatic aerial photographs and video will require new site assessments.

Capturing aerial imagery in a new location will necessarily involve flying *in a new location*. This means starting the assessment process all over again—identifying the local airspace and nearby airports as well as hazards specific to the site itself. In addition to examining aeronautical charts, professional drone pilots, including yours truly, will often spend time studying satellite images of locations where we intend to fly looking for the tell-tale signs of overhead utilities and other obstacles as well as roads and places where people might congregate.

CURIOUS BYSTANDERS

Being a remote pilot is undeniably cool—otherwise, why would you be doing it? There is a problem, however: Doing something cool in public can draw a lot of attention to you, and that is not necessarily conducive to the safety of your operations. Answering people's questions can be a lot of fun—to the point that it can turn into a career, if you're not careful.

It can also prove to be a potent distraction from what you really need to be doing while you've got a machine in the air, which is *flying the machine*. I'd be lying if I said that I hadn't wrecked more than one aircraft while dividing my attention between piloting and answering the questions of some adorable, towheaded tyke.

Even if you count yourself as a pretty good remote pilot and think you can handle it, well, that might not end up being the case. This is why professional drone pilots wear brightly colored vests that say "KEEP CLEAR" on them. That's an attempt to maintain what is referred to as a **sterile flight deck** in crewed aviation—a space where all you need to think about is flying, without distraction.

So, if you're approached by onlookers anxious to bask in how cool you are, I'd suggest saying something along these lines: "I'd love to talk to you. Give me a minute to make a safe landing, so I can give you my undivided attention." Then, of course, land the aircraft and give them your undivided attention.

If you're flying a drone with advanced position-hold capabilities, it *might* be acceptable to bring it to a hover 10 to 15 feet away, well clear of people and obstacles, and have a conversation then. This will allow your new friends to look at your video downlink and maybe even catch a glimpse of themselves on camera. That's always a hit with the kids—just make darn sure you don't actually *hit the kids*. Like pets, children don't always act with their own best interests clearly in mind while in the presence of a remote-controlled aircraft. Be prepared to fly it out of harm's way if they rush your machine.

Nothing is more discouraging than driving two hours to get an amazing shot only to find that the site is unflyable when you arrive. This is precisely the type of scenario that can tempt you to make a *bad decision*: flying against your better judgment because of the effort and expense it took to get there in the first place. Bad decisions can lead to *bad things* happening, and as pilots, avoiding bad things is our top priority.

Something else to keep in mind is the effect that the site will have on you personally. Heat, cold, thin air, and blazing sun,

Finally, if you find yourself overwhelmed at the moment a bystander approaches, it may be necessary to ignore them completely so that you can maintain all of your attention on your aircraft. Obviously, this isn't going to make a terrific first impression on that person, but your focus must always remain on the safe conduct of flight to the exclusion of every other concern.

By the way, this is one more good reason to fly at AMA fields: everybody else is at least as cool as you are, so the odds that you will be swarmed go way down.

The FAA recommends that professional remote pilots wear a high-visibility vest that discourages onlookers from asking questions.

along with other environmental factors, can adversely affect *you*. Dehydration, hypothermia, hypoxia, heat stroke, and hunger are not a benefit to either your judgment or your manual dexterity. Therefore, you should account for these hazards and take appropriate precautions, to include having ample supplies of water, food, appropriate clothing, and sunscreen on hand, as well as a means of calling for help if you need it. Check to be sure your phone has bars *before* you're in the middle of an emergency.

Next up, we will review the hazards associated with several different environments where you might want to go flying with your drone, including urban, desert, alpine, wilderness, coastal, and maritime. And, of course, you should recognize that these categories are not mutually exclusive: there are cities located in the mountains, wilderness that abuts the seashore, and so on.

URBAN ENVIRONMENT

Flying in a city is one of the gnarliest challenges that any remote pilot can ever contemplate, and yet the draw is undeniable: the architecture, the history, and the vibrant population all make for compelling subjects. You should have a great deal of experience before you even consider putting a machine over a city, because hazards abound. First, the urban environment is crowded with people and moving vehicles that both good sense and the regulations insist that we avoid. Indeed, these factors alone will likely be enough to eliminate many potential flying sites outright.

The key to finding a safe place to fly in the urban environment is to find a large open area devoid of people and vehicles. One good option is a body of water (Figure 7.7). I have logged quite a few hours over the Willamette River, which flows right through the middle of downtown Portland and, from a perch 400 feet above the water, provides commanding views of downtown and a large waterfront park where numerous events and festivals are held each year.

Of course, people and boats—which count as moving vehicles, in case you were wondering—can and do move across the surface of the water, so you must watch out for and avoid them with the same urgency as their land-dwelling counterparts. Still, unless you're in Venice, Italy, cars almost certainly outnumber boats, and flying over water can open up environments that would otherwise be foreclosed to drone operations.

Another key consideration when it comes to flying in the city is wind. To be sure, wind poses a potential challenge to remotely piloted aircraft operating in any environment, but its effects are magnified in cities. The sort of tall, square structures that we humans love to build in the urban environment can create powerful and unpredictable vortexes and eddies that can quickly overpower your drone and smash it into the side of a building. That will stop its propellers turning, and it will fall straight down along the facade until it hits the sidewalk—potentially teeming with pedestrians. It should go without saying by now that this is a *bad thing*.

7.7 / People, vehicles, and regulatory safegards in the urban environment would seem to make them nearly unflyable—unless you can get out over the water. Just remember: Your drone can't swim.

Finally, where humans go, their electronic gizmos and gadgets follow, and in cities there are plenty of both. Therefore, you are more likely to encounter EMI and RFI in the city other types of environments. Tall buildings can also obstruct or reflect the signals from GPS satellites, potentially making this important tool for maintaining aircraft stability unreliable. Always make sure you have a strong position fix before you launch.

As an aerial photographer, city flying should be on your list. Just make sure you have the experience and confidence to fly safely in such a challenging environment.

DESERT ENVIRONMENT

The desert presents another compelling venue for aerial photography but without the mad press of humans and vehicles that make flying in the urban environment so challenging. Wind-swept dunes, jagged rock formations, meandering streams and lonely roads can make excellent subjects for those of us fortunate enough to own a flying camera (Figure 7.8).

7.8 / Towering stone pillars, vivid blue skies, and a general lack of people make the desert ideal for aerial photgraphy as long as you prepare for the heat, the dust, and the sand.

However, the desert is not without its challenges for both you and your machine. First, like any other piece of electronic equipment, drones have a listed maximum operating temperature. Disregard it at your peril, and it's very real. Don't ask me how I know this. Also, if you store your aircraft's **lithium polymer (LiPo)** batteries in your car in the desert heat, you're just begging for them to catch fire and incinerate your ride home. Unclear on why? Think back to Chapter 5, and the possibility of **thermal runaway**.

Keep in mind that in 60 minutes on an 80-degree day, your car might reach temperatures in excess of 123 degrees, and at 100 degrees the car reaches 143 degrees in an hour. So, park in the shade, keep windows open, and make sure you are not storing batteries in those temperatures. Even if you don't reduce your car to a charred hulk, those kinds of temperatures will take a toll on your expensive batteries.

Of course, heat is a potent threat to you as well. I'm not here to teach a course in desert survival, but dehydration and sunstroke can be life-threatening conditions. Be sure to have plenty of water available—more than you think you will need—and lightweight clothing that covers as much of your skin as possible. Also, don't forget a wide-brim hat and sunscreen—plenty of sunscreen.

Finally, because you'll be spending much of your desert sojourn looking up into the bright, blue sky to maintain a **visual line of sight (VLOS)** with your aircraft, sunglasses are a great idea, as well.

The desert also poses one additional threat to your aircraft. Dust and sand—but especially sand—are the mortal enemies of electric motors like the ones that spin your propellers. Once you get sand into your motors, it can quickly degrade them and getting it out may require taking them apart. This is a circumstance to be avoided.

One possible solution is to take off and land using a launch pad. So long as you keep the surface of the pad clean, it should protect your aircraft from the grit that otherwise gets stirred up when its propellers start to spin. There are purpose-made launch pads that feature a weighted perimeter to help keep them in place, fold up neatly into a storage bag and generally look pretty snazzy—but a beach towel or a thick blanket will also work just fine in most cases (Figure 7.9).

7.9 / Sand, like you might find in the desert or on the beach, can damage your aircraft's motors if it gets inside them. Be sure to launch and land on a clean surface to avoid contamination.

Also, it's important that you never forget that your flying camera is a *camera*, and just like any other camera, an accumulation of dust on the lens can reduce the quality of the images you capture. There is plenty of dust in the desert and other places as well. Therefore, like any other photographer, you should have a cleaning kit with a microfiber cloth, a blower, a brush, and a lens pen.

ALPINE ENVIRONMENT

Ah, is there any sight in the world that elicits a greater sense of adventure than high, white-capped peaks? They are forbidding and yet simultaneously alluring, with dense stands of evergreen trees, snowfields, and ancient glaciers laid down thousands of years ago (Figure 7.10) To be sure, there are some great opportunities for aerial imaging to be found in the mountains, if you are prepared to endure the elements.

The first thing to know about mountains is that they are tall—really tall—and as elevation increases, atmospheric density decreases. Most drones handle elevations up to 10,000 feet above *mean sea level (MSL)* with only a negligible impact on performance. The same may not necessarily be true for you. The reduced

7.10 / The stark white snow in alpine environments can throw other details into sharp relief, making it unique and powerful for aerial imaging.

partial pressure of oxygen at altitude can affect your judgment and make you short of breath while engaging in activities that would be comfortable at lower elevation. You should also be alert for the symptoms of *altitude sickness*, which include dizziness, headache, muscle aches and nausea.

The next thing to know is that any place with snow on the ground is either below freezing or was recently, and it may well be below freezing again soon. Cold temperatures can have a significant impact on the performance of your aircraft and its batteries in particular. As the temperature of LiPo batteries drop, their internal resistance increases.

Don't bother trying to wrap your head around the science for the moment, just understand that you could get less flight time than usual out of your batteries when flying in cold weather—potentially a lot less. Furthermore, this limitation can sneak up on you, leading to abrupt drops in indicated battery power remaining, so always be especially conservative when flying in cold environments. I remember one incident in the cold when my indicated battery power remaining dropped from 90 percent to 20 percent in the time it took for me to ascend from the surface to 100 feet AGL. Be sure to keep your batteries warm, but not *too* warm.

The cold is no friend to the human organism, either. Hypothermia is real. People freeze to death every year. If you're heading into the cold, make sure you are well prepared. Bring warm clothing, a full tank of gas, and if possible, an alternative source of heat in case your first one—your car, presumably—fails. You may sweat more than you realize all bundled up like that, so have plenty of water available and nutritious food, as well.

Your hands pose a particular challenge when it comes to keeping warm. Manual dexterity is required to fly, but gloves may be necessary to keep warm. For me, flying in a full pair of gloves is difficult to the point of being dangerous. I can't feel my thumbs on the sticks, which has occasionally led to abrupt and unintended maneuvers when I try flying this way.

A good compromise I've found takes the form of gloves developed specifically for photographers, actually. The tip of the thumb and the index finger fold back to reveal bare skin, providing much finer control over the aircraft and easier access to knobs and switches (Figure 7.11). It may take some experimentation to find what works

7.11 / While flying in circumstances that require extra protection, fingerless gloves allow thumb tips to be in direct contact with the sticks.

best for you—but always remember that your health and physical safety come first. If you can't stay warm, you can't function as a pilot.

Monitoring the weather is especially important in the mountains. No matter how desolate a desert you might find yourself in, it never happens that *more desert* falls from the sky. In the mountains, additional snowfall can be an extremely serious threat, making the road that brought you to your flying site impassible. Like any good pilot, stay alert and err on the side of caution.

WILDERNESS ENVIRONMENT

What you call wilderness depends on where you live. In the Pacific Northwest, my home territory, it means endless, thickly forested hills and ridges, dotted with waterfalls and the unmistakable signs of ancient—as well as very recent—volcanic upheavals (Figure 7.12). In Hawaii, it could mean lush jungles as well as broken expanses of black lava rock. In the southeastern United States, it could mean a marsh or swamp, marked by soggy ground and dense, overhanging trees replete with dangling vines.

7.12 / A flying camera can capture a unique perspective on the majesty of the wilderness.

So, the advice in this section is going to be pretty general. One thing that many wilderness environments have in common is tall trees and other vegetation. This poses several challenges for the intrepid drone pilot. First, even before you take off, that dense canopy can make it difficult to obtain a reliable GPS fix.

A clearing amid the trees might seem like a perfect place to go flying—indeed, it can be—but bear in mind the need to maintain VLOS with your aircraft, so the circle of trees surrounding your launch and recovery site might prove to be much more limiting than you initially realized. Furthermore, it makes it difficult, or impossible, to monitor the surrounding airspace for other aircraft, which could suddenly appear in your narrow patch of sky without warning (Figure 7.13)

7.13 / One problem with trees is that you can't see through them.

Another problem with tall trees is that they make great obstacles for your aircraft to hit. You don't even need to fly at full speed into the trunk to cause serious damage. If you get one of your propellers tangled up in a thin branch—maybe too small to be seen at the distance you are flying—that will be enough to bring it down. Also, bear in mind that these are precisely the sort of obstacles that can evade detection

> ## "That tree wasn't there before!"
> – Simon Fischer,
> American Remote Pilot

by your aircraft's *collision avoidance system*. If you're lucky, it will tumble all the way down to the ground and land in a heap of broken parts. If you're unlucky, it will be stuck 100 feet up a tree. Then what?

If you happen to be a certified arborist and you have your climbing kit with you—great! Otherwise, you've got a significant problem. If you leave it up there, not only are you out the price of the drone, but the next windstorm that blows through is sure to dislodge it, causing it to fall battery-first onto a jagged rock, starting a wildfire that wipes out a highly endangered species of vole. And, of course, the investigators will find your registration number on the charred wreck of your aircraft using advanced forensic analysis worthy of a television crime drama. Yes, in case you were wondering, this is a *bad thing*.

So, you should have a contingency plan in place to retrieve your aircraft if it gets snagged halfway up a tree, which may indeed involve calling a certified arborist. However, it's better still to avoid this kind of situation in the first place by maintaining a high level of situational awareness, giving trees a wide berth, and never flying farther than you can see.

You should also be prepared to cope with whatever your particular wilderness environment throws at you: heat, cold, humidity, quicksand, poisonous plants, and maybe snakes. Or bears. Or snakes *and* bears if you're having a particularly bad day.

COASTAL AND MARITIME ENVIRONMENTS

Most often the seashore shares one factor in common with the desert: sand and plenty of it. As described under the Desert Environment heading, sand has the potential to quickly ruin your motors, so you should take appropriate precautions. The other key factor to consider when it comes to the coast is wind. To be sure, the wind can be a hazard in any flying environment, but it poses a particular threat at the beach (Figure 7.14).

If the wind carries your drone 1,000 feet across an open field, you can land, walk over, and pick it up. If the wind carries your drone 1,000 feet out to sea—well, that's another matter entirely. Also, the wind can be especially strong in coastal areas as well as being subject to rapid and unexpected changes.

The key to flying safely at the beach is understanding what your aircraft is and is not able to handle, monitoring the weather and weather forecasts, and always making the most conservative choice when deciding when and how to fly.

7.14 / Imagery of that liminal space where the sand meets the sea can be especially compelling if captured from an aerial perspective.

By my use of the word "maritime," I'm referring to conducting flight operations from a boat. Apart from a city, this is probably the trickiest type of flying that you can ever attempt—so you should only do so once you have built up some significant experience in other environments. Indeed, before your first effort, you might want to run a rehearsal from the boat while it's tied up at the dock, providing an alternative landing site if things start to get away from you.

Assuming that you are flying from a motorboat or some other small vessel, your first problem is going to be a lack of space. Finding a place to launch can be difficult. Finding a place to land can be nearly impossible. Between the pitching and rolling of the boat, its movement through the water, and the paucity of deck space, your best plan is to come up with an alternative to a conventional landing.

Professionals who confront this challenge will most often choose to *hand-catch* their aircraft, which is to say they pluck it out of the air. This will obviously entail putting your delicate fingers within an inch or two—and your face within a foot or two—of four propellers turning at 5,000 rotations per minute (RPM). This should therefore be regarded as a high-risk maneuver and should only be attempted by an experienced and properly equipped flight crew.

As a hobbyist, I don't think I can recommend you attempt this technique. You're flying for fun, not to save somebody's life or to perform critical scientific research, and no amount of fun is worth slicing up your fingers or grinding off your own face. If you are going to attempt it, make darn sure that you're wearing sturdy gloves and eye protection, at the very least, and get plenty of practice on dry land before you even think of attempting it on a boat.

Another problem with boats, as opposed to every other type of launch and recovery site, is that they move. In terms of your coordinates on the Earth's surface, the place you take off from and the place you land will not be the same. This can be a big problem if your drone's *return-to-home (RTH)* function works by flying back to its launch point—as many are programmed to do.

If the radio link between your controller and your aircraft is lost, or you lose track of your aircraft and have to activate RTH to get it back, it will make a beautiful, controlled descent directly into the water where the boat *was* located when you launched it. You can certainly have worse days flying a drone, but that isn't going to make for a good one.

KNOW WHEN *NOT* TO FLY

The simple truth is that there are some locations that are simply unflyable. Part of being a good pilot is learning to recognize and accept that fact. I have never gotten myself into more trouble than when I've attempted to "force" an operation that I should have known was a bad idea right from the outset.

A little voice inside your head will warn you before you do something dumb. Learn to listen to that voice—it will save you a lot of grief. I say that as a person who has ignored that voice more than I would care to admit. Because of that, and myriad other failures and mistakes, I've seen a lot of drone operations go wrong.

To be sure, that experience does eventually yield insight into how to fly safely and well, but at a high price. The whole reason for me to write this book, and presumably for you to read it, is so that you don't have to make those same mistakes yourself. When in doubt, fly tomorrow.

PARK IT

If you were to draw up a list of the most dramatic, the most compelling, the most beautiful landscapes across the entire United States, you would likely discover that list corresponds closely with our 63 national parks. Imagine capturing an aerial perspective of the sun rising over the Grand Canyon, or lava flows on the big island of Hawaii, or geysers erupting in Yellowstone, or the twilight world of Carlsbad Caverns.

Unfortunately for both you and I, imagining is likely all that we'll ever get the chance to do. All of the national parks are designated no-fly zones—and with good reason. People visit these sites to experience the majesty of nature, not to be perturbed by the buzzing of propellers. So, leave your drone at home and experience a little majesty yourself. There are plenty of other great places to fly.

8
How Do I Work This Thing!?

Now that we understand the rules and regulations and the philosophy as well as the theoretical and practical underpinnings, it may finally be a good time to discuss the subject that prompted you to pick up this book in the first place: How to fly! With that said, it was a deliberate choice on my behalf to hold back on this information because, once you put a machine in the air, there is a distinct possibility that things will not go as planned.

Knowing how to select the right time and place to begin flying is crucial, so that you don't get into trouble or—infinitely worse—hurt somebody. If you've been reading this book straight through, you should be well prepared on that score. If you just skipped ahead to the good part, at least consider going back and taking a look at the preceding content. The grief you save may well be your own.

> "I have often been asked what I think about at the moment of takeoff. [A pilot] has to be part of the machine. If he thinks of anything but the task in hand, then trouble is probably just around the corner."
>
> – Amelia Earhart,
> Pioneering American Aviator

WHICH WAY AM I GOING?

Perhaps the most critical thing to understand about remote piloting is that your aircraft will respond to your control inputs relative to the direction *it* is facing—not the direction *you* are facing. So, if the aircraft is flying directly away from you, commanding a left-roll input will cause it to move left and a right-roll input will, obviously, do the opposite.

However, if the aircraft is flying directly toward you, these responses will be reversed. And, if the aircraft is traversing from right to left in front of you, a left-roll input will cause it to move in your direction and a right-roll input will cause it to move away. If this sounds deeply counterintuitive, you are absolutely right (Figure 8.1).

8.1 / All of your control inputs are relative to the aircraft's facing, not yours. If your airplane is coming right at you, your roll and yaw inputs will be reversed from your perspective.

Learning to manage the confusing and ever-changing relationship between your location, your aircraft's location, and your aircraft's heading is probably the single most difficult skill that you will have to master to become a proficient remote pilot, as it combines both perception and manual dexterity. The good news is that you can, and will, master it. However, it's going to require time, patience, and *at least* a few crashes before you get there.

ISN'T THERE AN EASIER WAY TO DO THIS?

Constantly adapting your control inputs to account for your aircraft's relative position and heading is a real and fundamental challenge for new remote pilots. By now, you must be thinking, "But surely there must be an easier way to do this...What about all those sensors and the *flight control system (FCS)*, can't they help me do all this stuff?"

The answer, at least when it comes to drones, "Yes." The FCS is actually able to bridge this gap, making all control inputs relative to your position rather than the aircraft's heading. This capability is referred to as *intelligent orientation control (IOC)* or "headless" mode.

If your drone comes equipped with this ability, I understand that it is tempting—*oh, so tempting*—to enable it and just push your aircraft around the sky willy-nilly. However, I strongly urge you to resist this temptation. Sure, it will be easy at first, but you'll never be more than a mediocre remote pilot, at best, relying on a system like this. Furthermore, every minute you spend flying this way is building muscle memory that you will have to unlearn when you finally do decide to do it the right way.

And, what happens if you lose GPS lock while your machine is in the air, or you're flying from a boat and your position changes? Well, then you're flat out of luck. So, do yourself—and the rest of us—a favor and learn *orientation flying* from the beginning. By the way, model airplanes offer no such accommodations. You either fly them the right way or not at all.

Inevitable crashes are the main reason why I put so much emphasis in Chapter 6 on using a simulator and then a sturdy and inexpensive aircraft to begin your flying experience. Unless you are some kind of remote-piloting savant, it's going to take hours in the air for this process to become intuitive and reliable—and those hours will be punctuated by moments of panic, botched maneuvers and, yes, crashes.

So why bother at all? Because the final result, after 100 or 200 logged flight hours (or more) is glorious: Your thumbs and control sticks disappear, and you pilot the aircraft as if by mental telepathy. Your maneuvers follow one after the other like the choreography of a seasoned ballet troupe—elegant, assured and purposeful. You and your aircraft become one, and you experience flight without ever leaving the ground. It isn't an easy journey, but it is one well worth taking, I promise.

While it still involves challenges and the potential for mistakes, this process is easier if you are learning to fly a drone. Its sophisticated sensors and stationkeeping abilities mean that if you get confused, disoriented, or panicked, all you have to do is take your thumbs off the sticks, and the aircraft should settle into a hover, giving you a moment to collect yourself before resuming the flight.

Of course, this only works if you actually *take your thumbs off the sticks*. In these critical moments, many new drone pilots (including me) have felt compelled to keep giving control inputs even when they are likely doing more harm than good. In those moments, I find it best to rely on the wisdom that an old flight instructor used to share with his students, "Don't just do something, sit there!"

FIXED-WING OR ROTORCRAFT?

As we learned in Chapter 3, aircraft can be divided into many different types and categories. However, for the purposes of learning to fly, you are almost certain to begin either with a fixed-wing platform like an airplane or a rotorcraft like a drone or a helicopter. Both types use the same style of two-stick controller, and there is significant overlap between what each input on each stick will cause your aircraft to do. However, there are also *critical* differences, so we will consider each separately (Figure 8.2).

8.2 / The time of choosing is upon you, Padawan: Will you first learn to fly fixed wing or rotorcraft?

Even if you intend to fly both types eventually—and I'd argue it's impossible to be a well-rounded remote pilot unless you do—I'd urge you to pick one and stay with it until you master the fundamentals. Once you achieve competence—and confidence—with one type, learning to fly the others will be much easier. As a novice, trying to do both simultaneously is a recipe for heartache.

Which is easiest? Asking that question is a great way to start an argument among a group of remote pilots, if that is something you are interested in doing. However, once everybody settles down, they would probably agree a full-featured drone is the easiest for a new pilot to start flying. It will incorporate many different sensors and capabilities, including finding its own way home, that will make it easy to fly and hard to crash, especially when you are just getting started.

Having said that, two factors are important to keep in mind: First, drones with all of these capabilities will, at a minimum, cost many hundreds of dollars, so if you do crash it or lose it, the hit to your wallet is likely to be non-negligible. Second, if you manage to stumble upon a "blind spot" where these systems can't or won't help you, things can go bad quickly, and your nascent skills may not be enough to get everything back under control.

The next easiest to learn how to fly are fixed-wing airplanes, especially if you choose one with built-in "training wheels," like the **Sensor-Assisted Flight Envelope (SAFE)** system from Horizon Hobby, which we discussed in Chapters 5 and 6. Also, manufacturers will designate certain aircraft within their fleets as "trainers" or "beginner" aircraft. These aircraft will have much more stable and forgiving aerodynamic characteristics, even without an electronic copilot on board. If the box says "advanced" or "expert" on the outside, keep looking. You haven't found your first model yet.

Finally, conventional helicopters are the most difficult for new pilots to learn how to fly. While they are technically rotorcraft, like drones, and use the same basic control inputs, they can be finicky and vindictive flying machines, especially the larger ones. Setting aside the quirks of any particular model, when compared with drones and fixed-wing platforms, helicopters are subject to a whole range of subtle and occasionally counter-intuitive flight characteristics that can catch a new or unwary pilot off-guard.

Furthermore, they can be quite dangerous. It turns out that one large, spinning propeller can do a whole lot more damage than four small, spinning propellers. Of the bare handful of fatal accidents that have occurred with model aircraft over the decades, most have involved large helicopters. If flying them is your ultimate goal, seek additional education and experience before making the attempt—seriously.

So, in the style of a choose-your-own-adventure storybook, pick either fixed-wing or rotorcraft and read only the remaining portions of this chapter that cover that specific type. Again, there is just enough overlap between what the controls do when flying each type of aircraft that reading both could be a bit confusing. Don't worry. When the time comes to expand your flying horizons, those other sections will still be right here, waiting for you. I'm not going anywhere.

FIXED-WING CONTROL INPUTS

The **vertical axis on the left joystick** controls the aircraft's **throttle** (Figure 8.3). Move this stick up, and the aircraft's propeller turns more quickly, generating additional thrust. Move this stick down and the propeller turns more slowly or stops turning entirely. Think of it like the gas pedal in your car: As you apply pressure, the engine works harder, and your car goes faster.

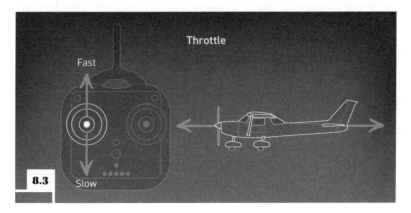

8.3

WHICH COMES FIRST: THE CONTROLLER OR THE AIRCRAFT?

When you're preparing to launch your aircraft for the first time, you will realize that you have a decision to make. What should you power up first—your controller or your aircraft? Fortunately, tradition and best practice have already made the decision for you: Turn on your controller first.

The original reason for this goes back to an earlier era of radio-controlled flight, which we learned about in Chapter 5. Those aircraft were controlled using a discrete radio frequency, so that any controller tuned to that same frequency could send it commands. Also, these systems were much more susceptible to *electromagnetic interference (EMI)* and *radio frequency interference (RFI)*, such that a random burst of static on the wrong frequency could be interpreted as a control input, like, say, "Go full throttle," while the pilot was leaning in to give the propeller a close inspection. Not good.

To help prevent these types of problems from occurring, pilots would always turn on their controller first, so that when they powered up the aircraft, a nearby source would already be sending it instructions—even if those instructions were to do nothing.

We still do that today, and for the same reason. Of course, with the advent of *frequency-hopping, spread spectrum (FHSS)* technology, the odds of a control input from another source or a random blast of static being interpreted as a command are vanishingly small, but not quite zero.

Yet one more example of how we stand on the shoulders of the aviators who came before us, they learned some lessons the hard way, so we don't have to—always respect and honor their wisdom.

Of course, just like your car, this ratio isn't fixed. If you're driving uphill, applying the same pressure on the gas pedal will result in less speed as your car works to overcome the force of gravity trying to drag it back down the hill. The same is true of an airplane, except that an airplane can go "uphill" any time it chooses, not only when the local geography demands it. Likewise, if you're going "downhill," that same throttle input will yield more speed as your motor and gravity are now on the same team.

When you're flying an airplane, speed has effects beyond how quickly you get from Point A to Point B, however. As airspeed increases, so does the flow of air over the wings and control surfaces, which generates more lift and makes the airplane more responsive to your control inputs. Fly more slowly and the control response becomes "soft" or "mushy." And, as we learned in Chapter 4, if an airplane's speed drops below a required minimum, it will experience an **aerodynamic stall**.

If that happens, and your aircraft's **center of gravity (CG)** is positioned properly, it's nose will drop and it will gain speed until lift is restored, unless it hits the ground first. All crewed aviators practice stall recovery as a routine part of their training, and you can, too. The main thing is to make sure that a stall doesn't sneak up on you, especially at low altitude.

The **horizontal axis on the left joystick** controls the aircraft's **rudder** and, nominally, aircraft **yaw** (Figure 8.4). However, give the rudder a heavy control input and, depending on the model you are flying, a roll maneuver might be the be the more noticeable outcome. As described in Chapter 4, you can do plenty of fixed-wing flying without ever actuating the rudder, and when you are learning how to fly, I'd suggest that's how you begin.

To be sure, the rudder will emerge as an important part of your repertoire as you gain experience. Some maneuvers are impossible to execute without it. However, for now, if your left thumb doesn't move side-to-side too much, that's nothing to worry about.

The **vertical axis on the right joystick** controls the aircraft's **elevators**, or stabilator, or whatever else it might have going on back there to control its **pitch** (Figure 8.5). Managing the pitch of your aircraft is crucial and has a direct correlation with its speed. Pitch down and you will begin descending, but you will also accelerate at a rate even faster than your current throttle setting would ordinarily deliver.

> "Always remember that you fly the airplane with your head, not your hands."
>
> – Aviation Aphorism

This maneuver can get away from you *very* quickly, especially at a steep pitch angle. You might want to get in the habit of pulling back on the throttle a little when you pitch down to avoid being caught off guard by your rate of descent. Furthermore, you aren't likely to stall while descending, so there is no reason to carry too much airspeed into a nose-down attitude.

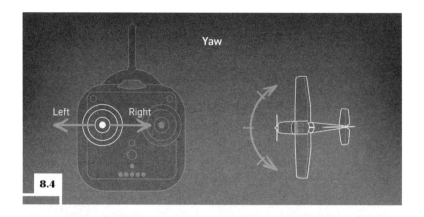

8.4

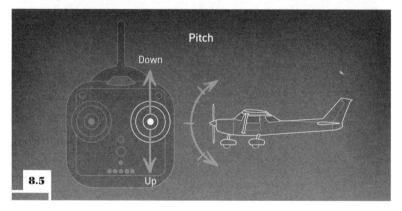

8.5

Pitch up, and your aircraft will begin to ascend, but you'll also start quickly bleeding airspeed. This is the classic set-up for a high *angle of attack* aerodynamic stall. Unless you're deliberately practicing stall recovery, you will want to avoid this. Therefore, it's advisable to add throttle simultaneously when you pitch up. This will give you a buffer in terms of your airspeed, providing a few extra seconds to realize what's happening if you inadvertently stray into a stall.

Most model airplanes, especially the ones you'll be flying as a beginner, have *thrust-to-weight ratios* that would leave their crewed counterparts blushing with envy. This means you can add airspeed much more quickly than a crewed aircraft can. You might even be able to accelerate while flying straight up, like a rocket ship. In crewed aviation, those who have experienced this form an elite club in which only a handful of high-performance jet fighters can claim membership. Consequently, you will generally have more latitude than a crewed pilot to avoid or address a stall, but you should never take it for granted.

Finally, the **horizontal axis on the right joystick** controls the aircraft's **ailerons**, and thus its movement in the **roll** axis (Figure 8.6). To be sure, some acrobatic maneuvers rely primarily on aileron input, but most of the time you'll roll to set up a **banked turn**. Especially as a beginning pilot, the ailerons will be your primary means of steering your aircraft.

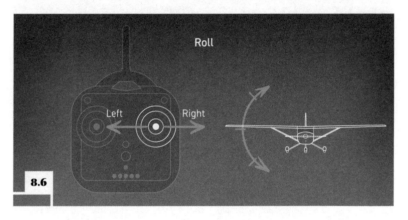

If you put your aircraft into a left roll, it will begin a gradual left turn while slowly descending. If you want to hurry the turn along, you can simultaneously pull down on the right stick. This will cause your elevators to pitch up, and the nose will come around faster as a result—because you are essentially pitching into the turn.

A banked turn, especially one that relies on aggressive elevator input, is going to cost you airspeed. Therefore, you must again be prepared to confront the possibility of an aerodynamic stall. Stay alert to the performance of your aircraft, and be prepared to add throttle, if needed (Figure 8.7).

8.7 / When changing heading in a hurry, use a steep roll combined with aggressive pitch input. Airspeed will be lost quickly, so keep the throttle up and watch out for a stall.

REMEMBER: SMALL MOVES

Although I can't explain the psychology behind it, all the brand-new, never-touched-the-sticks remote pilots that I have ever seen attempt their first flight always make their control inputs *WAY TOO BIG*. Maybe they figure that there wouldn't be so much travel in the stick if you weren't meant to use it all?

Occasions to give your aircraft full-stick inputs will happen, for example, the throttle when you are launching from a full stop or, once you've gained some experience, attempting an aggressive aerobatic maneuver. However, for the most part—and especially when you are just getting started—your stick movements should be so subtle that an untrained observer might not even be able to discern them.

If you go big on your first couple of flights, you'll quickly learn for yourself that this is not successful approach to remote piloting—and hopefully you had the good sense to do it in a simulator or with a stout little aircraft, as we discussed in Chapter 6.

As ever, I'm just trying to save you a little bit of grief by giving you the opportunity to learn from my experience, rather than your own. Don't worry, I've left plenty for you to learn on your own.

One final note: If you're flying a model that does not have ailerons, the horizontal axis on the right stick will control the rudder. As we learned in Chapter 4, this is not an uncommon configuration for training aircraft intended specifically for beginners. Don't give it too much thought: Just treat the rudder as if it were a pair of ailerons and you'll do just fine.

FIXED-WING LAUNCH

Now that we understand how to control a fixed-wing aircraft once it is aloft, we need to figure out how to get it there in the first place, and, more important still, how to get it back on the ground again. There are two fundamental ways to get a model airplane up into the sky: a *rolling takeoff* and a *hand launch*.

The rolling takeoff is what the big girls and boys do, so we'll start there. First of all, your airplane must have an undercarriage that allows it to move under its own power, at speed, on the ground for this to even be a possibility. Also, you must have sufficient space available for your aircraft to accelerate from a standing start to a speed that exceeds its stall speed. In crewed aviation, we refer to these facilities as *runways*.

If you're flying at an AMA club, you'll most likely have access to one. Otherwise, you're going to have to come up with an alternative. Something like a parking lot would be great—it's a smooth surface with plenty of open space—if only cars didn't have a habit of congregating on them. Most likely you'll end up on a grass field. These generally work pretty well, but they do have limitations.

Unless you are flying from a putting green, which would no doubt enrage the greenskeeper and result in an immediate telephone call to summon the constabulary, you will most likely find that the ground is a bit uneven. Small aircraft with small wheels will not be able to traverse it, so you'll need to select a model of sufficient scale to surmount the bumps and divots (Figure 8.8).

Now we find ourselves with a wheeled aircraft either on an improved runway, or of sufficient size to operate from a grass field. Next up, you want to ensure that your model is facing into the wind. You always want to take off, and land, for that matter, against the wind. With everything prepared, slowly advance the left stick in the vertical axis, causing your propeller to spin up. If you immediately push the throttle to the stop, especially on a grass field, your undercarriage might get stuck and your airplane flip over, nose first, hardly an auspicious beginning.

8.8 / One of these aircraft can make a rolling takeoff from a rough grass field and the other one cannot.

"When everything seems to be going against you, remember that the airplane takes off against the wind, not with it."

– Henry Ford

AGAINST THE WIND

Fixed-wing aircraft always take off, and land, into the wind—and there's a good reason for that. It stems from the fact that all aircraft have not one, but two, measures of speed—air and ground. Airspeed is the speed of the aircraft that is measured by instruments on board, like the **airspeed indicator (ASI)**. It reflects the movement of the aircraft through the air, regardless of whether or not it is flying into a headwind or with a tailwind. Ground speed, on the other hand, reflects the speed of the aircraft over the Earth's surface. It is the speed the aircraft's shadow would travel on a sunny day.

To help us better understand the distinction, imagine a crewed airplane that is flying at 120 knots in calm air. Its airspeed and ground speed are the same: 120 knots. Now, imagine that same airplane flying at that same speed is fighting a 10-knot headwind. Its airspeed is still 120 knots, but its ground speed is 110 knots. It's moving more slowly over the surface of the Earth because the wind is resisting its progress. Next, imagine that same plane is flying with a 10-knot tailwind. Its airspeed is still the same, but now its ground speed is 130 knots, because the wind is helping carry it along.

So, what does any of this have to do with taking off and landing? Let's assume you are flying a model airplane that stalls at 12 miles per hour (MPH). Let's further assume you're taking off into a 4 MPH headwind. Your airplane will begin to fly the moment its airspeed hits 12 MPH. However, with the headwind, its ground speed at that same moment will only be 8 MPH. That means you can take off on a shorter runway and your **undercarriage**—a significant source of friction—won't have to carry the weight of the aircraft as far.

Landing works the same way: A lower ground speed reduces the force of the impact on the undercarriage when the aircraft touches down and well as reducing the overall length of the **landing roll** required to bring the aircraft to a complete stop, meaning that, once again, you can get away with a shorter runway.

As you're advancing the throttle, simultaneously apply full down pressure on the vertical axis of the right stick, pitching the elevators up. As your aircraft starts to move forward, the wings will begin generating lift. At first, it won't be enough to actually fly, but it will reduce the load on the undercarriage and make your machine less susceptible to uneven ground.

After whatever distance your particular model requires for its *takeoff roll*, it will exceed its stall speed and lift off the ground. At this point, you want to back off on your elevator input, or you risk climbing too quickly and stalling out. If this happens, don't worry, we've all done it. Dust off your model and try again. Once airborne, continue a gradual climb and then transition to maneuvering as we discussed above once you have sufficient altitude and airspeed.

The alternative to a rolling takeoff is a hand launch. This is how you will get your machine into the sky if it makes *belly landings*. Again, make sure you are facing into the wind. Hold your controller in your left hand and your airplane in your right. Pause to acknowledge the danger inherent in the fact that you are holding a propeller capable of turning thousands of rotations per minute 18 inches from your face (Figure 8.9).

8.9 / If your airplane lands on its belly, it'll need help getting off the ground by means of a hand launch.

TRIM IT UP

Look closely next to the joystick gimbals on a model airplane controller, and you'll notice small buttons, switches, or levers—one for each axis of rotation. The exact configuration varies between manufacturers, but their function is the same. These are your *trim* inputs.

To understand what they do and why they are necessary, we must first take a step back and realize something fundamental about virtually all model airplanes and helicopters: They do not arrive from the factory as exemplars of aerodynamic perfection. Indeed, almost all of them will manifest some sort of quirk. For example, maybe your glider is always trying to roll off to the left just a little bit.

If this is happening, you'll need to constantly apply a little right pressure to the roll input so that it flies straight and level. No doubt this would leave you thinking to yourself, "Wouldn't it be nice if there was a way that I could just constantly apply that little bit of pressure without actually having to do it with my thumb?"

Before you start trying to rig something up using rubber bands and super glue, this situation is why you have those trim inputs. In the example mentioned above with a glider that veers to the left, just click the roll trim input—most likely located below the right joystick—to the right a few times and see how it performs. This is the same as putting constant pressure on the stick in the same direction.

Maybe after you make the adjustment it's still rolling slightly to the left, so it will need a few more clicks of right trim. Or, maybe you overcorrected and you need to click back to the left a couple of times. The point is that you can trim out those annoying little imperfections in your aircraft's performance so that it flies straight and level with the sticks centered, just the way it should.

One final note: Drone controllers don't have trim inputs because their multitude of sensors allow them to hold position despite any aerodynamic imperfections, in addition to external factors like turbulence and wind.

The trim inputs on a hobby controller allow small changes in the aircraft's pitch, yaw, and roll performance to correct for minor aerodynamic imperfections.

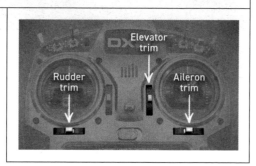

Hold the model at head level, its nose pointing at the horizon. Apply full throttle. You will feel the model tug at your hand, like a racehorse straining at the starting gate. Take a step forward while simultaneously tossing the aircraft straight ahead to give it as much airspeed as possible.

This next step can be a little panic-inducing, especially if your aircraft is headed toward the ground. As quickly as you are able, get your right hand back down on the controller and apply some back pressure on the elevators so that you begin a gentle climb while taking care not to stall the aircraft. Once you have sufficient altitude and airspeed, begin maneuvering.

An alternative hand-launch procedure is to have a friend fling the aircraft into the sky. This has the distinct advantage of allowing you to keep both hands on the controller throughout the sequence. However, you must also acknowledge the danger inherent in having a propeller capable of turning thousands of rotations per minute 18 inches away from *someone else's* face. The key to safety, and therefore success, is tight communication and making *darn* sure you don't touch the throttle until everyone is ready.

FIXED-WING LANDING

Congratulations! Your machine is aloft! Now comes the hard part—getting it back on the ground. Whenever I am flying a new model, the first thing I do once it's up is to start rehearsing the landing. I want to know how the machine behaves while gliding at low altitude, how it responds to control inputs at low airspeed, and so forth. Nothing is worse than trying to land an airplane without knowing the answers to those fundamental questions, so I try to figure them out straight away.

> **"Flying is the second greatest thrill known to man—landing is the first!"**
>
> – Aviation Aphorism

Hopefully you're conducting your first flights in a simulator or with a small, stout, and inexpensive model, so even bungling a landing or two—or 10—will be without significant consequences. The take-away here is that landing *is* difficult. In the following paragraphs, I'll describe the steps required and you may well come away thinking, "That sounds easy enough!"

However, mere words are insufficient to capture the difficulty, and the nuance, of the process. Much like the Matrix in the eponymous 1999 film, nobody can be told what landing is, you have to see it for yourself. Even professional, highly trained, and experienced crewed aviators occasionally have a landing that they wish they could take back. If it's enough to keep them on their toes, do you think it's going to be a challenge for you? The answer, in case you're wondering, is "Yes."

So, for whatever its worth, here is the procedure: Steer your aircraft into the wind and align it with the runway center line. If you're flying in an open field, just make sure you're facing into the wind and have plenty of open ground ahead of you. With any airplane you should be flying as a beginner, you'll want to reduce the throttle to zero, so that it is gliding in for a landing. Some larger and more complicated models land best with some minimum level of thrust—but those aren't anything you should be flying if you're still learning things from this book.

Pitch your aircraft slightly downward. You want a nice, slow descent. If you descend too abruptly, you're at risk of over-correcting and pulling back on the right stick so far that the plane noses up, then stalls. At that point, a crash is almost inevitable because you're only a few feet off the ground (Figure 8.10).

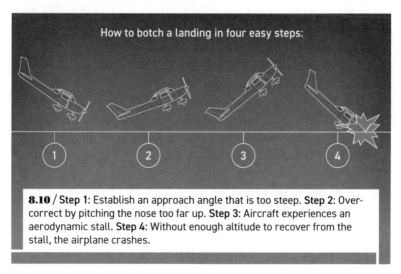

8.10 / **Step 1:** Establish an approach angle that is too steep. **Step 2:** Over-correct by pitching the nose too far up. **Step 3:** Aircraft experiences an aerodynamic stall. **Step 4:** Without enough altitude to recover from the stall, the airplane crashes.

Once you are less than a foot off the ground, apply gentle back pressure to the elevators, initiating a maneuver referred to as the *flare*. This will pull the nose up, and you'll start bleeding airspeed. Doesn't that put you at risk for a stall? Yes, and that's the whole point. Your goal is to stall the airplane at the precise instant it touches the ground. Easy, right? The truth is, landings take practice, they are not intuitive, and there is a lot of "feel" to getting it right (Figure 8.11).

The initial point of contact between the aircraft and the ground should be the *main gear*, the large pair of wheels below the wings. In either the tail dragger or tricycle configuration, the smaller wheel used for ground steering is typically too fragile to sustain the full force of landing, so your goal should be to hold it off the ground for as long as possible before gently setting it down.

If you're making a *belly landing*, you should aim to make contact at the spot on the airframe where the main gear would be— the space on the fuselage between the wings. Also, keep your wings level as far into the landing as you can. If the tip of one wing catches on the ground, the model can whip around into an abrupt stop, potentially causing damage in the process.

Now, you really have earned my congratulations: Your machine is back on the ground, and maybe even in a condition so that you'll be able to fly it again. That makes for a good day of aviation.

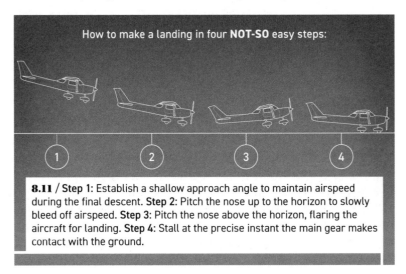

How to make a landing in four **NOT-SO** easy steps:

8.11 / **Step 1:** Establish a shallow approach angle to maintain airspeed during the final descent. **Step 2:** Pitch the nose up to the horizon to slowly bleed off airspeed. **Step 3:** Pitch the nose above the horizon, flaring the aircraft for landing. **Step 4:** Stall at the precise instant the main gear makes contact with the ground.

One more note: If at any time during the landing process you see something you don't like, you should always give yourself permission to perform a *go-around*. Crewed aviators (including me) do it, and you can, too. Advance the throttle, pull the nose up and resume flying. Then, circle the field and begin the process again. It's far better to go around than it is to carry a trash bag out onto the field to gather up the pieces of your machine. Begin your landing attempts with a healthy reserve of battery power, so that you have the option to waive off repeatedly, if necessary. Beginners "go around" a quite a bit: It's normal, it's part of practice. Do not be afraid to go around again, just watch your battery power.

ROTORCRAFT CONTROL INPUTS

Conceptually, rotorcraft are much easier to control than their fixed-wing cousins because, with airplanes, every type of input influences the machine's overall performance. Input yaw, and your aircraft will roll, as well. Roll, and it will also yaw. Increase the throttle and not only will it fly faster, but the wings will generate more lift, causing it to ascend and so on. With rotorcraft, each type of maneuver is separate from the others. Input yaw and all the aircraft does is yaw—and nothing else. This is absolutely true of drones, and to a certain extent, true of helicopters, as well. Keep this in mind as we discuss rotorcraft control inputs.

The *vertical axis on the left joystick* controls the aircraft's *throttle* (Figure 8.12). Push up, and a multirotor's propellers spin faster, or the pitch angle of a helicopter's blades increase, and the aircraft rises vertically into the air. Pull down, the opposite happens, and the aircraft descends. That's it.

The *horizontal axis on the left joystick* controls aircraft *yaw* (Figure 8.13) Push left and, owing to the *torque reaction* we learned about in Chapter 4, the aircraft yaws left. Push right, and it yaws right. A yaw maneuver that does not incorporate any other movement of the aircraft—essentially turning in place—is referred to as a *pirouette*, a name taken from a spinning ballet dancer.

The *vertical axis of the right joystick* controls aircraft *pitch* (Figure 8.14). Pitch the nose down, and the aircraft moves forward. Pitch the nose up, and the aircraft moves backward. In this axis of rotation, we begin to see some divergence between drones and

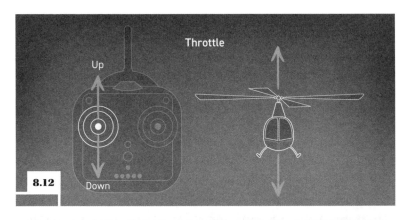

Throttle

8.12

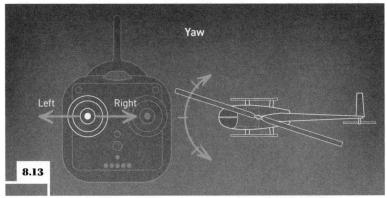

Yaw

Left   Right

8.13

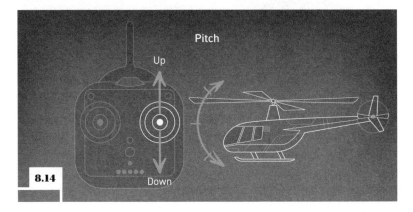

Pitch

Up

Down

8.14

helicopters. Again, as we discussed in Chapter 4, when rotorcraft pitch or roll, they do so by converting some of the *rotor disk's* lift into thrust. This creates a deficit of lift that will cause the aircraft to descend. Drones make up the difference as an automatic function of the *Flight Control System (FCS)*. However, to maintain a constant altitude while *translating*—fancy pilot talk for moving forward, backward, or side to side—with a helicopter, it is necessary to manually add throttle.

The *horizontal axis of the right joystick* controls aircraft *roll* (Figure 8.15). Push left, and the aircraft rolls left. Push right and, well, you get the idea . . . As we learned in Chapter 4, rolling a rotorcraft is essentially the same maneuver as pitching a rotorcraft—the only difference being the direction of the resulting movement.

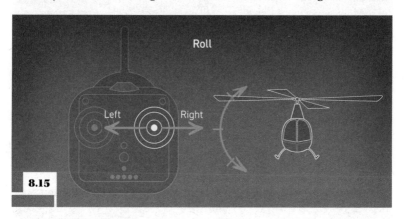

Now, just because a rotorcraft's movement in each axis of rotation is separate from the others doesn't mean that *we* can't combine them. Indeed, some of their most exciting capabilities—especially as aerial camera platforms—stem from their ability to execute multiple types of maneuvers simultaneously.

Let's imagine you are capturing aerial video of a solitary monument, like an obelisk or a column, in the middle of an open square. If you simultaneously input right roll and left yaw—or vice versa—your aircraft will move around your subject while it stays squarely in the center of the frame, while the surroundings slip past in the background. That makes for some compelling imagery!

Now, let's imagine you are capturing aerial video of a large vehicle (like a tugboat) moving across the water. If you simultaneously input pitch, roll, and yaw, you can achieve the same effect even though your subject is in motion. That makes for some *very* compelling imagery!

Of course, learning the precise combination of control inputs to achieve these effects requires practice, the kindly intervention of the FCS, or maybe some of both. However, the key point is that rotorcraft have remarkable maneuvering capabilities, and we can use them to achieve remarkable results.

ROTORCRAFT TAKEOFF AND LANDING

Befitting the overall simplicity of their maneuvering characteristics, launching and recovering a rotorcraft is a pretty straightforward process. Therefore, most of this discussion will focus on tangential matters related to the task at hand.

The first thing is to be aware of your surroundings. This is important while operating any type of remotely piloted aircraft, of course, but because rotorcraft can launch from such a small patch of ground, it's easy to start focusing only on what's right in front of you and neglecting the broader environment. So, remember to keep your head up.

Also, because drones are typically smaller and less flashy than model airplanes, it's easier for bystanders to walk right through your launch site without even realizing it. To guard against this possibility, professional drone pilots will use brightly colored landing pads and even traffic cones to alert everyone in the vicinity to their operations (Figure 8.16).

Something else to keep in mind is the surface where you are launching. Whereas airplanes will blow debris back and away from the aircraft, rotorcraft will tend to stir it up all around themselves once their propellers start spinning. As we learned in Chapter 7, dust and sand can have deleterious effects on your aircraft, so you'll want to take steps to make sure your rotorcraft doesn't contaminate itself at launch. This is a great argument for having a clean surface available, even if you have to bring it along yourself.

8.16 / This might be overkill for a small recreational operation, but not once since it was founded has the FAA levied a penalty for being too safe.

With the preliminaries out of the way, the process of launching a rotorcraft is actually pretty simple. One wrinkle is that most drones need to be *armed* before you can take off. Think of this like the safety on a firearm. Push up on the left stick before the aircraft is armed and nothing will happen. It will just sit there, blinking at you. This is designed to ensure that you don't start those four propellers turning at 5,000 RPM before you really, truly intend for that to happen. While there are variations between different manufacturers, the default arming sequence is to simultaneously push down and in on both sticks simultaneously—toward the bottom center of the controller (Figure 8.17).

8.17 / The most common arming sequence on a drone requires pushing both sticks "down" and "in" simultaneously.

At this point, the propellers will start turning at an idle speed, waiting for you to advance the throttle and lift it into the air. Push up on the left stick and the aircraft will ascend. Once you're clear of the launch site and any obstacles in the immediate vicinity, you are free to maneuver as you see fit. Small helicopters are essentially the same, except that they usually don't need to be armed before takeoff. Just be sure to give yourself some extra altitude, so you are prepared to lose a little when you start pitching and rolling.

Landing essentially requires you to complete the same steps in reverse. Bring the aircraft back to your launch and recovery site and establish it in a stable hover. Then, reduce the throttle until it settles on the ground. Drones will typically require you to maintain full down input on the left stick for a few seconds after touchdown to disarm them, at which point the propellers will stop turning. If you're flying a helicopter, do not reduce the throttle to zero until it is on the ground; otherwise, it will simply fall the remaining distance.

> **"Every landing is a controlled crash. Some are just better controlled than others."**
>
> – Aviation Aphorism

Once again, the complexities lie mainly in external factors related to safety. For whatever reason, bystanders tend to disregard the presence of small rotorcraft in their vicinity. There is a theory that over the millennia we humans evolved to disregard small, flying objects—like sparrows and finches—because they were neither a threat nor a potential source of food. Whatever the reason, I've seen it with my own eyes: People will quite happily walk right up to, or even into, a drone or other small rotorcraft in flight—buzzing propellers and all.

You need to be on guard against this type of behavior, even though in this case it would be the bystander doing something dumb, it's still your responsibility to keep it from happening, and it's your fault if it does. Be prepared to issue a verbal warning, waive off your aircraft's approach, or do both if that's what is required. Remember that humans, like crewed aircraft, have the right of way, so don't be a jerk about it, but always be ready. This, by the way, is another argument in favor of having a clearly marked and isolated launch site.

Finally, make sure that your aircraft is facing directly away from you when you land. Once again, the reason is rooted in evolution. Since before we shed our fur, our reflexes have been honed to push potential threats away from ourselves. If something goes wrong during landing and the nose of your aircraft is pointing out into the environment, reflexively pushing "away" (i.e., pushing up on both sticks) will cause the aircraft to move away from you. If, on the other hand, the nose of the aircraft is pointing toward you, pushing up on both sticks will likely cause it to fly directly into your face. Hopefully, by now, there is no need for me to explain that this is a *bad thing*.

CONTROLLER MODES

In another one of those "Who thought this was a good idea!?"-type developments in remote piloting, controllers can operate in different "modes." A controller's mode determines which joystick does what. You are (almost certainly) learning to fly with a Mode 2 controller—so the vertical axis on the left stick controls throttle, the horizontal axis controls yaw, and so forth.

In Mode 1, pitch and yaw are controlled with the left stick, and throttle and roll are controlled with the right stick. If you're a Mode 2 pilot, and someone hands you a Mode 1 controller, the result would almost certainly be an immediate crash, because all your experience would be working against you. Oh, and for good measure, Mode 3 and Mode 4 also exist because...why not?

Mode 2 has long been the standard here in the United States, while our friends across the pond have always relied on Mode 1 for their aeronautical adventures. However, the advent of drones upended this arrangement as virtually all of them ship from the factory with their controllers configured for Mode 2.

Thus, Mode 2 is slowly but inexorably becoming the global standard.

Still, if you happen to meet a remote pilot with a posh accent that would sound right at home on *Downton Abbey*, and she asks if you would like to fly her machine 'round the field, you might want to verify what mode she flies, lest you fall victim to Sod's law. Pip-pip, wot!

9

An Aerial Imaging Primer

If I've done my job correctly, you will have learned (more or less) everything you need to know to become a competent, novice remote pilot over the preceding eight chapters. However, it occurred to me that you might want to put these newfound skills to some specific use—even if you are still flying for fun at this point. Providing you with some suggestions along those lines will be the subject of these final two chapters.

In this chapter, we'll take a look at aerial imaging—the breakthrough application that separates drones from virtually all of the other small, civilian remotely piloted aircraft that have existed for the past 80 years or so (Figure 9.1). In Chapter 10, we'll look at everything else.

As you read these last two chapters, bear in mind that, as an industry, remote piloting is still new, and there are likely many useful applications that have not yet been discovered. In a little more than a decade, this technology has morphed from the exclusive domain of intrepid weirdos—including yours truly—to a burgeoning mainstream technology that will only make increasing beneficial contributions to our lives in the decades ahead.

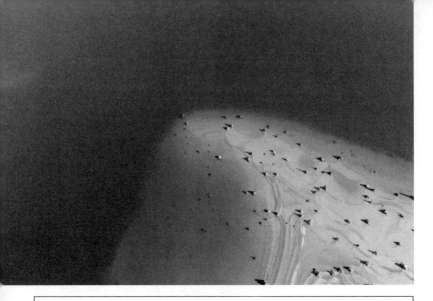

9.1 / The beauty and power of aerial imaging was once limited to people who could afford aircraft and cameras. However, the development of small, civilian drones has made it much more widely available.

People are coming up with new ideas and applications for drones all the time, and you might be one of them. Don't think of the topics we will be discussing as limiting what can be done, only describing what has been done. The past shapes the future, but it need not define it.

A WHOLE NEW WORLD

Before going any further in our discussion of imaging, it's worthwhile to take a moment and realize that photography is an entire field of human endeavor. In the same way that it takes years of training and practice to become a professional aviator, it also takes years of training and practice to become a professional photographer, or even a decent one. Obviously, no immediate risk of physical harm typically attaches to the practice of photography in the same way as it does to aviation, and the two share no fundamental skills or knowledge in common—but they are nevertheless similar.

Both are recent developments in human history, with photography having emerged as a practical tool around 1840—roughly halfway between the advent of lighter-than-air and heavier-than-air flight. Both are technical pursuits, impossible to perform without specialized equipment, and both rely on a highly developed understanding of scientific principles.

I note all this only to bring your attention to the fact that our discussion of aerial imaging will be almost comically deficient. In this book, I've sought to distill all of aeronautics to its most fundamental level, and it's taken me about 50,000 words to accomplish that. This chapter, addressing an equally complicated and nuanced subject, is only about 6,000 words long. Do you see the problem?

This won't be the last word on imaging—aerial or otherwise. Heck, it'll barely be the first word. My only goal is to familiarize you with the most basic concepts and ideas.

Another thing to keep in mind is that imaging necessarily involves aesthetic judgments. You might love a particular photograph that I hate, or vice versa, and that's fine. Neither of us is, nor can be, "right." Each of us has walked our own unique path on this world, which has shaped our perspective on what is "beautiful" or "ugly," and there can be surprising variation across the human population in this regard.

This makes imaging fundamentally different than everything else we have learned about in this book, like aerodynamics, for example. When it comes to the design of an airplane wing, the only question that matters is how it interacts with air moving across its surfaces, and how much lift it generates as a result. The universe couldn't care less what you or I think of the wing, because physics gets the final word.

A FLYING CAMERA IS A CAMERA

Much like aviation, imaging technology has made startling gains in recent decades. These have determined not only what we are able to accomplish but who is able to accomplish it. Half a century ago, producing high-quality images—or any images at all—was the exclusive domain of trained professionals using expensive gear. Today, each of us walks around with a smartphone that far exceeds the capabilities of the cameras that have recorded our entire history from the Civil War to the mid-1990s. The pioneers of cinema would have wept for the capabilities that all of us take for granted today.

Yet, when you watch video captured by an amateur, like an incident recorded by witnesses to a newsworthy event, you can always see the difference between that, and video captured by the professionals. To be sure, this is in part because the professionals have access to even better equipment, but it is also because the professionals know how to make the most of it. My goal for the rest of this chapter is to give you some small insight into that know-how so you can make the most of your drone's camera.

Of course, much like the camera on your smartphone, you can simply stick with the default settings and achieve acceptable results under most circumstances. However, if that is all you are interested in doing, I suspect you would have skipped over this

chapter entirely. So, let's dig a little deeper and look at what your camera can do once you begin to assert some manual control over its functions.

We'll begin by familiarizing ourselves with two of the most fundamental concepts in photography: *focus* and *exposure*. If an image is out of focus or improperly exposed, most people will regard it as a failure, because they won't be able to discern its subject: It will be blurry or obscured by too much darkness, or light. Like the *flight control system (FCS)* in a drone, virtually all modern cameras incorporate features that are designed to prevent these types

> # "Your first 10,000 photographs are your worst."
>
> – Henri Cartier-Bresson, French Photographer

of failures, like auto-focus and auto-exposure settings. Indeed, these are typically engaged by default.

In the realm of aerial imaging, we can typically take focus for granted. There are a couple of reasons for this. First, modern auto-focus systems work quite well. Second, drones typically carry cameras equipped with wide-angle lenses best suited for capturing large subjects, like landscapes (as opposed to portraits of individual people, for example), and focus is much easier to maintain in this type of application. We will briefly revisit focus later in this chapter, but we'll be giving most of our attention to exposure moving forward (Figure 9.2).

For an image to be properly exposed, an appropriate amount of light must fall upon the sensor

9.2 / For a variety of reasons, ranging from the capabilities of modern autofocus systems to the science of optics, you can generally expect that almost all of your aerial photographs will be in focus.

that is responsible for capturing it. In the old days, this took the form of a clear strip of plastic coated with a gelatin emulsion bearing light-sensitive silver halide crystals. That's a mouthful, so we just called it "film" for short. It's still around, but today most cameras are digital and rely on an electronic sensor to perform this task.

However, despite this fact, many of the terms and concepts that we use in the image-making process are left over from the film era, which is why it is helpful to understand the history. As a photographer, you have three basic tools available to you that influence the exposure of your images: *shutter*, *ISO*, and *aperture*.

GIMBAL MACHINE

Every drone intended for aerial photography that is not merely a novelty will incorporate a *camera gimbal*. This is essentially a self-leveling platform that supports the camera and keeps it steady while the aircraft is maneuvering. It accomplishes this task by controlling the pitch, roll, and yaw axes of the camera, independent from the aircraft.

For example, if you roll left, the gimbal will roll the camera right to precisely the same degree. Consequently, the horizon will remain steady in the camera's field of view, despite the aircraft's movement. These are incredibly powerful tools for capturing stable aerial images—most especially video.

For the most part, this is a completely automated process that will take place without your direct input. While there are variations, most manufacturers give the pilot manual control over only one axis of rotation—pitch. This means you can tilt the camera up and down using a knob or lever on your controller.

Although the term "gimbal" is often used to refer to the entire assembly, it actually refers only to the mechanism that keeps the camera stable in spite of the movement of the aircraft.

SHUTTER FLUTTER

In a film camera, the *shutter* is a mechanical device that exposes the film to the light coming through the lens for an extremely precise interval, referred to as the *shutter speed*. This can range from a tiny fraction of a second to, in the case of long-exposure photography used in astronomy and night photography, minutes or hours. Think of the shutter as a perfectly opaque window blind that snaps open, exposing the film to light, and then snaps shut again.

GLOBAL SHUTTER VS. ROLLING SHUTTER

Start shopping for drones, and you'll soon notice that shutters come in two flavors—*global shutters* and *rolling shutters*. In terms of their overall impact on image exposure and motion blur, they both do basically the same thing and deliver similar overall results. However, there are differences that can be important in some specific applications.

A global shutter is like the shutter in a film camera: It moves aside in an instant, exposing the entire sensor to the light coming through the lens for the entire interval established by the shutter speed you select. This essentially guarantees clear, undistorted images—as opposed to rolling shutters, which can create visual artifacts under certain circumstances.

You see, a rolling shutter isn't really a shutter at all but rather a specific means of capturing the data being generated by the imaging sensor. As an example, consider a high-definition video image: It is 1,920 by 1,080 pixels, meaning there are 1,080 rows of pixels, each one 1,920 pixels wide. While a global shutter captures all 2 million of these pixels simultaneously, a rolling shutter captures each row of pixels, one after the other, from the top of the frame to the bottom.

This process is stupid fast, but it's not quite the same as capturing them all in the same instant. As a result, rapidly spinning objects, like propellers, will be distorted into unrecognizable—and unnatural—shapes. Straight lines, like a column or the edge of a building, skew diagonally in the direction of the camera's movement, and so forth.

Again, most of the time, this won't make much difference. However, high-end users—like surveyors and aerial cinematographers—rely on global shutters to deliver the best-possible quality in their finished images. And, as you might expect, cameras that incorporate global shutters are generally more expensive than those with rolling shutters.

Although some digital cameras still make use of a mechanical shutter, these days it largely exists as a concept to help us understand how the sensor accomplishes its mission of gathering light to create an image. Obviously, the longer the shutter is open, more light falls on the sensor or the film behind it. If the shutter isn't open long enough, the result will be an under-exposed image that appears dark and muddy (Figure 9.3). If the shutter is open for too long, the image will appear blown out, like what happens when you take your sunglasses off at the beach (Figure 9.4). Like Goldilocks, we are looking for a shutter speed that is "just right" and yields a correctly exposed image. However, shutter speed can have other consequences for the final image.

9.3 / If, for whatever reason, an insufficient quantity of light reaches the camera's sensor, the result will be an underexposed image. While this may find favor with a particular audience, an underexposed image is conventionally regarded as a failure.

On a bright, sunny day, a shutter set to 1/1,000th of a second may be sufficient to achieve an appropriate exposure. Because this is such a short interval, the resulting image will "freeze" the world we see in the resulting image (Figure 9.5). Assuming that the image is in focus, everything will appear extremely crisp and clear. Now, as a mental experiment, let's imagine you leave the shutter open for one-half second. That isn't a whole lot of time in daily life, but it is enough time for things to move, at least a little bit. Imagine a speeding freight train or the legs of a running dog.

Getting Started With Drones and Model Airplanes

9.4 / On the other hand, if too much light reaches the sensor, the result will be an overexposed image which obscures the subject. In the right circumstances, this could lead to the creation a compelling image—but this one clearly doesn't qualify

9.5 / This photograph was captured with a shutter speed of 1/8000th of a second. Notice how the propellers are frozen, mid-turn. This doesn't reflect the way we see the world with our own eyes, so it appears to be unnatural.

As a result of the longer exposure, those fast-moving objects will appear blurry because they physically moved while the shutter was open. As a rule, we regard "blurry" as the enemy of good imaging. However, this isn't always the case. The specific phenomenon we are describing here is known as "motion blur" and can be used to create dramatic effects (Figure 9.6).

Look at basically any photograph in this book, and you'll see that all the propellers of the aircraft in flight appear as an indistinct, disk-shaped blur, which mimics how our eyes perceive a turning propeller in real life. An extremely brief exposure, like 1/1,000th of a second, will "stop" the propeller blades midturn, creating an unnatural effect in the resulting image. By using a slightly longer exposure, we achieve a result that better reflects how we actually see the world. Motion blur can also be used to add drama and energy to an image, like a sports car roaring down a racetrack.

9.6 / While "blurry" isn't an attribute that we generally associate with high-quality photography, in the right context a little motion blur can add drama and energy to an image.

For all its potential to create more dynamic images through motion blur, holding the shutter open for an extended period of time creates a new problem for us: What happens if the camera moves? If that happens, then everything in the image will be blurry, almost like the lens was out of focus.

This is why professional photographers use a tripod to take long-exposure photographs. It eliminates the possibility that the camera will move while the shutter is open. That's all well and good if you're taking pictures on the ground, but if you're mounting your drone on a tripod, you clearly aren't using it to its fullest potential, and you're probably going to get some strange looks while you're at it, besides.

If you're in a situation where you need a long exposure to capture a particular image using a drone, you clearly want the aircraft to move as little as possible. Obviously, the FCS and the camera gimbal are going to help with this, but you can improve your chances of capturing a usable image by flying in calm air, so that your aircraft isn't being buffeted by winds and turbulence.

Go ahead and play around with your camera under different conditions and see how it performs. Unlike aviation more generally, it's okay to make gratuitous mistakes with your camera. I mean, not every image will be Ansel Adams worthy, but at least nobody will get hurt in the process.

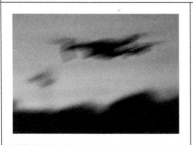

One way to capture a photograph in low light is to leave the shutter open for an extended period of time—half a second, or longer. However, if the camera itself moves during this interval, the entire image will suffer from motion blur, as seen in this example.

The shutter setting that we select has not one, but two, effects on the final image—its exposure and the presence of motion blur—and this may necessitate some trade-offs. Let's say it's a sunny day and you want to take a picture of an airplane that renders its propeller with a nice motion blur. You leave the shutter open long enough to achieve that effect, but you find your image is overexposed as a result. It turns out that no shutter speed will result in both a properly exposed image and a motion blur on the propeller.

To be sure, you could address this problem using the ISO or aperture settings, which we'll be discussing next, or you could reduce the light level using a *neutral-density (ND) filter*. These diminish the light entering the lens equally across all wavelengths, making the image darker but without affecting its color or other properties (Figure 9.7). Now, you can achieve the motion blur you want while still capturing an image that is properly exposed.

9.7 / Neutral Density (ND) filters are available for some drones, to prevent images from becoming overexposed in brightly lit environments. Typically, ND filters come in sets, allowing the photographer to choose how much light to eliminate from a particular scene.

I TOLD YOU ISO

ISO, which is sometimes referred to as *gain* in the context of digital photography, is another concept left over from the film era. Basically, ISO measures the sensitivity of the film—or a sensor—to light. It is represented by numbers that, generally speaking, range from 100 to 3,200, or more. This numerical value for light was set by the International Organization for Standardization (hence, ISO). In the context of film, ISO numbers correspond with the size of the silver-halide crystals used in the creation of the stock. The smallest crystals, indicated by a low ISO number, are the least sensitive to light. In other words, the scene must be brightly lit—like the outdoors on a sunny day—to achieve appropriate exposure.

On the other hand, a high ISO number indicates larger crystals that are more sensitive to light, meaning that they can be used to capture darker scenes—at twilight or indoors, for example. However, as usual, there is a price to be paid for this increased sensitivity. Because the crystals are larger, the resulting image is grainy.

While you aren't likely to see many grainy images on the covers of high-fashion magazines, you will in plenty of other applications: Like gritty, action-packed Hollywood blockbusters about soldiers and spies. Indeed, most photo- and video-editing software allows you to *add* grain retroactively to achieve this aesthetic. So, a grainy image in and of itself is "good" (or "bad") depending on the context of the image and the mood you are trying to capture (Figure 9.8).

Of course, those silver-halide crystals are long gone, but the same fundamental principles hold true even in the digital era. As you increase the sensitivity of your sensor, more and more grain will appear in the resulting images because of increasing electronic "noise" in the signal as the camera tries to make the most of the available light.

9.8 / This low-light image includes some grain, which can be a side-effect of very high ISO settings. Full disclosure: This image originally did not include any grain. I added it afterward so you can see what it looks like. Modern cameras are getting pretty good at wringing clear images out of challenging environments.

Again, this may or may not be a problem based on the tone of the image you are aiming for, but grain is not considered an enhancement in the context of most imaging applications. You probably don't want the photos from your family vacation looking like the middle third of a Jason Bourne movie—or maybe you do. I'm not here to judge. However, you do need to know one thing: While you can easily add grain to existing imagery, it's almost impossible to remove after the fact. The road to Grainyville only runs in one direction, so choose your on-ramp carefully.

Also, increasing your ISO setting means that you don't have to leave the shutter open as long to capture an equivalent degree of exposure. That means you have another trade-off available to you: If you want to reduce motion blur in a dimly lit location, you can crank up the ISO to compensate. Experiment to find what combination of these settings will yield results that are acceptable to you.

The good news is that digital cameras allow for grain-free imagery at much higher ISO settings than were ever possible using film. While your typical drone can't deliver this type of results (yet), a professional handheld camera can capture clean images at ISO settings in excess of 10,000. The very notion of an ISO rating that high, let alone using it to produce usable images, would have seemed absurd to previous generations of film photographers.

CONTROLLING THE LIGHT

Your final option for controlling the amount of light that hits the sensor is the size of the opening it comes through to reach the sensor: Smaller hole, less light; bigger hole, more light. Of course, in the context of photography, this opening has a special name—the *aperture*. The size of the aperture is referred to as the *f-stop*. A low number, like "2" means a great big aperture, whereas a high number, like "22," means a tiny aperture.

Like pilots, I suppose, photographers never miss a chance to make everything just a little bit more obscure. Consequently, they put "f/" in front of these numbers, so the examples above would be referred to as "f/2" and "f/22." With some cameras, you can adjust the f-stop, making the hole larger or smaller as needed to achieve correct exposure in a particular environment. However, adjusting the f-stop will also affect the final image's *depth of field*.

Depth of field defines the distance from the lens at which objects will be in focus. A very wide, or "deep," depth of field means that objects just a few inches from the lens all the way to the horizon will be in focus. A "shallow" depth of field means that only objects within a very narrow range will be in focus. Objects that fall outside this range, because they are closer to or farther from the lens, will be out of focus. (Figures 9.9, 9.10, 9.11, and 9.12 illustrate this concept.)

9.9 / Notice that in this photograph, all three model airplanes are in focus, despite the differing distance between each of them and the camera's lens. This is a "deep" depth of field shot, and was accomplished using a pinhole aperture setting of f/22.

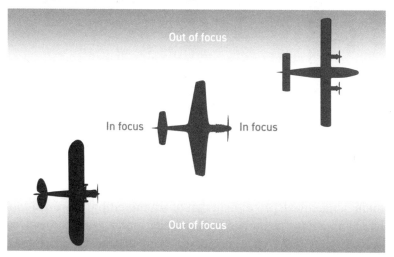

9.10 / This illustration shows how the "deep" depth of field includes all three airplanes, so that all three are in focus.

9.11 / Unlike the previous example, notice how in this photograph, only the middle airplane is in focus, while the other two are blurry and indistinct. This is an example of a "shallow" depth of field shot, and was accomplished with an aperture setting of f/2.8.

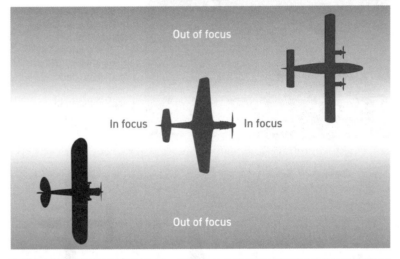

Out of focus

In focus

In focus

Out of focus

9.12 / In this illustration, we can see how the use of a "shallow" depth of field leaves only one of their aiplanes in focus, and thereby naturally focuses the viewers attention on it.

In the hands of a skilled photographer with the right equipment, a narrow depth of field can be an incredibly powerful tool for shaping how the audience of an image perceives its subject, so much so that the f-stop is considered as much a tool for controlling the depth of field as exposure. By now, you can probably sing along with me: This is necessarily going to involve some trade-offs.

Specifically, if you want a narrow depth of field, you're going to need to crank the aperture wide open, which is going to let in *a lot* of light, possibly enough to over-expose the resulting image. As a result, you may need to dial back the ISO and reduce the shutter speed. That will work, but what if you want to capture some motion blur in this same image? Unless you're taking pictures in the dark, this will basically guarantee your image comes out overexposed. Consequently, you'll need to break out the *ND filters* to create an image that is properly exposed and combines all these elements. By the way, this is exactly what I did for almost all the images that depict an aircraft in flight on the pages of this book.

One thing to be aware of is that, like smartphones, almost all small drones—anything you are likely to fly as a first, or a second, or even a third, aircraft—will have a fixed aperture. It left the factory set at f/2.8 (or whatever), and that's never going to change. This will be less of an impediment to your adventures in aerial imaging than it might appear at first. As I mentioned above, drones typically incorporate cameras that capture a wide field of view, and the effects of a narrow depth of field become most pronounced when you are using a lens with a narrow field of view, like a telephoto or a long zoom lens.

> **"There are always two people in every picture: the photographer and the viewer."**
>
> – Ansel Adams,
> American Photographer

So, tuck away this knowledge of apertures and f-stops for when you are shooting with a serious handheld camera or a much more sophisticated drone camera—or, when you need to impress your friends.

I'VE BEEN FRAMED!

Congratulations! Now you understand the fundamentals of focus and exposure, which puts you miles ahead of the people mashing the "Take Picture" button on their smartphones and relying on a computer to do all of the real work. Next up, we'll turn our attention to what most people think of when they discuss the art of capturing still photos or video, the *composition* of a shot. In this context, composition describes how the different elements are arranged within an image.

WHITE BALANCE!

Noodle around long enough in your drone's camera menu and in addition to shutter speed, ISO, and (possibly) aperture controls, you'll also find something called **white balance**. The purpose of this tool is to ensure your camera captures true-to-life colors. If you have ever successfully navigated an intersection in an automobile, then you are aware the light comes in different colors, red, yellow and green, at the very least.

What is less obvious is that the light we encounter in everyday life, emitted by the sun or a light bulb, also comes in different colors, ranging from "warm" tones, red and orange, to "cold" tones, blue. The differences are subtle compared to a traffic light, so you could be forgiven for not having noticed this fact before now.

We discern these differences by relying on the concept of **color temperature**, which is measured in degrees **Kelvin (K)**. If you paid attention in high school physics (or you watched the first installment in J.J. Abrams' "Star Trek" reboot) you will recognize that Kelvin is a temperature scale where "zero" equals absolute zero, the temperature at which all molecular activity ceases. Rendered in degrees Fahrenheit, this equals a brisk −459.67 degrees.

It's a credit to you if you were aware of this fact, but unfortunately, it will be of no help whatsoever in this application. The Kelvin scale that is used to measure color temperature has nothing to do with the Kelvin scale used to measure actual temperature. I know, why didn't they just pick a different name?

At first, this may seem like a peculiar notion. If you take a picture of a building, for example, you can't move parts of it around to make it more pleasing. All you can do is capture an image of the building as it exists, right? Of course, that's true at the most fundamental level. However, when photographers speak of composition, they don't mean re-arranging the physical world but selecting which parts of it to show and what parts to obscure or place outside the camera's field of view, also known as the *frame*.

Returning to our example of photographing a building: You could choose to put the building at the center of the frame, which is what most untrained photographers will do. The building is the subject of the image, they figure, so it should be in the center.

right? However, the building could also be positioned at the left or right side of the frame, which is a choice a professional photographer might make. If you want to emphasize how tall a building is, it helps to see it next to something short, for example.

Also, professional photographers tend to be guided by various aesthetic theories, such as the *rule of thirds* and the *golden mean*, which suggest that certain arrangements of subjects within a frame are intrinsically pleasing to the human eye. Let's take the rule of thirds as an example (Figure 9.13). This idea states that a rectangular frame should be evenly divided by two horizontal lines and two vertical lines, kind of like a tic-tac-toe board. The subject or essential element of the image, like the horizon, should be placed along one of these lines or at one of the four points where two of them cross.

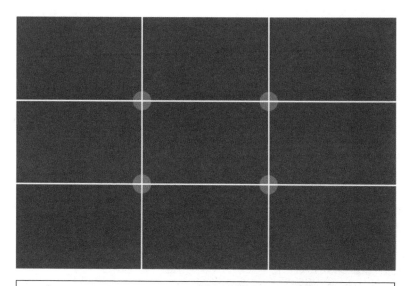

9.13 / The rule of thirds is a concept widely held by photographers and other visual artists, which suggests that important elements of an image should be aligned with vertical or horizontal lines which divide the frame into thirds— and in particular the locations where those lines cross. It is not, however, an actual rule, like staying below 400 feet or not flying over people.

"To me, photography is an art of observation. It's about finding something interesting in an ordinary place ... I've found it has little to do with the things you see and everything to do with the way you see them."

– Elliott Erwitt, French Photographer

After you learn about the rule of thirds, you'll start seeing it everywhere: on the covers of books and magazines, in TV shows and movies, in drawings and illustrations, and so forth (Figure 9.14). It becomes inescapable. Of course, unlike the rules that govern aviation, aesthetic rules are made to be broken. Millions of brilliant images have been created over the centuries that put the subject dead center or otherwise ignore this rule (Figure 9.15). The only real test of whether or not an image is successful is how that image makes you, and other people, *feel* when they look at it. And, of course, feelings are subjective.

9.14 / Uh oh...Can you see the rule of thirds peeking out at you in the composition of this photograph?

9.15 / Is this a good photograph? As ever, it's a subjective question, meaning that you and I can disagree regarding the answer and neitiher of us is "right." However, I took it and made the choice to include it in this book, so it's a fair bet that I like it. Now, notice the fact that the rule of thirds is nowhere to be seen. Is that a problem?

One perspective you should embrace as an aerial photographer is the *nadir* orientation. And, yes, "nadir" is definitely a vocabulary word, so let's pause for a moment and explain what it means. Imagine that your drone is hovering at the center of a giant, clear beach ball—just don't ask me how it got in there. The surface of the beach ball is marked with latitude and longitude lines, like a globe. The point at the bottom of the beach ball where all of the longitude lines converge, which we would refer to as the South Pole on a globe, is the nadir point: It's as low as you can go within a sphere before moving in any direction necessarily means moving upward. If you're standing at the South Pole, literally the only direction you can go is north. Incidentally, the point at the top of the beach ball where all of the longitude lines meet (i.e., the "North Pole") is referred to as the *zenith*.

So, establishing your drone's camera in a nadir orientation is just a fancy way of saying that it is pointing straight down at the ground directly underneath it. What makes this perspective so special is that it can only be achieved using a drone or some other type of aircraft, which means it can take a familiar landscape and make it look very unfamiliar indeed. It can show us the world as we have never seen it before, and that is one of the greatest accomplishments that any artist can hope to achieve (Figure 9.16).

9.16 / Pointing your camera straight down from an elevated perspective can create some unique images. Here, the shadow of a forest appears to be the forest itself as it falls across a sand dune that evokes the sky.

AFTER YOU LAND

Probably one of the most common mistakes that novices make is thinking that photography is something you do with a camera in your hands. In truth, the most consequential part happens afterward, when you sort through all the images you captured and pick out only the very best ones to share with other people. This idea is perfectly encapsulated in one of my favorite jokes:

Q: "Do you know the difference between a professional photographer and an amateur?"

A: "The amateur shows you all of his photos."

Choosing which images to keep—and which ones should be banished forever from human sight—is what really distinguishes the professionals from everyone else. Once you fully embrace this fact, your process for capturing images with a camera (or a controller) in your hands will change forever. Rather than fretting about whether to put the building on the left side of the frame, the right side of the frame, or in the center of the frame, you'll just take three photos and figure it out later (Figure 9.17).

9.17 / The secret to success in photography is to take dozens, or hundreds, of images while you are on site and then pick and choose the best ones afterward. Do you think I rolled up on the banks of the Columbia River, launched my drone, captured this one single image, and called it a day? Hardly. I captured maybe 50 different exposures of this kite surfer, picked out this one, and manipulated the heck out of it in Photoshop. Then—and only then—did I let anyone else see it.

I cannot tell you how many times I've taken a photo that I thought was brilliant, only to realize later that it was garbage. Likewise, I've captured a whole bunch of images that I was sure were trash when I pressed the shutter release, only to realize that it was some of my best work upon further consideration. You will also receive an additional, hidden benefit from learning how to discern your most successful images from the rest: It will refine your understanding of photography so that when you are tasked with capturing a specific image, you will be much better prepared to meet that challenge.

One more thing to be aware of is that almost all professional images are manipulated before they are published. In the most extreme cases, this can include fundamental alterations, such as adding or removing major elements, making an image captured in daylight appear as though it was taken at night, and so on. No doubt the recent advances in *artificial intelligence (AI)* will radically advance these capabilities in the years ahead.

Most of the time, these are relatively minor tweaks, comparable to what traditional film photographers were able to accomplish in the dark room, such as brightening or darkening the image or enhancing the color and contrast so that the subject stands out more clearly against the background. All the photos that I contributed to this book have been re-touched in precisely this way. It is such a common practice that if you saw an image in a book or magazine that hadn't been manipulated, you probably would think that something went wrong in the printing process.

Of course, using a digital camera means that digital tools are required to change or enhance the resulting images. Far and away the best known—and most expensive—among these is Adobe Photoshop, which has become nearly synonymous with the process of image editing itself. Teaching you how to use these sorts of tools goes well beyond the scope of this humble tome, but there are plenty of books and online resources you can consult to further your knowledge.

BE ALERT

At the beginning of this chapter, I pointed out that "A flying camera is a camera." Now, I'd like to conclude by turning that notion on its head and reminding you that *a flying camera is an aircraft.* You must never allow your pursuit of the perfect image to compromise your focus on the safety of flight. Unfortunately, it's easy to do, so easy, in fact, that pilots have a word for it—*target fixation.* Okay, so that's two words, but you get the idea.

The concept is simple enough to understand. Basically, you get so wrapped up in one aspect of your mission, capturing a compelling image, in this case, that you begin to neglect everything else. You stop paying attention to how much battery power you have remaining. You fail to maintain visual line of sight (VLOS) with your aircraft. You don't notice that a school bus just pulled up and disgorged 30 rowdy fourth graders into your landing zone.

Rest assured that these facts will assert themselves eventually, most likely at the absolute worst moment for you. As with almost every other type of error you can make as a pilot, I'm speaking from hard-won experience here when I tell you to always, always, always maintain *situational awareness (SA)* when you have a machine in the air. Doing anything else is foolish and dangerous. Learn from my mistakes so you don't have to learn from your own (Figure 9.18).

9.18 / Aerial imaging requires you to manage two separate roles simultaneously: pilot and photographer. Never forget that you are a pilot first.

10

More Ways to Fly (and Have Fun)

In the previous chapter, we looked at how you can use a drone to capture aerial video and still images. As promised, in this chapter we're going to consider everything else you can do with remote-control flying machines. That's a lot, obviously, so think of this as a tasting menu: just a few little nibbles to whet your appetite and see what piques your interest. Many of the specific recreational activities I'll be describing below are represented by *special interest groups (SIGs)* within the *Academy of Model Aeronautics (AMA)*. Visit the organization's website (modelaircraft.org) to find a complete list of these groups and connections to additional resources. (Figure 10.1)

TURNING PRO

As we learned in Chapter 2, conducting commercial operations—that is, those that offer a tangible benefit to you or someone else, beyond pure enjoyment—requires you to become a *remote pilot-in-command (RPIC)*. A number of steps are involved, but the most crucial is passing a 60-question *FAA Airman Knowledge Test (AKT)* administered at an FAA-approved testing center. The knowledge you have gained from this book has given you a good foundation, but you are not yet prepared to take the test.

10.1 / Whether you fly recreationally or professionally, remote piloting will always present you with new opportunities and adventures. You might be surprised by the places you'll end up—I certainly have been.

Since each attempt will cost you $175+, it's a good idea to expand your knowledge further before you try. You will need to deepen your understanding of most of the topics we covered in this book—with the remarkable exception of how to actually operate an aircraft—while paying particular attention to the rules and regulations that govern commercial operations and the *National Airspace System (NAS)*.

Those rules are contained within *14 CFR Part 107*, and while they broadly mirror the recreational rules we discussed in Chapter 2, there are some crucial differences and even a few contradictions. You need to understand them in detail, both because they represent the standard to which you will be held as a professional remote pilot, and because they are a key subject covered by the test.

Likewise, the NAS is a bedrock topic that you will have to understand in depth before you're able to pass the test. Your ability to interpret sectional charts should be on par with a private pilot, and that is going to take some significant effort on your behalf. Also, these charts are so dense with information that they can be hard to tease out on your own. You might consider sitting down with a living, breathing human being who already has a good handle on them to begin your own exploration.

Finally, when you do decide to take your test, be aware: The FAA is *really good* at designing questions that truly test your knowledge. They hire those expert test makers, so a good class, or the ASA

Remote Pilot Test Prep book or ASA Online Ground School could be a real beneficial start to your Part 107 training (Figure 10.2).

Once you pass the test and earn your RPIC credential, you will need to maintain it. This follows a well-established precedent. Crewed aviators are required to undergo a ***biannual flight review (BFR)*** once every two years with a qualified flight instructor to verify that they are still able to fly safely. In the not-so-good old days, professional drone pilots like me had to show up at a testing center every two years, pay another $175+ and pass another AKT. Fortunately, the FAA now allows us to take recurrent training online for free once every two years. The course is titled ***ALC-677*** and is available on the ***FAA Safety Team (FAAST)*** website. Don't worry, by the time you need it, you'll have an easy time finding it, and an even easier time passing it as long as you keep up with your credentials, and the more credentials you have, the more money you can demand for your services as a professional.

As I've mentioned previously, the strangest thing about becoming an RPIC is that you are not required to touch the aircraft you intend to fly. This is, to the best of my knowledge, unique in the universe of aeronautical credentials and sets the United States

10.2 / Taking the test to become a remote-pilot-in-command requires that you know Part 107 rules inside and out. ASA's *Remote Pilot Online Ground School* is a great place to find the knowledge (and the practice tests) you need. Also, you'll get to see me—I'm one of the presenters in this course!

apart from most other countries, which do require a hands-on proficiency demonstration—called a *check ride* by aviation types—in addition to a knowledge test.

At first, you may think to yourself, "This is great! Think of all the time I'll save by not actually learning how to fly!" Your buoyant attitude will last right until the moment you start looking for a job. You see, a lot of other would-be pilots had the same thought as you, and the people handing out the jobs are in on the joke too. Therefore, showing up with your shiny, new credential in hand likely won't be enough to get you any paid work. After all,

10.3 / Earning a Trusted Operator Program (TOP) certificate beyond the most basic level will require you to complete a practical flight demonstration, AKA check ride.

you will be competing with hundreds of thousands of newly minted pilots, so it's going to be your other credentials and flight experience and hours that make you marketable, not the Part 107 certificate.

Clearly, this is where maintaining a detailed and accurate flight log pays dividends, but you may also want to consider earning a third-party certificate. At the time of this book's publication, the most well-established one is the *Trusted Operator Program (TOP)*, developed by the *Association for Uncrewed Vehicle Systems International (AUVSI)*. Through a painstaking, multi-year process of consultation with industry educators and accomplished professional drone pilots, AUVSI developed a standard of knowledge and practical flying skill that goes beyond Part 107, to include a check ride at more advanced levels of certification.

Ironically, AUVSI itself does not offer a TOP certification program but made the standard available for educational and training organizations to implement for their own students and customers. The list of providers changes over time, but the certification manual and current certification centers can be found on the AUVSI website (auvsi.org/topoperator).

CLIMB ABOARD

This next section does not involve seeking certification as a crewed aviator—though that certainly has its own rewards for those who can afford it—but rather engaging in a unique form of remote piloting called *first-person view (FPV)* flying. As has been well established at this point, drones have cameras on them and transmit video in near real-time to a display on the pilot's **ground control station (GCS)**. What if, instead of a small display, you watched that video through a pair of high-resolution video goggles? That would be as close to flying as you are ever likely to get with your feet still on the ground (Figure 10.4).

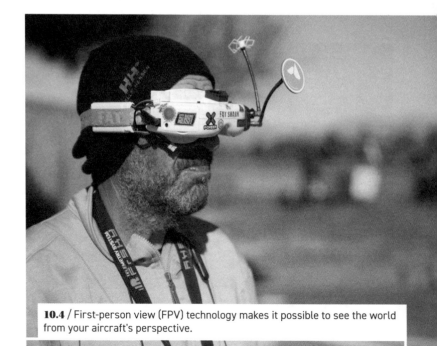

10.4 / First-person view (FPV) technology makes it possible to see the world from your aircraft's perspective.

This approach is referred to as "FPV" flying because you view the world from the perspective of your aircraft: a first-person view. This is in contrast with watching your aircraft from the outside, a third-person view, although nobody calls it that. FPV flying is a heck of a lot of fun, but there is a lot to unpack from both a regulatory and a technical perspective.

First, I hope it goes without saying that if you're wearing a pair of video goggles on your face, you absolutely cannot maintain a *visual*

A CRASHING SUCCESS

Provided that you employ a visual observer (VO) and good judgment, FPV flying does not especially increase the risk that you will crash and smash your aircraft into a thousand tiny pieces. However, some of the things you might want to do while flying FPV will make crashing almost inevitable. Specifically, **drone racing** and **freestyling** involve aircraft traveling at high speeds—sometimes 50 miles per hour or more—while maneuvering aggressively a few feet off the ground and punching through narrow gates and gaps. Even with supremely skilled pilots, this process is going to involve *a lot* of crashing.

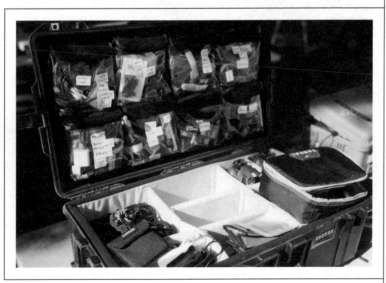

Drone racing and freestyling pilots are well-advised to keep a comprehensive stockpile of spare parts close at hand.

line of sight (VLOS) with your aircraft, which is a strict requirement for all remote piloting operations, as we learned in Chapter 2. Therefore, it is necessary that you have a *visual observer (VO)*, also referred to as a *spotter* in the hobby community, standing right next to you throughout the flight, keeping an eye on your aircraft as well as the surrounding airspace. This is nonnegotiable. As we discussed previously, it is impossible to maintain meaningful *situational awareness (SA)* looking at the world through a camera.

Therefore, if this is a path you choose to walk, you should anticipate you are going to wreck your machine, over and over and over again. Invariably, this leads to competitive FPV pilots also becoming skilled aircraft repair technicians, just as handy with a soldering iron as they are with an aircraft controller. Also, they will typically bring multiple aircraft to each event, so that after they wreck one, they can immediately resume flying with another one, making repairs at the end of the day. Oh, and propellers? Plan on buying those by the pound once you get into aggressive FPV flying.

Crashing is such an expected part of competitive FPV flying that pilots bring multiple aircraft to events, so that they don't need to make repairs immediately when one is wrecked.

People have all kinds of good fun while flying FPV, such as *drone racing* and *freestyling*, which involves making complex aerobatic maneuvers inside confined spaces. Both require a very high degree of skill as well as specialized gear.

While all drones worthy of the name can send video to their pilot on the ground, it usually isn't *quite* real time. Typical **latency** is less than one second, which is negligible when you are trying to frame a picture of a city's skyline. However, if you're hurtling 40 miles an hour through a dense forest, a half-second delay in your video signal is the difference between a cool clip to share with your friends and wrecked aircraft.

Therefore, FPV pilots use downlink technology that reduces latency as close to zero as physics will allow. The first variety involves an **analog** video transmitter and receiver, the same technology that makes AM and FM radio possible and brought television broadcasts to our homes through a roof-mounted antenna before the advent of cable, satellite, and streaming services. Go ask your parents. I'll wait.

With analog systems, latency is basically determined by the speed of light, the time it takes for the signal to travel from the aircraft to the pilot's video goggles, which at any range you are likely to be flying a drone FPV means it is essentially instantaneous. Another advantage is that analog systems are relatively inexpensive, and it's easy to mix-and-match gear between different manufacturers, provided they can broadcast and receive the same frequencies.

Analog systems have a few critical drawbacks as well. First, they rely on a single, discrete frequency to carry the video signal. That's exactly like the old-school model airplane controllers we learned about in Chapter 5. If someone else starts transmitting on the same frequency as you, your video signal will become a garbled mess, which doesn't make for a good day of flying. Therefore, FPV drone racing pilots using analog gear have to carefully **deconflict** their video frequencies before they start flying. Also, even if you are alone on your frequency, you'll still see occasional breakup or sparkle in your signal based on random interference in the environment.

As you have likely guessed by now, the alternative to analog FPV systems is *digital,* and their strengths and weaknesses are essentially the opposite of their analog brethren. Digital hardware tends to be proprietary, meaning that all the components in the system must come from the same manufacturer, and it is typically more expensive as well. However, because it uses the same *frequency-hopping spread spectrum (FHSS)* technology as a modern controller (again, see Chapter 5) it is not as susceptible to interference from other video transmitters in the environment.

While it is essentially negligible, digital FPV systems also create a tiny degree of latency because the video must be converted into a digital signal before it can be sent. It's darn fast but still not as fast as the speed of light. Also, while the clarity can be startling under optimal circumstances, you can still expect to see some signal degradation while flying with a digital FPV system, at least occasionally.

THE NEED FOR SPEED

Wherever it is possible to distinguish between two human beings in terms of their knowledge, skill, or intrinsic capacity, it seems inevitable that a competition will ensue. Seriously. What else could possibly account for the rise of the "caber toss," the Scottish sport of hurling logs for distance? This competitive instinct certainly holds sway among various groups of remote pilots.

> "It is possible to fly without motors, but not without knowledge and skill."
>
> – Wilbur Wright,
> Pioneering American Aviator

As someone who is just beginning your journey into aviation, if you choose to compete, you probably shouldn't expect to win all that often. However, competing against your fellow pilots will sharpen your skills faster than almost any other type of flying, and there is no shortage of opportunities to test yourself within the model aviation community.

10.5 / Racing drones are highly specialized aircraft that inevitably suffer nearly constant abuse, even in the hands of skilled pilots. A crash isn't just possible, it's a normal and expected part of the process.

We already touched on drone racing as one form of competition. These races do not involve the conventional aircraft you might use to capture aerial photographs while on vacation but rather highly specialized machines that prioritize speed and maneuverability above all other considerations. At a typical drone race, perhaps half a dozen pilots wearing video goggles will fly simultaneously, pushing their machines relentlessly through a series of narrow gates and obstacles.

One way or the other, each heat lasts less than three minutes, on average, with time between races set aside for the competitors who wrecked their aircraft to clear the debris off the field. If this all sounds like fun to you, be sure to check out the AMA's MultiGP special interest group (SIG) (Figure 10.5).

Of course, people have been racing radio-controlled aircraft since long before the advent of drones and FPV technology. These competitions generally resemble the world-famous crewed air racing championship, held each year in Reno, where the aircraft circle miles-long courses defined by 50-foot pylons. Naturally, the pylons aren't quite as tall or far apart when the airplanes are models, and the pilots are standing on the sidelines, but basically everything else is the same.

The *National Miniature Pylon Racing Association (NMPRA)*, another AMA SIG, hosts competitions that feature four aircraft flying simultaneously on a course defined by either two or three pylons. To qualify for an official race, aircraft must meet a variety of specifications, including wingspan (typically between 50 to 60 inches), weight (between four and five pounds), and various other technical requirements. While NMPRA does have categories for battery-powered aircraft, the majority require gasoline-fueled engines as the primary power source (Figure 10.6).

If you're looking for a bigger challenge—literally—the **Unlimited Scale Racing Association (USRA)** offers the same basic format but with even larger aircraft. For its premier races, the aircraft must be approximately a 1:2.4 scale model of a real airplane that has qualified for the crewed races in either Reno or Cleveland. I'll spare you the effort of reaching for a pocket calculator: That

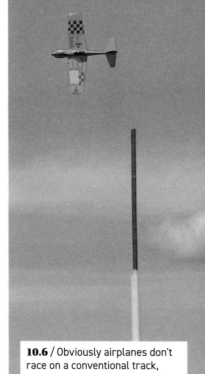

10.6 / Obviously airplanes don't race on a conventional track, so pylons are used to define the contours of the course.

works out to a wingspan of 100 inches or more, with a takeoff weight approaching 55 pounds. As you may have guessed, gas-powered engines are standard equipment on these beasts, and they can approach speeds of up to 200 MPH during competition.

YANKIN' AND BANKIN'

Of course, racing isn't the only way to compete. If grace rather than speed is your preferred measure of achievement, several AMA SIGs will likely appeal to you. The **International Miniature Aerobatic Club (IMAC)** top-level competitors must fly airplanes that are scale models of full-sized aircraft flown in previous International Aerobatic Club (IAC) competitions. However, beginners are not held to this requirement and are allowed to pilot any airplane that they are able to operate safely (Figure 10.7).

10.7 / Remote-control aerobatic models can bear an almost uncanny resemblance to their crewed counterparts.

Like figure skating, aerobatics is a judged competition. During each round, pilots fly one at a time, completing the same sequence of 8 to 10 maneuvers. If a maneuver is executed perfectly, as determined by a panel of judges, the pilot receives a score of 10, with points deducted for deviations and errors. This process is repeated for every maneuver in the sequence and every pilot in the round to establish a ranking. After multiple rounds of flying, an overall winner is determined.

The *National Society of Radio Controlled Aerobatics (NSRCA)* promotes precision aerobatic competition, otherwise known as *pattern flying*. Again, this entails flying a prescribed series of maneuvers under the watchful eyes of judges who determine an overall score for each sequence. While more experienced pilots will often build their own custom airplanes specifically for pattern competitions, people using store-bought models do enter, and even win, these contests. The NSRCA also has a program for indoor aerobatic flying and competitions. Naturally, these aircraft are much smaller and less powerful than their outdoor counterparts, and activities range from flying basic maneuvers for fun to international competitions involving specialized aircraft that weigh less than 100 grams, including the flight battery.

An entirely separate type of competitive flying involves both staying aloft as long as possible and flying as fast as possible, though not at the same time. The *League of Silent Flight (LSF)* specializes in gliders, which can stay aloft for many hours without the benefit of thrust from a motor or an engine. Like their crewed counterparts, these glider pilots become experts at seeking out *thermals*, rising columns of warm air they are able to harness to carry their machines farther aloft.

In this task, they are sometimes assisted using a *variometer*, also known to crewed aviators as a *rate of climb and descent indicator (RCDI)*. No surprise, this is a device that tells you how fast your airplane is ascending or descending. In the context of model aviation, this information is usually conveyed by a series of rising or falling tones, as opposed to a gauge, to allow these pilots to keep their eyes fixed on their machines. In its simplest form, glider competitions are won by the pilots who manage to keep their machines airborne the longest (Figure 10.8).

10.8 / The gliders used in competitve soaring events are substantial aircraft in their own right.

However, some of these competitions are truly epic in scale, such as cross-country races that cover miles of open country with pilots and their support teams piling into cars to keep pace with their aircraft.

Given their silent grace and lack of propulsion systems, you could be forgiven for not realizing that the fastest civilian remote-control aircraft ever to fly was a glider, which substantially exceeded 500 miles per hour. This pursuit is known as *dynamic soaring* and involves specialized aircraft flying in unique environments, as well as steely-eyed pilots with the reflexes of a hummingbird.

Of course, dogfighting is the ultimate form of head-to-head aerial competition, pitting one pilot directly against another. Given the prohibition against weaponizing remote-control aircraft that we learned about in Chapter 2, it should come as no surprise that this doesn't involve shooting down other airplanes. Rather, it mimics the fighter pilot's imperative to get behind an opponent's aircraft (i.e., in its *six o'clock position)* by attaching a streamer to each competing aircraft (Figure 10.9).

If you manage to drive your propeller into another pilot's streamer, thereby cutting it, metaphorically if not literally, you are awarded the victory. Obviously, at a minimum this requires

10.9 / In radio-controlled combat flying events, each of the competing aircraft trails a streamer behind it, with the victory being awarded to the pilot who first "cuts" the opponent's streamer.

two airplanes, two willing pilots, and a length of party-streamer, but formal competition involves aircraft that meet specifications and requirements promulgated by the **Radio-Control Combat Association (RCCA)**.

LOOK, MA! NO RADIO WAVES!

Next up, we will discuss a few aeromodelling activities that can be found at the farthest reaches of the sport, so much so that they cannot be fairly described as "remote piloting" at all. These include *free flight (FF)* and *control line (CL)* flying. Apart from a fundamental grasp of the aerodynamic principles we studied in Chapter 4, almost nothing you have learned from this book is applicable to either of these activities, so be sure to expand your knowledge before embarking upon them.

If you have ever folded a paper airplane and set it upon the wind, you already have some limited experience with free flight. Like the name suggests, FF involves launching an aircraft with no external control mechanisms and no power source, apart from maybe a tightly wound rubber band or a motor that is designed to shut off after a few seconds, and seeing what happens next (Figure 10.10).

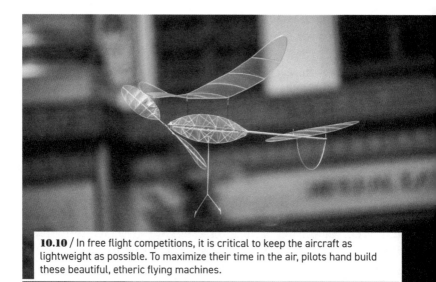

10.10 / In free flight competitions, it is critical to keep the aircraft as lightweight as possible. To maximize their time in the air, pilots hand build these beautiful, etheric flying machines.

These are inevitably fixed-wing airplanes, and the challenge lies in staying aloft for as long as possible. While you can get started with a store-bought balsa kit costing just a few dollars, serious FF enthusiasts take great pleasure in building their own aircraft by hand and attempting to optimize their aerodynamic potential. If you want to gain a deep appreciation of how design choices and things like the *center of gravity (CG)* affect aircraft performance, FF will surely provide you with a worthwhile education.

As an organized recreational activity, there are two flavors of FF available: indoor and outdoor. Typical indoor settings include gymnasiums, auditoriums, and other large, open spaces. The international championship is held in a cavernous, decommissioned salt mine beneath the Romanian countryside. Clearly, there are people for whom this is a very serious undertaking.

Indoor aircraft tend to be small, lightweight, and powered by a rubber band turning a large propeller, or they are simply gliders, launched either by hand or using a slingshot. Outdoor aircraft are typically larger and heavier than their indoor cousins, and they are capable of impressive performance. Some even have electric motors or gas-powered engines that incorporate a timer to stop the propeller turning at a set interval after launch. Only five seconds of thrust will allow a well-built model to fly for ten minutes or more.

If launching a paper airplane represents the distillation of FF into its most basic form, control line might be best understood by its similarity to flying a kite, if your kite had an engine on it. Like FF, CL flying is the exclusive domain of fixed-wing aircraft. The CL pilot holds a handle that is physically connected by two (or more) wires to the aircraft through *lead-outs* threaded through one of its wings. Control is maintained using essentially the same technique as a puppeteer manipulating a marionette: Applying more or less tension on the different wires *actuates* the airplane's *control surfaces* (Figure 10.11).

It is critical to note that the pilot only has direct control over the airplane's *pitch* axis. *Yaw* and *roll* are dictated not by the aerodynamic characteristics of the aircraft but by the fact it is tethered to the pilot. To better understand how this works, imagine that the pilot is the Earth, the airplane is the Moon, and the wires are their mutual gravitational attraction for one another.

10.11 / In control line flying, the pilot's only means of actuating the aircraft's control surfaces are wires attached to lead outs, seen here emerging from the model's wing.

If the law of gravity was abruptly repealed, the Moon would fly off into space on a straight-line course, which is exactly what a CL airplane would do if its wires were cut. However, so long as the law of gravity holds sway, the Moon will remain in orbit. Likewise, so long as the wires remain intact, the airplane will continue to fly in circles, always rolling and yawing toward the pilot but forever prevented from arriving by its desire to continue in a straight line (Figure 10.12).

10.12 / Control line airplanes are tethered to their pilots by two or more wires, making them something akin to flying puppets.

As a result, the CL pilot must constantly spin in the same direction that the airplane is flying or be wrapped in the wires, lose control, and potentially end up with a face full of propeller. If spinning around and around like a top maybe sounds like it might make you dizzy, there is an alternative, using only pitch-axis input, you can command the airplane to loop and fly inverted, that is, upside down and in the opposite direction, thereby keeping it in the same general quadrant of the sky.

Here are a few more things for you to consider: First, CL enthusiasts only use gasoline engines to power their models, so you'll need to be prepared for the expense and complexity that entails. Second, there are several safety concerns unique to CL flying, such as ensuring that the wires are strong enough to restrain the model, and if the pilot fumbles the handle, a safety strap makes sure it doesn't fly off out of control.

As ever, take the time to understand the risks involved and how you can mitigate them, just like any good pilot would when engaging with a new and unfamiliar activity.

SHARING WHAT YOU HAVE LEARNED

By now, I'm sure it won't come as a terrible shock that I find sharing aeronautical knowledge a worthwhile and enjoyable activity in and of itself, and I'd like to suggest that you might as well. As we discussed in Chapter 7, it's almost inevitable that you'll be doing some of this simply because of the attention you will bring to yourself while flying in public.

Flight safety must always be your top priority, of course, but with that obligation fulfilled, don't be shy about sharing your experiences with people you meet. You might inspire them to pursue it for themselves, and you could even make a new friend in the process. That has certainly been my experience.

However, right now I want to suggest that you participate in more formal aeronautical training, as a teacher. Maybe you are already a professional educator who wants to help your students enhance their understanding of *science, technology, engineering, and math (STEM)* subjects using drones and other remotely piloted aircraft. If so, blessings and peace be upon you. Even under optimal circumstances, teaching is a difficult job. However, it seems to be an especially fraught proposition these days. I, for one, salute you!

Even if you don't work as a teacher, I hope you will consider sharing what you have learned. Your first inclination may be to protest, saying: "I haven't even finished reading a book for the beginning-est of beginners, and this guy expects me to go start teaching other people!? How's that supposed to work?"

That's a fair question. First, I'll point out that what is true today will not necessarily be true tomorrow. All experts began as novices. Furthermore, I would argue that, even at this point, you have more to offer than you realize—and that will only become truer as you continue to gain experience and explore different facets of remotely piloting.

Second, knowledge matters less than you might think for being an effective teacher. Of all the people I have met during my own flying career, only a few of them have told me that they are impressed by the depth of my knowledge. Instead, they nearly all praise me for my passion for this technology, and the benefits that I believe it can provide for all of humankind. This has been a revelation for me, as I have always believed encyclopedic knowledge was the prerequisite for being a good teacher.

We have, however, entered an era where information is cheap. Our ancestors had to travel hundreds or thousands of miles to visit a library that housed a few dusty scrolls written centuries before. Today, the entire breadth of human understanding is never more than a few keystrokes away. As a potential instructor, your real gift lies not in the knowledge that you possess, but in your ability to inspire others to acquire that knowledge for themselves. If it happens that you are prepared to share some relevant information with them yourself, that's just a bonus.

In short, by putting you to work as a teacher, I'm not relying on your specialist insight into the laws of aerodynamics but on the fact that *you love flying as much as I do*. Believe me. That love, and the willingness to share it with others, is the most important contribution you can make to this community.

So, how should you go about it? If you're not a professional educator, you can volunteer at a local school or youth group. Even if you just fly a model airplane around for a class of grade-school students and answer a few basic questions about how it flies, you may end up inspiring the first astronaut to set foot on Mars or the engineer who builds a probe that finds life in the oceans of Europa. It matters that much.

In addition, plenty of formal programs seek to use this technology to enhance STEM education, and any one of them could use your help. Our friends at the AMA have a number of ongoing initiatives, *UAS4STEM* and ***U.S. Drone Soccer*** among them (Figure 10.13). Apply yourself to these or any of the other countless, worthwhile programs that are available across the country, and you will find that time, not knowledge, is the only thing you lack.

Did I mention there's an additional bonus for being a teacher? If you teach a subject to someone else, you yourself will come to understand it better than anyone, even people who do it every day. If you are greedy for knowledge, share it. There is no more reliable means of increasing your own stockpile.

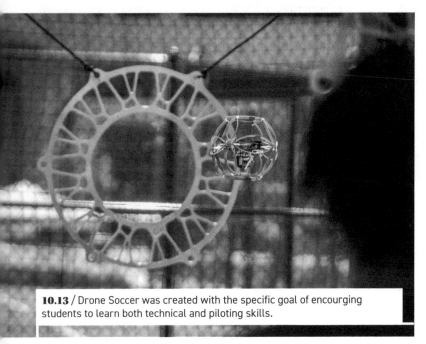

10.13 / Drone Soccer was created with the specific goal of encourging students to learn both technical and piloting skills.

Getting Started With Drones and Model Airplanes

Conclusion

Whew! So, you waded through all of that, and you still want to be a remote pilot!? Good for you! Please remember that this was the easy part. So far, you've been sitting comfortably (I hope) turning pages in a book and looking at pretty pictures. That doesn't take much effort on your behalf, nor does it involve putting anything at risk.

Now, you need to begin making decisions and taking action. Have you joined the *Academy of Model Aeronautics (AMA)* yet? When are you planning to complete *The Recreational UAS Safety Test (TRUST)*? If you're going to become a *remote pilot-in-command* flying under *Part 107*, how will you acquire the additional knowledge that is required to pass the test and earn your certificate?

What about actually flying? Are you going to start out with a simulator? If so, which one? Are you going to fly a *fixed-wing* platform or a *rotorcraft* to begin with? How much will it cost to replace the aircraft you've selected when you wreck it? How will you prevent its *lithium-polymer (LiPo)* batteries from burning your house to the ground?

Where will you fly? An AMA field or a public park? Is it in controlled or uncontrolled airspace? Are there any airports nearby? What obstacles and hazards does it present to your operations?

How will you mitigate them? Who can you learn from and where will you find them?

Most important of all: *How will you ensure that your aircraft never causes injury or damage to any person or their property?*

You may not have the answers to all these questions right now, and that's fine, but I'm hoping that after the time we have spent together, you understand *why* you need to answer each of them, and that you have a solid foundation of knowledge upon which to base your answers. I'd like to thank you for taking the time to prepare yourself to be a safe remote pilot. You've made the effort to do it the right way and, because of that, I'm a big fan of *you*, and your continued effort to gain knowledge and expertise.

Moving forward, I would exhort you to continue learning, because there is still plenty more for you to learn. Indeed, I would argue that even if you could recite every word written in this book, you only possess a small fraction of the knowledge you will require to be a competent, well-educated remote pilot. This is the beginning, not the end, of your aeronautical education—but the understanding of the fundamentals you have gained from this experience means you are now prepared to engage with more advanced subjects.

Read everything that you can about flying, meet other people in your local community who share your passion for aviation, and if you are able, attend regional and national events dedicated to this subject. These offer great opportunities to hear directly from leaders and experts and ask them questions, as well as seeing the very latest technology. Sometimes these lectures are even free! Look for events at your local university and community college, they will often bring in guest speakers that are free to attend.

Although civilian remote piloting began nearly a century ago, the past decade has seen unprecedented advances in the capabilities of these systems and that is going to continue in the years ahead. Just keeping up with it all can feel like a full-time job, but one made easier by attending industry conferences and trade shows.

Throughout this book, I have urged you to share what you have learned with others, but now I'd like to suggest one circumstance in which you should restrain yourself: When you see someone else doing something wrong. If we were to look back across the entire sweep of human history, we could probably count on one hand the number of times a stranger walked up to a somebody and said, "You're doing that wrong!" and that person replied, "Wow! Thank you! Can you please explain the correct way to do it?"

This probably goes back to the distinction I made between knowledge and wisdom in the introduction, but it seems like the default human response to critical feedback from a stranger is to become defensive, even if the stranger is friendly, sincere, and correct. I almost never comment on the performance of other remote pilots unless they are enrolled as a student in a class that I'm teaching.

If I do choose to share some advice, I phrase it in terms of a benefit to the pilot, by saying something like this, "You might find it easier if you try doing it this way." In my experience, strangers will reject criticism but welcome help.

Of course, if you see someone doing something reckless or which otherwise poses a legitimate risk of harm to yourself or other people or property, notify the local authorities and let them deal with it. You're a remote pilot, not a junior air marshal. You are responsible for the safety of your operations—not anyone else's.

So, with that final piece of advice, there really is nothing left for you to do except get out there, fly safe, and have fun.

I'll see you on the flight line.

Patrick Sherman

Acknowledgements

None of us achieves anything worthwhile on our own. At a minimum, all of us had to rely on our parents or caretakers, at least until we were old enough to forage for ourselves. So, I'd like to thank my family and friends, especially my wife Lisa for her boundless support and encouragement. I'd also like to recognize my good friend Brian Zvaigzne, without whom I never would have embarked on this journey in the first place, and also Erik Mayne, for his tireless and ongoing support of this long, strange trip.

Beyond my immediate social circle, I am a citizen of an interconnected, technologically advanced society. I've benefited enormously from the efforts of countless individuals: My teachers, of course—Ellen Spitaleri and Dick Trtek principle among them—but also all of the people who work hard every day to provide me with good food, clean water, and 120-volt electricity, along with other amenities of modern life. I will never get the opportunity to meet all of you and tell you this directly so, "Thank you! Your efforts are recognized and appreciated!"

When it comes to the publication of this book, in particular, there are some people who deserve special recognition. At the top of that list are Jackie Spanitz, Jennifer Moore, and the entire team at Aviation Supplies & Academics (ASA). I remember reading ASA publications 30 years ago when I was earning my private pilot's certificate. To think that I am now writing for ASA seems more than a little surreal. I don't think I'll believe it's actually true until I'm holding a printed copy of this book in my own hands.

I also owe my thanks to Rich Hanson, the president of the Academy of Model Aeronautics (AMA), and the organization's executive director, Chad Budreau, as well as Matt Ruddick.

At Embry-Riddle Aeronautical University (ERAU), I'd like to thank Dr. David Thirtyacre who—for some reason that still defies easy explanation—decided to take a chance on a drone nerd who wandered in from the Internet with essentially no formal training in aeronautics to join the Worldwide Department of Flight. I'd also like to recognize all of my university colleagues—Dr. Scott Burgess and Dr. Joe Cerreta among them—for their advice and support.

Special thanks also goes to Dr. Will Austin, the president of Warren Community College in Washington, New Jersey. I honestly have no idea what I could have done to earn the friendship and esteem of such an accomplished individual, but I am thankful for his encouragement and his efforts on my behalf. I am also grateful for the steadfast support of Wendie Kellington, without whom this journey would have ended before I could possibly have reached this point—and thanks also to Rick and Beth Bohlman of GoProfessional Cases.

Finally, I would like to recognize the efforts of my mother, Barbara Sherman, who deployed her considerable talent as an eagle-eyed copy editor to the manuscript for this book. Because of her efforts, you won't have to endure my confusion of contractions and possessives, nor my failure to properly hyphenate my compound adjectives. Thanks, Mom!

About the Author

Patrick Sherman is a pioneer in the drone industry, with more than a dozen years of operational experience flying small uncrewed aircraft systems (UAS). An award-winning speaker, writer, and educator, Patrick is an Assistant Professor of the Practice at the Embry-Riddle Aeronautical University Worldwide Campus, College of Aviation, Department of Flight. He shares his knowledge and insights around the world.

Patrick Sherman

Recognized for his contributions with an individual Xcellence Award as the "Drone Instructor of the Year" by the Association for Uncrewed Vehicle Systems International (AUVSI), he has been quoted in the *New York Times* and the *Washington Post* as a drone expert. He is a certified Level 3 Remote Pilot Instructor (RPI) through the AUVSI Trusted Operator Program (TOP) and a

DronePro serving with the Federal Aviation Administration Safety Team (FAAST). Patrick has logged more than 500 hours of UAS flight time.

Patrick is the author of more than 200 published articles about drones and their applications, which have appeared in magazines including *RotorDrone Pro*, *Drone360*, *Drones*, and *Drone* in the UK, as well as the *International Journal of Aviation, Aeronautics, and Aerospace*. For the past decade, he has also been a regular contributor to Model Aviation, as the author of the Advanced Flight Technology column, read by the more than 250,000 members of the Academy of Model Aeronautics (AMA).

Patrick is also the author of several current and forthcoming books, including *Drones: How They Fly*, a STEM-education coloring book for children ages 6 to 9, and a co-author of *Using Drones in Planning Practice*, published by the American Planning Association in 2020. In addition to this volume, he is the lead author of *Understanding Drones: Safety, Operations and Professionalism* under development for publication by Aviation Supplies and Academics (ASA) in 2025.

A top-rated speaker, he has given presentations at events across the United States and around the world, including: CES, AUVSI Xponential, Commercial UAV Expo, InterDrone, the Drone World Expo, Drones Data X, the Drone User Group Network National Conference, the International Drone Expo, and AMA Expo West. In 2017, he was invited to the Middle East to speak at the Drones Oman conference in Muscat and to interview the deputy director of the United Arab Emirates (UAE) civil defense UAS program.

Always seeking opportunities to support the acceptance and growth of the drone industry, Patrick serves as the secretary of the AUVSI Cascade Chapter board of directors and the chair of its government affairs committee. He is also a founding member of the AMA's sUAS Task Force and the Oregon State Legislature's Drone Working Group. Patrick is a technical adviser to the DRONERESPONDERS public safety alliance, as well as an advisory committee member and brand ambassador for the AUVSI TOP program.

Known to fans worldwide as "Lucidity," Patrick is the public face of the popular Roswell Flight Test Crew YouTube channel, which has more than 45,000 subscribers and more than 10 million video views. Sharing their adventures online since 2011, the crew promotes the safe, beneficial, and nonintrusive use of drone technology.

A master scuba instructor and licensed private pilot, he holds an undergraduate degree *summa cum laude* from the University of Southern California in sociology and English, as well as an MBA with honors from Willamette University. He also holds a Part 107 Remote Pilot-in-Command (RPIC) certificate and is a certified Level 2 Thermographer.

Glossary

Below you will find an abbreviated glossary of terms used in this book. For the extended version, please see the Reader Resources on the ASA website at asa2fly.com/modelair.

above ground level (AGL). The altitude of an aircraft above the terrain, as opposed to its altitude above mean sea level (MSL). In drone operations and the rules which govern them, altitude above ground level (AGL) is referenced most often. On the other hand, crewed aviators typically refer to their altitude MSL, which is displayed on standard aircraft altimeters. This distinction is critical because if you're flying 9,000 feet MSL at Pikes Peak, Colorado, your aircraft is a mile underground. *See* mean sea level.

airfoil. A specific shape that exploits the Bernoulli Principle to generate lift: one of the four forces of flight. Seen in airplane wings and propeller blades, the airfoil in its most basic form is curved across its upper surface and flat on the bottom. This causes a pressure differential in the air moving past it, which creates lift.

angle of attack. The angle of attack, despite its aggressive-sounding name, is simply defined as the angle at which the leading edge of an airfoil (or, more specifically, that airfoil's chord line) meets the oncoming air. As the angle of attack increases, so does the lift generated by the airfoil—right up to the moment it crosses the critical angle of attack, at which point the smooth flow of air over its upper surface collapses. This results in a sudden and dramatic loss of lift known as an aerodynamic stall.

antitorque rotor. The antitorque rotor—referred to by unschooled as the "tail rotor"—is the little propeller mounted on a boom at the back of a conventional helicopter that rotates on a geometric plane perpendicular to the ground. It serves two basic functions: it counteracts the torque reaction created by the rotation of the main propeller on top of the helicopter and allows the pilot to control the aircraft's maneuvering in the yaw axis.

arresting gear. While virtually unknown in small, civilian drone and model airplane operations, arresting gear refers to a system that captures an aircraft and immediately terminates its flight. These are typically used when the aircraft is incapable of landing safely on the ground and must therefore be caught in midair, or when it is necessary to stop the aircraft in a short distance—as with high-performance jets landing on an aircraft carrier. No surprise, systems and spaces that require arresting gear often also require the use of launch catapults. *See* launch catapults.

attitude. In aviation, the word attitude describes the relationship between a part of an aircraft in flight and the horizon, such as a nose-high or nose-low attitude. If a more experienced pilot tells you to "watch your attitude" while you are flying, they are most likely not criticizing your surly disposition, but rather trying to help you avoid a crash.

binding. In remote piloting, binding is the process of connecting an aircraft to the hand-held controller that the pilot will use to direct its maneuvers in flight. The procedure is similar to pairing a Bluetooth accessory to a smartphone.

center of gravity (CG). In physics and engineering, the center of gravity (CG) is an imaginary point associated with an object where, for purposes of analysis, the total weight of that object can be assumed to be concentrated. Alternatively, the CG is the point around which the object will rotate in freefall, as in zero gravity.

Managing the location of the CG is critical for the safe operation of aircraft. If the CG moves beyond a range defined by the aircraft's designers, the aircraft can become unpredictable or even uncontrollable in flight.

center of pressure (CP). Just as the weight of an aircraft can be said to act at its center of gravity (CG), the total lift generated by that same aircraft's wings can be said to act at its center of pressure (CP). The relationship between the CG and CP is crucial in determining the stability of the aircraft. Fortunately, establishing the CP in the correct position is pretty much the exclusive concern of the aeronautical engineers who design aircraft—not the pilots who fly them.

chord line. An imaginary line that connects the leading edge of an airfoil to its trailing edge. Do not cut open the wing of your airplane looking for the chord line—you won't find it. It's imaginary, remember? The reason the chord line is important is that a wing's angle of attack is measured from its chord line, not any physical feature of the wing itself.

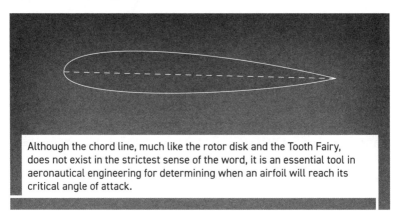

Although the chord line, much like the rotor disk and the Tooth Fairy, does not exist in the strictest sense of the word, it is an essential tool in aeronautical engineering for determining when an airfoil will reach its critical angle of attack.

community-based organization (CBO). A designation mandated by Congress and implemented by the Federal Aviation Administration (FAA), a community-based organization (CBO) is a private, nonprofit group that publishes a safety code for recreational small uncrewed aircraft systems (sUAS) operations and oversees their operations by its members. The oldest and most well-established CBO is the Academy of Model Aeronautics, founded in 1936.

control line (CL) flying. A type of aeromodelling activity entirely separate from conventional, radio-controlled flight. In control line flying, the pilot is tethered to the aircraft by—you guessed it—control lines. By manipulating these lines, the pilot can actuate control surfaces on the model, allowing it to perform aerobatic maneuvers.

control surfaces. Control surfaces are moveable panels that are generally located on the trailing edges of an airplane's wings and stabilizers. The most common among these are the elevator, the ailerons and the rudder—which nominally allow the pilot to control the aircraft's pitch, roll, and yaw, respectively.

deconflict. Deconfliction describes any process or procedure that seeks to avoid potential conflicts among participants operating in the same space at the same time or relying upon a common resource, such as radio frequencies. For example, early aeromodelling enthusiasts used controllers that employed discrete, fixed frequencies. If two pilots transmitted on the same frequency at the same time, the aircraft would receive simultaneous—and contradictory—control inputs, likely resulting in a crash. To prevent this, each flying field had a board with tags corresponding to each available frequency. Before powering up, a pilot would claim the tag corresponding to their frequency, and no other pilot using a controller tuned to that same frequency was allowed turn on their system until the tag was returned to the board. Today, first-person view (FPV) pilots using analog video transmitters must rely on similar procedures.

dihedral angle. In fixed-wing aviation, the dihedral angle reflects the degree to which the wing of an airplane slopes up from the point where the wing is attached to its fuselage. The steeper this angle, the greater the intrinsic aerodynamic stability of the aircraft.

FAA-Recognized Identification Areas (FRIAs). A defined geographic space within which drones and model aircraft are allowed to operate without a functioning Remote Identification (RID) system. Such sites must be affiliated either with a recognized Community-Based Organization (CBO) or with an educational institution, such as a primary school, secondary school, trade school, college, or university. The CBO or educational institution must apply to the Federal Aviation Administration (FAA) to establish an FAA-Recognized Identification Area (FRIA), and its authorization must be renewed every four years.

FAA Safety Team (FAAST). A volunteer organization sponsored by the Federal Aviation Administration (FAA) that relies on its members to provide counseling and education to their fellow pilots with the goal of improving safety. Professional remote pilots who serve as members of the FAA Safety Team (FAAST) are known as "DronePros."

first-person view (FPV). Rather than maintain a direct visual line of sight with their aircraft, remote pilots who fly first-person view (FPV) wear a set of video goggles that provide them with a real-time video feed from an on-board camera. This creates an immersive experience that can be likened to sitting on the flight deck of a crewed aircraft. However, because the pilot is not able to see their aircraft directly, both commercial and recreational rules require that a visual observer (VO) be employed to keep the aircraft, and the surrounding airspace, in sight for the duration of the flight.

flaps. A control surface located on the trailing edge of an airplane's wings, inboard from the ailerons. Unlike the ailerons, flaps move symmetrically and are employed to increase lift, reducing the speed at which a fixed-wing aircraft will experience an aerodynamic stall. They can be used to decrease the length of the aircraft's takeoff and landing roll.

flare. The flare is a maneuver that immediately precedes the landing of a fixed-wing aircraft. The moment before the undercarriage contacts the ground, the pilot applies slight back pressure to the elevators, pitching the nose upward and bleeding off airspeed, such that the aircraft experiences an aerodynamic stall at the precise instant it touches down. Nobody—and I mean *nobody*—can pull this off correctly every single time.

flight line. Within the Academy of Model Aeronautics (AMA) safety code, the flight line is a boundary that separates soft, fleshy humans from the fast-turning propellers of their radio-controlled flying machines. The goal is to ensure that people and aircraft under power never occupy the same space at the same time, which should—theoretically, at least—preclude the possibility of injuries.

free flight (FF). A specialized aeromodelling activity that is entirely separate from radio-controlled flight. Free flight is much like making and launching a paper airplane, if your paper airplane was a meticulously crafted exemplar of aerodynamic perfection. Aircraft are launched either by hand or using a slingshot. These models can be unpowered, powered by wound rubber bands, or by electric motors or gasoline engines designed to shut down after providing a few seconds of thrust. As a competitive activity, the plane that stays aloft the longest wins—but the real winners are the people who build them and thereby gain a deep understanding of aerodynamics.

freestyling. A specific type of first-person view (FPV) flying not dissimilar to an aerobatic demonstration or competition. Pilots, wearing a pair of video goggles, push their aircraft through a series of extreme maneuvers. Much like drone racing, doing this—and learning to do it—will result in frequent crashes. Expect to become an expert aircraft repair technician along with an expert pilot if you choose to participate in this type of flying.

go-around. In aviation, to "go-around" is to abort a landing. Rather than continue an attempt to land in unfavorable or unsafe circumstances, the pilot applies throttle to gain airspeed and climbs away from the approach. Unless they are flying an unpowered glider, all pilots should be prepared to perform a go-around on any landing attempt—and that goes double if you're a new remote pilot still figuring out how to fly.

hand launch. The act of launching a small uncrewed aircraft system (sUAS), most often a fixed-wing airplane, by hand: throwing it like a javelin into the air. Great care needs to be taken while hand-launching an aircraft owing to the immediate proximity of the aircraft's propeller, which could inflict serious injuries to the person doing the launching.

infrared range finder. A device that sends out a pulse of invisible infrared light and watches for its reflection from an object in the environment. This allows the infrared range finder to determine the distance between the object and the sensor. Previously, these types of sensors were occasionally used for collision avoidance, but today they are used almost exclusively as precise, low-altitude altimeters.

intelligent orientation control (IOC). Also known as "headless mode," intelligent orientation control (IOC) is a flight mode incorporated into some drones that allows the pilot to make control inputs based on their own position relative to the aircraft, rather than the aircraft's direction of travel. While IOC is a tempting alternative for new pilots, it will only limit the growth and development of their skills as remote pilots. As they said when I was coming of age, "Friends don't let friends fly using IOC."

landing roll. The minimum distance a fixed-wing aircraft requires to reach a full stop after its initial contact with the ground. If an aircraft's landing roll exceeds the length of the runway available, that's a bad day for everyone involved. *See* takeoff roll.

latency. Latency is a measure of the time required for a sensor, such as the video camera on board a drone, to capture data and transmit it to the ground-based pilot. As data is carried by electromagnetic waves traveling at the speed of light, some tiny degree of latency is inevitable. When time to encode and decode the data is added at each end of the process, the latency with conventional drones can be half a second, or more. This is perfectly serviceable for ordinary aerial photography applications. However, a half-second delay would mean disaster for first-person view (FPV) pilots engaged in drone racing or freestyling. To overcome this hurdle, these pilots either use analog systems—which are nearly instantaneous but subject to interference—or more expensive digital systems that drastically reduce the time required for the encoding/decoding process.

launch catapult. A surface-based device used to hurl a fixed-wing aircraft into the sky in a short distance. Apart from free flight (FF) competitors drawing back slingshots to launch their unpowered gliders, launch catapults are essentially unknown in drone and aeromodelling activities. Larger military and civilian drones that are incapable of a rolling takeoff will use launch catapults to get airborne, as will crewed aircraft operating from a confined space, such as the deck of an aircraft carrier. No surprise, systems and spaces that require a launch catapult often must also rely on arresting gear. *See* arresting gear.

mean sea level (MSL). Altitude above mean sea level (MSL) is the standard measure of altitude in crewed aviation and reflects the height of the aircraft above the average level of the oceans world-wide. Altitude MSL is distinguished from altitude above ground level (AGL) (the altitude of the aircraft above the local terrain). AGL is the measure typically referenced in drone and model aircraft operations. This distinction is critical, for example, because under most circumstances these operations are limited to an altitude of 400 feet. Therefore, operating a drone or model aircraft at 14,515 feet MSL would get you in big trouble in some places, but if you're flying over Pikes Peak, Colorado, you're still only flying at 400 feet AGL. *See* above ground level.

monoplane. A fixed-wing aircraft with one wing, a design that constitutes the overwhelming majority of airplanes, both crewed and uncrewed, in service today. The monoplane is distinguished from multi-wing airplanes, the most common being the biplane which dominated in the first few decades of powered flight.

multirotor embed. A type of vertical takeoff and landing (VTOL) aircraft employed exclusively in uncrewed system design that effectively embeds a multirotor—most often a quadcopter—within a conventional fixed-wing aircraft. While a relatively inefficient design when compared with other types of VTOLs, the multirotor embed offers a robust, mechanically simple design which makes it appealing to certain users, the armed services principle among them.

multirotor. A type of rotorcraft that employs four, or more, propellers spinning parallel to the ground for lift, thrust and maneuvering. Multirotors were the first type of crewed rotorcraft to fly, but their mechanical and aerodynamic complexity severely limited their practical applications. However, the advent of small, extremely reliable brushless electric motors, inexpensive low-power computing solutions for flight control systems (FCS) and micro electro-mechanical systems (MEMS) sensors resurrected this aircraft type that is today universally recognized as a drone.

multi-wing. A fixed-wing aircraft with more than one wing, the most common example being the biplane. Because multi-wing airplanes are significantly slower than a comparable monoplane, they quickly fell out of favor once structural engineering and materials science enabled the development of single-wing airplanes.

Notices to Air Missions (NOTAMs). A Notice to Air Missions (NOTAM) is a bulletin that alerts airspace users to temporary circumstances with the potential to affect flight operations. Most NOTAMs are irrelevant to remote pilots, as they concern on-airport or crewed aircraft operations such as the closure of a particular taxiway or the erection of a crane along an approach or landing corridor. However, NOTAMs can also apply to remote pilots, as well, such as when a Temporary Flight Restriction (TFR) is established. Professional remote pilots will also post NOTAMs to alert crewed aviators when drones will be operating in a specific area.

orientation flying. Orientation flying is the conventional approach to remote piloting: the pilot directly observes the aircraft's movements and performance from the ground and gives control inputs relative to its attitude and heading. As the relationship between the pilot and the aircraft's heading is constantly changing, this is a skill that requires considerable practice to master.

relative wind. When an airfoil exceeds its critical angle of attack—that is, when the angle at which the oncoming air meets the airfoil (or, more accurately, its chord line) exceeds a limit defined by its aerodynamic properties—the result will be an immediate and dramatic loss of lift known as an aerodynamic stall. However, if you've ever been to an airshow, you've likely seeing airplanes flying straight up into the sky, their wings at a 90-degree angle to the horizon. It certainly seems like this kind of maneuver should exceed any airfoil's critical angle of attack. The reason it doesn't is the phenomenon known as "relative wind." Fixed-wing aircraft are themselves responsible for creating most of the wind, i.e., the moving air, that they encounter in flight, due to the thrust developed by their motors or engines. If an aircraft is traveling fast enough, even if it is pointing straight up, the motion of the air around the airfoil will still not exceed its critical angle of attack, because of the resulting relative wind. Of course, unless that airplane has rocket engines powerful enough to lift it into orbit, this is necessarily going to be temporary.

The truth is, unless they are flying directly into a hurricane, fixed-wing aircraft are themselves responsible for generating most of the "wind" they encounter in flight through the thrust developed by their engines or motors, a phenomenon known as "relative wind." Thus, if an airplane is flying fast enough, it can appear to make a mockery of the critical angle of attack, at least for a while

remote identification (remote ID or RID). A requirement put in place in September 2023 by the Federal Aviation Administration (FAA) that requires all small uncrewed aircraft systems (sUAS) weighing more than 250 grams, or any sUAS used for a commercial operation, to carry a short-range electronic beacon that transmits a unique identification code tied to its registration number, speed, altitude and other basic flight information.

remote pilot-in-command (RPIC). The formal title given to an aviator certificated under 14 CFR Part 107 to operate small uncrewed aircraft systems (sUAS) in commercial applications. It is derived from the title given to crewed aviators, being pilot in command (PIC).

rotorcraft. One of four major types of heavier-than-air flying machines—along with fixed-wing airplanes, VTOLs and ornithopters. Rotorcraft, which include helicopters and multirotors, are distinguished by their use of propellers turning parallel to the ground as their primary source of lift.

runway. A flat, unobstructed surface built for the purpose of launching and recovering fixed-wing aircraft. To be viable for this purpose, the runway must be at least as long as the takeoff and landing rolls of the airplanes that intend to operate from the facility, plus a safety margin.

situational awareness (SA). Situational awareness (SA) is a foundational concept in aviation, but it defies an easy explanation. Much of what I've tried to teach you throughout this book has focused on developing your capacity for SA, although I've avoided using the term for the most part because it can be confusing. Here's my best definition: Every time you go out to fly, you are actually flying two aircraft. The first one is the aircraft in the real world, and the second one is the aircraft inside your head. SA is the art of ensuring that the second aircraft resembles the first aircraft as much as possible in all respects: its location, its performance, and its condition. If you lose SA, for example, the aircraft in your head may have 50 percent battery power remaining, while the aircraft in the real world has 20 percent battery power remaining. Guess which one will determine how long the real-world aircraft keeps flying? Sitting comfortably, reading a book, this seems like a trivial challenge—barely even worth mentioning. However, in actual flight operations, maintaining SA can be a serious problem: one that bedevils even experienced crewed aviators and has accounted for a surprising proportion of fatal accidents over the years. Here is an old-timey aviation aphorism that I think does a good job of illustrating SA and its importance: "Never let your airplane take you anyplace your brain didn't arrive five minutes beforehand."

small uncrewed aircraft systems (sUAS). An uncrewed aircraft system (UAS)—a category that includes both drones and model aircraft—that weighs less than 55 pounds at takeoff.

stationkeeping. A maneuver that allows a vehicle—such as an aircraft or a boat—to maintain a fixed position despite the influence of external forces, such as the wind or currents. In the early days of small, civilian drones, stationkeeping required considerable skill and constant pilot input to achieve. However, with the advent of more sophisticated flight control systems (FCS) with global navigation satellite system (GNSS) receivers, this has become an automated function of the aircraft itself. In short, if you're just getting into flying drones right now, you've got no idea how easy you've got it! Also, when I was young, we had to walk to school in the snow—uphill in both directions, no less!

sterile flight deck. The concept of a sterile flight deck developed in crewed aviation and has nothing to do with preventing the spread of communicable diseases. Rather, the idea is that during high-risk phases of flight—such as takeoff and landing—the aircrew should be focused exclusively on piloting the aircraft. Idle chit-chat and other distractions are prohibited, rendering the flight deck a "sterile" environment. As this requirement was implemented in the interest of safety, an effort has been made to extend the concept to remote pilots. This is the primary motivation behind professional drone pilots donning those garish vests with "Drone Pilot: Keep Away" written across the back. Based on my own personal experience while flying in public, these seem to draw as much attention as they deflect, so I suppose we'll have to wait and see whether they are the best solution available to us in the long term.

sUAS. *See* uncrewed aircraft system.

takeoff roll. The minimum distance a fixed-wing aircraft requires when accelerating from a full stop to attain sufficient speed to achieve flight. It should go without saying that any flight you are hoping will end successfully should begin from a runway that exceeds your airplane's required takeoff roll, plus a safety margin. *See* landing roll.

ultrasonic range finder. A device that sends out a pulse of ultrasonic sound, inaudible to humans, and listens for its echo after it reflects off an object in the environment. This allows the ultrasonic range finder to determine the distance between the object and the sensor with a high degree of precision. Some drones incorporate these systems on the underside of the aircraft as low-altitude altimeters.

uncrewed aircraft system (UAS). Uncrewed aircraft system (UAS) is the term used almost universally in industry and professional circles to describe drones and model aircraft. This term refers not only to the aircraft itself, but also the ground-based hardware—like the controller, battery charger, and so forth—necessary to enable it to fly. UAS that weigh less than 55 pounds are specifically described as small uncrewed aircraft systems (sUAS). It is also worth noting that the term "UAS" is predominant only in the United States. Elsewhere in the world, they are known as remotely piloted aircraft systems (RPAS).

vertical takeoff and landing (VTOL). One of four major types of heavier-than-air flying machines—along with fixed-wing airplanes, rotorcraft and ornithopters. Vertical takeoff and landing (VTOL) aircraft are capable of ascending directly from a small, unprepared patch of ground like a rotorcraft, then transitioning into fixed-wing flight, like an airplane—thereby attempting to capture the flexibility and efficiency of both aircraft types.

visual observer (VO). A member of the flight crew of a drone or model airplane, the visual observer (VO)—also referred to as a "spotter" in the recreational flying community—is responsible for maintaining visual line of sight (VLOS) with the aircraft, as well as monitoring the surrounding airspace for emergent hazards, such as low-flying crewed aircraft. The VO must be located near enough to the remote pilot to facilitate easy communication. There is never a good reason not to have a VO, but they are advisable or even mandatory, if the pilot is engaged in certain especially distracting activities, such as aerial photography or first-person view (FPV) flying.

visual line of sight (VLOS). In the context of remote piloting, maintaining visual line of sight (VLOS) is a requirement for most small uncrewed aircraft system (sUAS) operations, including all recreational activities involving drones and model aircraft. Effective VLOS goes well beyond being able to discern the aircraft as a tiny point in the sky. Instead, it is defined by a six-point test developed by the Federal Aviation Administration (FAA) using the acronym "LAADON." VLOS can only be adequately maintained if the remote pilot can determine:

Location: The position of the aircraft, including distance and direction.

Altitude: The elevation of the aircraft above the surface of the earth at its current location, as opposed to the surface where it was launched (which is what virtually all small UAS telemetry reports).

Attitude: The aircraft orientation in the pitch, roll, and yaw axes.

Direction of flight: The aircraft's current heading and anticipated movement through the air.

Observe airspace: Keep watch for other aircraft or hazards in the vicinity of the operation.

Not pose a hazard: Ensure the aircraft does not endanger people or vulnerable property not directly involved in the operation.

Image Credits

Unless otherwise specified, photos are by the author, Patrick Sherman, and illustrations by ASA.

Foreword

Image 1. istockphoto.com/JanakaMaharageDharmasena

Chapter 1

Figure 1.1. Illustration by Pieter Philippe for Hippocrates, *Magni Hippocratis Coi opera omnia*. Van der Linden, J.A., editor. 1665. From Wellcome Collection, London. Accessed at: wellcomecollection.org/works/mn9vkqm4.

Figure 1.3. U.S. Air Force photo by Bobbi Zapka - http://www.af.mil/shared/media/photodb/photos/070301-F-9126Z-229.jpg

Figure 1.6. Photo by James Galloway

Sidebar Image 1. United Kingdom War Office Second World War Official Collection

Chapter 2

Figure 2.3. Federal Aviation Administration (FAA)

Figure 2.6. Federal Aviation Administration (FAA)

Figure 2.7. Federal Aviation Administration (FAA)

Figure 2.10. National Aeronautics and Space Administration (NASA)

Chapter 3

Figure 3.3. Nationaal Archief/Spaarnestad Photo

Figure 3.8. Photo courtesy the Academy of Model Aeronautics (AMA)/ Matt Ruddick

Figure 3.10. Photo by James Galloway

Figure 3.17. Photo by Andrew Schmidt

Figure 3.19. NASA/JPL-Caltech

Figure 3.21. pixabay.com/tragiccharacter

Figure 3.22. U.S. Naval Forces Central Command/U.S. Fifth Fleet

Figure 3.24. San Diego Air & Space Museum

Sidebar Image 2. National Park Service

Sidebar Image 3. Photo courtesy the Academy of Model Aeronautics (AMA)/Matt Ruddick

Chapter 4

Sidebar Image 1. Portrait of Daniel Bernoulli, c.1720-1725. Oil painting on canvas, Height 90.6 cm, Width 73.8 cm. inventory number 1991.156 (Basel Historical Museum, Peter Portner). No modifications have been made.

Chapter 5

Sidebar Image 2. U.S. Air Force

Chapter 8

Figure 8.1. Photo by James Galloway

Figure 8.7. Photo by James Galloway

Chapter 9

Chapter 10

Figure 10.6. Photo courtesy the Academy of Model Aeronautics (AMA)/ Matt Ruddick

Figure 10.7. Photo courtesy the Academy of Model Aeronautics (AMA)/ Matt Ruddick

Figure 10.8. Photo courtesy the Academy of Model Aeronautics (AMA)/ Matt Ruddick

Figure 10.9. Photo courtesy the Academy of Model Aeronautics (AMA)/ Matt Ruddick

Figure 10.10. Photo courtesy the Academy of Model Aeronautics (AMA)/ Matt Ruddick

Figure 10.11. Photo courtesy the Academy of Model Aeronautics (AMA)/ Matt Ruddick

Figure 10.12. Photo courtesy the Academy of Model Aeronautics (AMA)/ Matt Ruddick

Figure 10.13. Photo courtesy the Academy of Model Aeronautics (AMA)/ Matt Ruddick

Sidebar Image 2. Photo courtesy the Academy of Model Aeronautics (AMA)/Matt Ruddick

Glossary

Image 2. U.S. Air Force

Index

Code of Federal Regulations
(CFR), 23. *See also* 14 CFR, Part
107
collision avoidance system, 118–120,
181
color temperature, 228
commercial drone operator, 10, 79
commercial operations, 21, 23, 35, 43
Common Traffic Advisory
Frequency (CTAF), 44
community-based organization
(CBO), 24–26, 39
compass. *See* magnetic compass
composition in
photography, 227–232
computer-generated imagery
(CGI), 150
Congress, United States, 23
control horn, 129
control inputs, 191
  fixed-wing, 190–196
  rotorcraft, 204–207
  rudder, 192
  size of, 195
  trim, 200
controlled airspace, 27, 39, 45, 161
controller, 13, 61, 132–136, 139,
153–154, 156, 158, 165, 184, 191,
199, 200–201, 208, 216, 242, 245
  binding, 134
  channel, 135
  joystick, 132
  modes, 187, 210
  two-stick, 152, 188
control line (CL) flying, xii, 28,
252–254
control receiver, 110
control surfaces, 98–102, 129, 132,
252
control tower, 44
Convair XFY-1 Pogo VTOL, 78
coordinated turn, 102
crashing, 148–149
critical angle of attack, 91

D

da Vinci, Leonardo, xi, 4
Day, Harry, 22
de Bothezat, George, 74
de Bothezat helicopter, 74
De Havilland Tiger Moth biplane, 9
depth of field in
photography, 224–227
desert environment
imaging, 174–176
Diehl, Aaron, 127
digital camera, 234
dihedral angle, 63–64
dirigible, 51, 53
  thrusters, 53
DJI Phantom 4 drone, 2–3
drag, 59, 84–85
drone, 4–9, 13, 25, 56, 109–110, 112,
114, 117–119, 127, 132, 136, 138,
148, 155, 157, 162, 169, 189
drone racing, 242, 244, 246
drone soccer, 14
  U.S. Drone Soccer, 256
dynamic soaring, 250

E

Earhart, Amelia, 185
Eisenhower, Dwight D., 78
electric-ducted fans (EDFs), 67–69
electric motor, 110, 122–123
electromagnet, 122, 125
electromagnetic interference
(EMI), 139, 164–165, 174, 191
electromagnetic spectrum, 133
electronic copilot, 153–156
electronic speed controller
(ESC), 110, 126–128
elevator, 98–102, 109, 129
Embry-Riddle Aeronautical
University, 33
energy density, 141
engine, 124
engineering, structural, 93–94
envelope, 51, 53